Contents

--A-- 1
--B-- 18
--C-- 43
--D-- 66
--E-- 84
--F-- 95
--G-- 104
--H-- 119
--I-- 137
--J-- 141
--K-- 146
--L-- 159
--M-- 176
--N-- 201
--O-- 208
--P-- 216
--Q-- 231
--R-- 232
--S-- 249
--T-- 278
--U-- 290
--V-- 292
--W-- 297
--X-- 311
--Y-- 311
--Z-- 313

--A--

Aalto, Alban (furniture designer)
Aalto, Alvar (architect--Finlandia House; Fin.)
Aames, Willie (actor--Charles in Charge, Eight is Enough)
Aaron, Hank (baseball)
Abba (musical group--Voulez-vous, S.O.S., Waterloo, Fernando)
Abbas the Great (politician--Shah of Iran)
Abbas, Mahmoud (politician) (Arafat's successor)
Abbott, Bernice (photographer)
Abbott, Bud (comedian/actor--Here Come the Co-eds)
Abbott, Jack (author--In the Belly of the Beast)
Abbott, Jacob (author--children's--Rollo)
Abbott, Roger (comedian--Air Farce)
Abdul, Paula (actress/dancer/T.V. personality/singer--Forever Your Girl, Straight Up)
Abdul-Jabbar, Kareem (a.k.a. Lew Alcindor) (basketball)
Abe, Shinzo (politician; Jap.)
Abel, Elie (journalist/Dean of Journalism at Stanford & Columbia/author--The Missile Crisis, Hold Back the Dawn)
Abel, Frederick Augustus (chemist/co-inventor with Dewar--cordite)
Abel, Iorwirth Wilbur (labor leader--United Steel Workers of Am.)
Abel, Walter (actor; Am.)
Abel/Abell, Thomas (priest) (Henry VIII's foe)
Abelard, Peter (intellectual/author--Sic Et Non) (Heloise's lover)
Abels, Rudolf (spy)
Abercrombie, David (businessman--Abercrombie & Fitch)
Abercromby, Ralph (Sir) (General--French Rev. Wars)
Abner (Norris Goff's pseudonym) (actor) (Lum's partner)
Abraham, F. Murray (actor--Amadeus)
Abram, Norm (handyman--This Old House)
Abramovitz, Max (architect--Lincoln Center)
Abrams, Jeffrey Jacob (J.J.) (producer/director--Star Trek)
Abzug, Bella (feminist)

AC/DC (musical group--The Black Ice, Hell's Bells)
Aces, Paul (actor--There Will Be Blood)
Achebe, Chinua (author--Things Fall Apart)
Acheson, Dean (author/diplomat)
Acheson, Edward (chemist)
Ackles, Jensen (director/singer/actor--Supernatural)
Ackroyd, Dan (actor)
Aco, Michel (explorer; Fr.)
Acorn, Milton (poet)
Acuff, Roy (singer--country)
Adair, Deborah (actress--Dynasty)
Adair, Gilbert (author--Love and Death on Long Island)
Adair, Jean (actress--Arsenic & Old Lace)
Adair, Red (oilwell firefighter)
Adam, Adolphe (author--Giselle)
Adam, Elina (composer--Cantique de Noel)
Adam, Robert (architect/furniture designer; Sc.)
Adams, Abigail (First Lady) (John's wife/John Quincy's mother)
Adams, Alice (author--Careless Love)
Adams, Amy (actress--Enchanted)
Adams, Ansel (photographer)
Adams, Bryan (singer/songwriter)
Adams, Cecil (author--The Straight Dope)
Adams, Edie (actress/singer) (Ernie Kovac's wife)
Adams, Franklin P. (newspaper columnist--The Conning Tower)
Adams, Henry (author/autobiographer--The Education of Henry Adams)
Adams, John (composer--Nixon in China)
Adams, John (politician) (Abigail's husband/John Quincy's father)
Adams, John Quincy (politician) (John & Abigail's son)
Adams, Lee (lyricist)
Adams, Louisa (J. Q.'s wife)
Adams, Maud (model/actress--Octopussy; Swed.)
Adams, Maude (actress--Peter Pan; Amer.)
Adams, Neile (actress) (Steve McQueen's wife)
Adams, Oleta (singer--soul--Get Here, All the Love)

Adams, Richard (author--Watership Down)
Adams, Samuel (statesman/philosopher)
Adams, Sarah (songwriter--Nearer My God to Thee)
Adams, Scott (cartoonist--Dilbert, Catbert)
Adams, William Taylor (pseudonym--Oliver Optic) (politician/author)
Adamson, Joy Friederike Victoria (author--Born Free)
Aday, Marvin Lee (pseudonym--Meatloaf) (musician--Bat Our of Hell)
Addams, Charles (Chas.) (cartoonist--The Addams Family in New Yorker & T. V.)
Addams, Jane (reformer/pacifist; Am.) (Ellen Gates Starr's partner) (Hull House founder)
Adderley, Nat (musician-cornet/sax)
Addison, Joseph (author--Ode to Creation, The Tatler, Spectators) (Steele's co-author)
Addy, Mark (actor)
Ade, George (humorist--slang/author--Fables in Slang, The Sultan of Sulu, Artie,   The College Widow, Doc Horne)
Adela (St. Adela) (William the Conqueror's daughter)
Adele (nee Adkins) (singer--Rolling in the Deep, Someone Like You, Skyfall, Send My Love)
Adelina, Patti (singer--soprano)
Adenauer, Konrad (Der Alte) (politician; Ger.)
Adjani, Isabelle (actress--Adeleh, Camille Claudel)
Adler, Alfred (psychoanalyst) (contemporaries--Freud & Jung)
Adler, Felix (educator/founder of Ethical movement; Am.)
Adler, Larry (musician--harmonica)
Adler, Lou (music producer)
Adler, Luther (actor)
Adler, Mortimer (philosopher/educator/author--How to Read a Book)
Adler, Pearl (Polly) (brothel madam--New York/author--A House is Not a Home)
Adler, Stella (actress)
Adler, Warren (author--The War of the Roses)
Adolfo (nee Adolfo Dominguez) (fashion designer)
Adoree, Renee (actress--The Bog Parade)

Adrian (Pope)
Adriano (soccer)
Adu, Fredua Koranteng (Freddie) (soccer)
Aduba, Uzo (singer/actress--Orange is the New Black--Crazy
Eyes)
Aerosmith (musical group--Cryin, Love In An Elevator)
Aeschylus (playwright--Oreteia, Seven Against Thebes)
Aesop (fabulist--The Two Pots, The Lion, The Bear and the
Fox, The Frog and the Ox)
Affleck, Ben (actor--Gigli, Argo)
Agamemnon (King--Trojan War)
Agar, John (actor--Sands of Iwo Jima)
Agassi, Andre (The Punisher) (tennis/author--Open)
Agee, James (film critic/poet--Permit Me
Voyage/author/screenwriter--African Queen, The
          Morning Watch, The Night of the Hunter, A Death in the
Family)
Agee, Philip (author--C.I.A. expose)
Agee, Tommie (baseball)
Ager, Milton (songwriter--Ain't She Sweet, Happy Days Are
Here Again)
Aglukark, Susan (singer)
Agnes (martyr)
Agnew, Spiro (politician)
Agnon, Shmuel Yosef (author)
Agricola, Julius (Gen.) (Roman governor of Britain)
Agrippina (Nero's mother)
Aguilera, Christina (singer)
a-ha (musical group; Oslo)
Ahern, Bertie (politician; Ir.)
Aherne, Brian (actor--Night to Remember, Juarez)
Ahmadinejad, Mahmoud (politician; Iran)
Ahmed, Ali (author)
Ahmose (Egyptian king)
Ahn, Philip (actor--Kung Fu)
Aiello, Danny (actor--Radio Days, Do the Right Thing)
Aiken, Conrad (poet)
Aikman, Troy (football)
Ailes, Roger (media exec.)

Ailey, Alvin (choreographer--ballet--Revelations)
Aimee (Sister Aimee) (evangelist--Foursquare Church)
Aimee, Anouk (actress--A Man and a Woman)
Ain, Noa (composer)
Ainge, Danny (basketball)
Aislin (Terry Mosher's pseudonym) (cartoonist--political)
Aivazavsky, Hovhannes (artist--seascapes)
Ajar, Emile (Romain Gary's pseudonym) (author--Momo)
Akbar (The Great) (emperor--Hindustan)
Akers, Karen (singer/actress--Nine)
Akers, Michelle (soccer)
Akers, Thomas (astronaut)
Akhenaten (a.k.a. Amenhotep IV) (pharaoh)
Akihito, Heisei Tenno (Emporer of Japan)
Akihito, Meguro K. (Emperor of Japan)
Akihito, Michiko (Heisei's wife)
Akihito, Tsugu (Emporer of Japan) (Showa Hirohito's son)
Akins, Claude (actor--Lobo)
Akins, Zoe (playwright/poet/author)
Akio, Morita (inventor--founder of SONY)
Akira, Kurosawa (director--Ran)
Akon (singer--Locked Up, Smack That)
Alabama (musical group--If I Had You, Christmas in Dixie)
Alagna, Roberto (singer--opera--tenor)
Alajuwon, Hakeem (basketball)
Alaman, Lucas (historian; Mex.)
Alaric (Visigoth king)
Alastair, Sim (actor--Scrooge)
Alba, Jessica (actress--Dark Angel, Into the Blue, Valentine's
Day, Barely Lethal) (The   Honest Company's
co-founder)
Albanese, Licia (singer--opera)
Albani, Emma (Marie Louise Cecile) (Dame) (singer--soprano-
-Elsa in Lohengrin)
Albano, Lou (wrestler)
Al-Bashir, Omar (politician; Sud.)
Albee, Edward (playwright--Tiny Alice, Three Tall Women, The
Goat or Who is Sylvia,   A Delicate Balance,
The Sandbox, Zoo Story, Fam and Yam)

Alben, William (politician)
Albeniz, Isaac (pianist/composer--Tango in D, Cantos de Espana)
Albers, Josef (artist--Op Art)
Albert, Eddie (actor/activist) (Margo's husband)
Albert, Margo (actress) (Eddie's wife)
Albinoni, Tomaso (composer)
Albom, Mitch (author--Tuesdays with Morrie)
Albright, Lola (actress)
Albright, Madeleine (politician/diplomat)
Alcindor, Lew (nee Kareem Abdul-Jabbar) (basketball)
Alcorn, Allan (computer scientist--Pong)
Alcott, Louisa May (author--Little Women, Jo's Boys, Eight Cousins, Little Men)
Alda, Alan (nee Alphonso D'Abruzzo) (actor--M.A.S.H., Betsy's Wedding, Jenny, Four Seasons,   Paper Lion, Sweet Liberty, The Aviator, Blacklist/ host--Scientific America Frontiers)
Alda, Frances (diva)
Alden, John (politician) (Plymouth Rock settler) (Priscilla's husband)
Alden, Priscilla (Plymouth Rock settler) (John's wife)
Aldiss, Brian Wilson (author--Frankenstein Unbound)
Aldrich, Ames (C.I.A. spy, fink)
Aldrich, Thomas Bailey (author--Marjorie Daw)
Aldridge, Ira (actor)
Aldrin, Edwin (Buzz) (astronaut)
Aleichem, Sholom (author--Tevye)
Aleman, Mateo (author--Guzman de Alfarache)
Aleman, Miguel (politician; Mex.)
Alexander the Great (Greek/Macedonian king) (Roxana's husband) (Roxana's husband)
Alexander, Erika (actress)
Alexander, Grover Cleveland (baseball)
Alexander, Lamar (politician)
Alexander, Shana (journalist/T.V. personality--60 Minutes/author--Astonishing   Elephant, Anyone's Daughter)
Alexis, Kim (model)

Al-Fayad, Dody (businessman/producer--Chariots of Fire)
Alfiero, Vittorio (Conte) (playwright; It.)
Alfonso (first Portugal king)
Alfonso's queen (Ena)
Alfred the Great (King of Wessex) (Ethelred's son, Egbert/Echberht's grandson)
Alger, Horatio (author--Ragged Dick, Luck & Pluck, Risen from the Ranks, Tattered Tom, Sink or Swim, Phil, the Fiddler)
Alget, Eugene (photographer)
Algren, Nelson (author--The Man with the Golden Arm)
Ali (7th century Arab caliph)
Ali, Laila (boxer)
Ali, Mahershala (actor--Moonlight, Green Book)
Ali, Muhammad (boxer)
Ali, Tatyana (actress--Fresh Prince of Bel Air)
Alicia, Ana (actress)
Alighieri, Dante (poet--Purgatorio, La Vita Nuova; It.)
Alioto, Joseph Lawrence (politician; San. Fran.)
Alito, Samuel (Supreme Court Justice) (O'Connor's successor)
Allah, Baha (prophet/founder of Baha'l faith)
Allan, John (merchant) (Edgar Allan Poe's adoptive father)
Allan, Ted (author--Love is a Long Shot)
Allegret, Marc (director)
Allegret, Yves (director)
Allen, Barbara Jo (a.k.a. Vera Vague) (actress)
Allen, Debbie (actress)
Allen, Ethan (soldier)
Allen, Fred (comedian)
Allen, Irwin (Master of Disaster) (director/producer--Time Tunnel, Lost in Space)
Allen, Jared (football)
Allen, Joan (actress)
Allen, Kris (musician/singer--American Idol)
Allen, Mel (sportscaster)
Allen, Red (trumpeter)
Allen, Steve (comedian/singer) (Jane Meadow's husband)
Allen, Tim (actor--Home Improvement)

Allen, Woody (actor/director--Radio Days, Scenes from A Mall, Zelig, Hannah, Anything Else, Sleeper, Crimes and Misdemeanors) (Soon Yi's husband)
Allende, Isabel (author--The House of the Spirits, Ines of My Soul)
Allende, Salvador (politician; Chili)
Alley, Kirstie (actress--Cheers)
Allgood, Sara (actress)
Allison, Francis (Fran) (singer/comedian/actress--Kookla, Fran & Ollie)
Allison, Mose (pianist--jazz)
Allman Brothers (musical group--Eat A Peach)
Allman, Duane (musician)
Allman, Gregg (singer) (Cher's ex.)
Allred, Gloria (attorney)
Allyson, June (actress—Two Girls and a Sailor, Little Women)
al-Maliki, Noari (politician; Iraq)
Almodovar, Pedro (director/screenwriter--Talk to Her)
Almond, Marc (singer)
Alomar, Roberto (baseball)
Alomar, Sandy (baseball)
Alonso, Alicia (dancer--ballet)
Alonso, Maria Conchita (singer-songwriter/actress--Caught)
Alou Felipe (baseball)
Alou, Jesus (baseball)
Alou, Matty (baseball)
Alou, Moises (baseball)
Alpert, Herb (trumpeter)
Alsop, Joseph (journalist/biographer--F.D.R./columnist--Matter of Fact)
Alsop, Stewart (journalist/columnist--Matter of Fact)
Alsop, Susan Mary (author--biographer)
Alston, Walter (Smokey) (baseball) (La Sorda's predecessor)
Alt, Carol (model/actress)
Altman, Robert (director--M.A.S.H., The Player, Nashville, Dr. T & The Woman, Welcome to L.A.)
Alto, Juhani (Johannes Brofeldt's pseudonym) (author)
Alvarado, Trini (actress--Little Women)
Alvarez, Juan (politician: Mex) (deposed Santa Ana)

Alvarez, Luis (physicist/nobelist)
Alver, Betti (poet)
Alzheimer, Alois (phychologist)
Amado, Jorge (author--Gabriela, Clove & Cinnamon, The Violent Land, Dona Flor and Her Two Husbands; Braz.)
Amati, Andrea (violin maker)
Amati, Nicolo (violin maker)
Amato, Pasqale (singer--opera--baritone)
Ambler, Eric (author--Journey Into Fear, Epitaph for a Spy)
Ambrose, Lauren (actress)
Ameche, Don (actor--Cocoon)
Amechi, Alan (football)
Amend, Bill (cartoonist--Fox Trot)
Amenhotep IV (a.k.a. Akhenaten) (pharaoh)
Ames, Aldrich (spy)
Ames, Ed (singer--My Cup Runneth Over/actor--Daniel Boone's Mingo)
Ames, Fisher (orator)
Ames, Leon (actor--Life with Father)
Ames, Louise Bates (psychologist) (co-authors Gesell & Ames)
Ames, Nancy (singer--T.W.3)
Amiel, Henri (poet; Swiss)
Amiel, Jon (director)
Amin, Idi (Wild Man of Africa) (dictator; Uganda) (Obote's predecessor)
Amis, Kingsley (author--Lucky Jim, Jake's Thing, The Old Devils, I Like It Here, Alteration, One Fat Englishman, The Green Man)
Amis, Martin (author--Night Train, London Fields, Yellow Dog, The Information, House of Meetings, Time's Arrow, The Rachel Papers, The Pregnant Widow) (Kingsley's son)
Amith, Anthony Terrell (nee Tone-Loc's) (actor/singer--rap)
Amory, Cleveland (animal rights activist/author--The Proper Bostonians)
Amos (preacher--8th century B. C.)
Amos, John (actor--Roots, Good Times)

Amos, Tori (singer—Under the Pink)
Amos, Wally (Famous) (entrepreneur--baking/literary advocate/host--Learn to Read)
Ampere, Andre (physicist)
Amsterdam, Morey (comedian)
Amundsen, Roald (explorer--North Pole)
Anders, William (astronaut)
Andersen, Adolf (chess champion)
Andersen, Eric (singer--folk)
Andersen, Hans Christian (author--The Red Shoes)
Andersen, Ivar (singer--basso)
Anderson, Brad (cartoonist--Marmaduke)
Anderson, Gillian (actress--X-Files)
Anderson, Ian (singer--Jethro Tull Band)
Anderson, Ivie (singer--jazz)
Anderson, Judith (actress--Medea)
Anderson, Laurie (singer/musician/artist)
Anderson, Leroy (conductor/composer--The Syncopated Clock, The Typewriter, Belle of the   Ball, Sleigh Ride0)
Anderson, Loni (actress) (Bert's ex)
Anderson, Louie (nee Louis Perry Anderson) (comedian/author--Letters from an Adult Child)
Anderson, Marian (singer--opera)
Anderson, Mary (inventor--windshield wiper)
Anderson, Maxwell (poet/author/playwright--High Tor, The Bad Seed/lyricist--   September Song, journalist)
Anderson, Neil (politician)
Anderson, Pamela (actress)
Anderson, Sherwood (author--Winesburg, Ohio)
Anderson, Wes (director--The Royal Tenenbaums, Isle of Dogs)
Anderson, Willie Lee (Flipper) (football)
Andersson, Arne (runner)
Andersson, Bibi (actress—I Never Promised You a Rose Garden, Wild Strawberries)
Andre, John (Major) (Br. officer/spy) (Benedict Arnold's accomplice)

Andresen, Ivar (singer--basso)
Andress, Ursula (actress--She)
Andretti, Mario (race car driver)
Andrews Sisters (musical group--Say Si Si, Bei Mi Bist Du
Schoen)
Andrews, Dana (actor)
Andrews, Erin (journalist/sportscaster/T.V. personality--Fox
Sports)
Andrews, Julie (actress/singer--The Sound of Music, S.O.B.)
Andrews, Laverne (singer--Andrews Sisters)
Andrews, Naveen (actor)
Andrews, Tige (actor--Mod Squad)
Andric, Ivo (author--The Bridge on the Drina)
Andropov, Yuri (politician; Ru.)
Anet, Claude (Jean Schopfer's pseudonym) (author) (Pierre
Loti's contemporary)
Anet, Jean-Baptiste (musician--violin)
Anfuso, Nella (diva--soprano--Gianni Schicchi)
Ange, Michel (Fr. translation of Michelangelo)
(sculptor/painter/architect/poet--High
        Renaissance)
Angeli, Pier (actress)
Angelico, Fra Giovanni (nee Guido di Pietro) (painter)
Angelil, Rene (manager) (wife--Celine Dion)
Angelou, Maya (poet--Gather Together in my Name, All God's
Children Need Traveling Shoes,   And Still I Rise)
Angle, Criss (illusionist)
Angstrom, Anders (physicist; Swed.)
Anheuser, Eberhard (beer brewer)
Aniston, Jennifer (actress--Friends, The Good Girl)
Anka, Paul (singer--Eso Beso, Lonely Boy, Dance On Little
Girl, Crazy Love, My Way,   Diana)
Anker, Samuel Albert (artist)
Ann (Eugene's aunt)
Anna (Freud's daughter)
Anna (Grandma Moses' first name)
Annan, Kofi Atta (politician) (U. N. Secretary; Ghana)
Anouilh, Jean (playwright)
Anouk, Aimee (actress)

Ansara, Michael (actor--Broken Arrow, Cochise)
Ansari, Aziz (filmmaker/comic/actor--Master of None)
Anselm (Saint) (founder of Scholasticism)
Ansermet, Ernest (conductor)
Anson, Cap (baseball)
Anspach, Susan (actress--Five Easy Pieces)
Ant, Adam (musician/singer)
Anthony, Carmelo Kyam (basketball)
Anthony, Earl (bowling)
Anthony, Marc (singer)
Anthony, Susan B. (activist--civil rights/ feminism)
Antin, Mary (author--The Promised Land)
Antoine, Herbert Jon (Tex) (weatherman)
Anton, Susan (actress/singer)
Antonioni, Michelangelo (director--La Notte)
Antuofermo, Vito (boxer)
Anu, Christine (singer)
Aoki, Hiroaki (Rocky) (wrestler/restauranteur--Benihana
founder)
Aoki, Isao (Tower) (golfer)
Aoki, Sass (golfer)
Aparicio, Luis (baseball)
Aparicio, Yalitza (actress--Roma
Apatow, Judd (comedian/producer/screenwriter/director--
Knocked Up, Bridesmaids, Trainwreck)
Apel, Johann August (jurist/author--ghost stories)
Apple, Fiona (singer/songwriter)
Apted, Michael (director--Gorillas in the Mist)
Aquinas, Thomas (Saint) (philosopher)
Aquino, Corazon (politician)
Arafat, Yasser/Yasir (politician--P.L.O. leader) (Mahmoud
Abbas's predecessor)
Arbuckle, Fatty (comedian)
Arbus, Diane (photographer)
Arcand, Denys (filmmaker)
Arcaro, Eddie (jockey)
Archer, Anne (actress--Fatal Attraction, Patriot's Game)
Archer, Beverly (actress--Mama's Family--Iola)
Archer, Jeffrey (author)

Archeys (musical group--Sugar Sugar)
Archibald, Nate (basketball)
Archilochus (poet--epodes)
Arcos, Rene (poet--Le Mal)
Arden, Elizabeth (nee Florence Nightingale Graham)
(cosmetologist)
Arden, Eve (actress)
Arden, Jann (singer)
Arendt, Hannah (author--Men in Dark Times, The Human
Condition/philosopher)
Arens, Moshe (politician; Isr.)
Arensky, Anton (composer)
Argento, Isia (actress)
Argerich, Martha (pianist)
Argote, Luis de Jonjora Y. (poet; Sp.)
Arias, Oscar (politician; Costa Rica)
Arie, India (singer--soul)
Arion (poet--dithyramb; Gr.)
Arista, Mariano (politician; Mex.)
Aristophanes (comic playwright--Wasps)
Aristotle (philosopher/polymath/author--Metaphysics, Treatise-
-Ethics)   (Plato's student,
Alexander's teacher)
Arius (theologian--Greek Christian)
Arkin, Adam (actor--Chicago Hope) (Alan's son)
Arkin, Alan (actor--Havana, Popi, Argo, Little Miss Sunshine,
The In-Laws) (Adam's father)
Arledge, Rune (Roone) (sportscaster)
Arlen, Harold (composer--Stormy Weather, Over the Rainbow,
I Love a Parade, Let's Fall in Love,   Right As Rain, I've
Got the World on a String, Hooray for Love, Blues in the Night,
                    That Old Black Magic, Green Hat, Wizard
of Oz)
Arlen, Michael (author)
Arlen, Richard (actor)
Arliss, George (actor--Disraeli)
Armani, Giorgio (fashion designer)
Armantrout, Rae (poet)
Armas, Tony (baseball)

Armen (singer--Stop the Music)
Armendariz, Pedro (actor)
Armey, Dick (politician)
Armisen, Fred (actor)
Armour, Tommy (golf)
Armstrong, Bess (actress)
Armstrong, Lance (cyclist)
Armstrong, Louis (musician--trumpet/composer/singer--How High the Moon)
Armstrong, Lucas (sportscaster--basketball)
Armstrong, Neil Alden (astronaut)
Armstrong, Otis (football)
Arnaz, Desi (singer--Dino, Desi & Billy) (autobiography--A Book)
Arnaz, Desiderio (Desi) (comedian/actor/musician)
Arne, Thomas (composer--Rule Brittania, Artaxerxes, Dido and Aeneas, Judith, Comus, A Hunting We Will Go)
Arness, James (actor--Gunsmoke, How the West Was Won)
Arnett, Peter (reporter)
Arno, Peter (cartoonist)
Arno, Sig (actor)
Arnold, Benedict (military officer/spy) (John Andre's co-conspirator)
Arnold, Eddy (actor)
Arnold, Edwin (Sir) (poet)
Arnold, Henry Harley (Hap) (Gen.--W. W. II)
Arnold, Matthew (critic/poet--Empedocles on Etna)
Arnold, Tom (actor)
Arnott, Peter (journalist)
Arone, Shidane (Somali youth beaten to death by Can. Airborne Regiment)
Aronofsky, Darren (director--Black Swan)
Arouet, Francois Marie (pseudonym--Voltaire) (author)
Arp, Jean (nee Hans) (author--Dreams and Projects/sculptor--dadaist/surrealist--Human Concretion, Head and Shell, Der Blaue Reiter, Leotard, Silhouette, Cloud Shepherd, A Navel, Birds in An Aquarium, Leaves and Navels)

Arpel, Adrien (cosmetologist)
Arquette, Patricia (actress)
Arrau, Claudio (pianist--Chilean) (Beethoven's interpreter)
Artest, Ron (basketball)
Arthur, Bea (actress)
Arthur, Chester Alan (Chet) (politician)
Arthur, Jean (actress--You Can't Take It With You)
Arundhati, Roy (author/activist; India)
Asada, Mao (figure skater)
Asahara, Shoko (Chizuo Mastsumoto's pseudonym) (cult figure--gas attacks)
Asch, Sholem (author--The Nazarene, Moses, Chaim Lederer's Return, The Apostle, Uncle Moses)
Ashanti (singer--Foolish)
Ashby, Alan (baseball)
Ashe, Arthur (tennis/author--Days of Grace, Hard Road to Glory, Off the Court)
Ashe, Rosalind (author--Moths)
Ashe, Samual (politician)
Asher, Peter (musician--Peter and Gordon)
Ashley, Laura (designer; Am.)
Ashman, Howard (lyricist)
Ashmore, Aaron (actor)
Ashton, Frederick (dancer--ballet/choreographer--Ondine)
Asia (musical group--Heat of the Moment)
Asimov, Isaac (author--sci.fi.--I Robot, The Stars, Like Dust, Murder at the Aba, Nemesis,   Puzzles of the Black Widowers, The Robots of Dawn, Nightfall, Foundation)
Asner, Ed (actor--Roots, Up)
Asoka (Buddhist king of India)
Asper, Izzy (entrepreneur--Can West Global)
Asperger, Hans (pediatrician)
Aspin, Les (politician--Clinton cabinet)
Asquith, Ros (author)
Assange, Julian (editor/publisher/activist--WikiLeaks)
Assante, Armand (actor--Gotti, The Funeral, The Mambo King)
Asser, Tobis (legal scholar/international lawyer)
Association (musical group--Cherish)

Astacio, Pedro (baseball)
Astaire, Adele (dancer) (autobiography--Steps in Time) (Fred's sister)
Astaire, Fred (nee Frederick Austerlitz) (dancer/actor--Daddy Longlegs, Second Chorus)
        (Adele's brother)
Asther, Nils (actor)
Astin, John (actor--Adams Family, Viva Max)
Astin, Mackenzie (actor)
Astin, Sean Patrick (director/actor--Lord of the Rings, Rudy, Stranger Things)
Astley, Rick (singer--Never Gonna Give You Up)
Astor, Brooke Russel (philanthropist)
Astor, John Jacob (Colonel) (fur trader/Titanic passenger)
Astor, Mary (actress--Maltese Falcon)
Astor, Nancy (politician)
Astor, Violet Elliot (Lady) (politician; Br.)
Atahualpa (Inca emporer)
Ataturk, Mustafa Kemal Pasha (Father of the Turks) (politician)
Ates, Roscoe (actor/comedian)
Atkins, Chet (singer--country)
Atkins, Coral (actress)
Atkinson, Rowan (actor--Mr. Bean)
Atkov, Oleg (cosmonaut)
Atli (a.k.a. Attila) (Hun king/Gudrun's victim)
Attell, Abe (boxer)
Attell, Dave (comedian)
Attenborough, Richard (actor/director--Chaplin, Ghandi)
Attila (a.k.a. Atli) (Scourge of God) (Hun king/Gudrun's victim)
Attlee, Clement Richard (politician--P.M.; Br.)
Attucks, Crispus (patriot)
Atwal, Arjun (golfer)
Atwood, Margaret (author--Bluebeard's Egg, Alias Grace, Oryx and Crake)
Auber, Daniel-Francois-Esprit (composer--Fra Diavolo)
Auberjonois, Rene (actor--Benson, Star Trek--Odo)
Auden, Wystan Hugh (poet--The Age of Anxiety, Homage to Clio, Funeral Blues,   As I Walked Out One

Evening, Look Stranger, The Shield of Achilles, For the Time
              Being, Another Time)
Audubon, John James (ornithologist/painter--wildlife)
Auel, Jean M. (author--Clan of Cave Bear, Earth's Child)
Auer, Leopold (violinist; Hung.) (Efrem Zimbalist's/Mischa
Elman's/Jascha Heifetz/   Yehudi Menuhin's
teacher)
Auer, Mischa (actor--You Can't Take It With You)
Auerbach, Artie (actor/comedian)
Auf der Maur, Nick (journalist)
Augmon, Stacey (basketball)
Augustus (politician) (Tiberius successor)
Aulette, Ken (author)
Aulin, Ewa (actress)
Aurelius, Marcus (author)
Austen, Jane (author--Northanger Abbey, Emma, Mansfield
Park)
Austerlitz, Frederick (a.k.a. Fred Astaire) (dancer/actor)
Austin, Gene (author--My Blue Heaven)
Austin, Stephen F. (Father of Texas) (politician/settler--Brazos
R.)
Austin, Teri (actress--Knot's Landing)
Autry, Gene (singer--Here Comes Santa Claus/actor)
Avedon, Richard (photographer--In the American West)
Averback, Hy (director)
Avery, Tex (cartoonist--Bugs Bunny)
Avila, Bobby (baseball)
Avildsen, John G. (filmwriter/director)
Avital, Mili (actress)
Avogadro, Amedeo (physician/mathematician)
Avon, Earl of (name Eden, Anthony) (Lord) (politician)
Awkwafina (singer/actress--Crazy Rich Asians)
Axl Rose (singer--Welcome to the Jungle)
Axton, Hoyt (singer--country)
Aybar, Erick (baseball)
Ayckbourn, Alan (playwright)
Ayer, Alfred Jules (Freddie) (philosopher)
Ayer, Nat (composer)
Ayesha (Mohammed's favorite wife)

Aykroyd, Dan (actor)
Ayme, Marcel (author/essayist/playwright)
Ayres, Lew (actor--Dr. Kildare, All's Quiet on the Western
Front)
Azalea, Iggy (singer--rap--Fancy)
Azaria, Hank (direcftor/actor/voice actor--The Simpsons (Apu))
Aziz, Tariq (politician; Iraq)
Azuma, Atsuko (singer--soprano)

--B--

B Cardi (singer--Bodak Yellow)
B-52 (musical group) (Kate Pierson's group)
Babatunde, Obba (singer/dancer)
Babbitt, Tabitha (inventor--circular saw)
Babel, Isaak (author--Odessa Tales)
Babilonia, Tai (figure skater)
Bacall, Lauren (actress--Key Largo, The Big Sleep, Applause,
Clap Clap)
Bach, Johann Sebastian (composer--toccata/masses--Passion
According to St. John,   Partita, Sheep May
Safely Graze, Goldberg Variations, Jesu, Joy of Man's
                    Desiring, St. Matthew's Passion, The Art
of Fugue, Coffee Contata, St. John's
          Passion, Mass in B Minor) (P. D. Q.'s father)
Bach, P.D.Q. (composer--masses--Oedipus Tex, A Little
Nightmare Music) (Johann's son)   (pseudonym--
Peter Schickele)
Bacharach, Burt (musician--
composer/pianist/singer/songwriter) (Hal David's partner)
Bachardy, Don (painter--portraits) (Christopher Isherwood's
partner)
Bacheller, Addison Irving (journalist/author--Eben Holden)
Bachman, Tal (singer--pop)
Backstreet Boys (musical group--Yes I Will)
Backus, Jim (actor--Gilligan's Island, Mr. Magoo)
Bacon, Francis (painter)

Bacon, Francis (Sir) (author/philosopher)
Bacon, Kevin (actor--The Air I Breathe, Animal House)
Bacon, Roger (Admirable Doctor Mirabilis)
(friar/philosopher/scientist/
        theologian--Franciscan)
Badel, Alan (actor)
Badu, Erykah (singer--On & On)
Baeda (Saint) (scholar)
Baer, Arthur (Bugs) (journalist)
Baer, Buddy (boxer)
Baer, Max (boxer)
Baer, Max Jr. (actor--Beverly Hillbillies)
Baerga, Carlos (baseball)
Baez, Joan (singer--Farewell Angelina, Diamonds and Rust,
We Shall Overcome)
Baeze, Braullo (jockey)
Bagnold, Enid (author--Serena Blandish)
Baha Men (musical group--Who Let the Dogs Out)
Bahau'llah (religious leader; Persia)
Bahr, Matt (football)
Bai, Li (poet)
Bai, Matt (author--politics)
Bailey, F. Lee (lawyer)
Bailey, Pearl Mae (singer)
Bain, Barbara (actress--Mission Impossible)
Baio, Scott (actor--Happy Days, Bugsy Malone)
Baird, Bil (puppeteer)
Baird, Cora (puppeteer)
Baird, John (inventor--television)
Baird, Zoe (lawyer/activist--Markle Foundation Pres.)
Baiul, Oksana (figure skater)
Baker, Anita (singer--Sweet Love)
Baker, Chet (trumpeter--jazz--Let's Get Lost)
Baker, Diane (actress/producer)
Baker, Etta (musician--blues)
Baker, Howard (politician--Reagan's Chief of Staff)
Baker, Janet Abbott (singer--opera)
Baker, Joe Don (actor)
Baker, John Franklin (Home Run) (baseball)

Baker, Mark Linn (actor--Perfect Strangers)
Baker, Norma Jean (pseudonym--Marilyn Monroe)
(actress/singer)
Baker, Russell (author)
Bakker, Jim (P.T.L. evangelist)
Bakula, Scott (actor--Enterprise)
Bal Geddes, Barbara (actress--Dallas)
Balaban, Liane (actress)
Balakirev, Mily (composer--Thamar/Tamara)
Balanchine, George (choreographer--Roma, Agon (ballet)
Balau, Horst (ski jumper)
Balbo, Italo (politician/soldier/aviator) (Mussolini's heir)
Baldwin, Alec (actor--Match Game)
Bale, Christian (actor)
Balfe, Michael William (composer--Arline)
Balfour, Arthur James (politician; Br.)
Balfour, David (politician; Can.)
Balin, Ina (actress)
Ball, Alan (director/producer/writer--Six Feet Under, American
Beauty)
Ball, Lucille (comedian)
Ballantine, Ian (publisher)
Ballard, Florence (singer--Supremes)
Ballesteros, Seve (golfer)
Balli, Melvin (lawyer)
Balogh, Erno (musician--piano)
Balsam, Martin (Marty) (actor--Tora, Tora, Tora)
Balzac, Honore (playwright/author--Une Tenebreuse Affaire (A
Shadowy Affair),   Adieu, Cesar
Birotteau, Le Pere Gariot, La Tulipe Noire)
Bana, Eric (actor--The Incredible Hulk, Troy)
Banana Rama (musical group--Venus)
Banchieri, Adriano (composer)
Bancroft, Anne (nee Anna Maria Italiano) (actress--Golda
Meir, Miracle Worker)
Banderas, Antonio (actor)
Bandy, Moe (singer)
Bangles (musical group--Eternal Flame)
Bani-Sadr, Abolhassan (politician; Iran)

Bankhead, Tallulah (actress)
Banks, Ernie (baseball)
Banks, Leanne (author--Some Girls Do)
Banks, Tyra (model)
Banky, Vilma (actress)
Baquet, Dean (journalist)
Bara, Theda (actresss--vamp--Cleopatra)
Barak, Ehud (politician; Isr.)
Baraka, Amiri (a.k.a. Everett LeRoi Jones) (poet--The Black Experience)
Barbeau, Adrienne (actress--Maude)
Barber, Red (sportscaster)
Barber, Samuel (composer)
Barbusse, Henri (author)
Barca, Hannibal (Carthaginian general)
Barcelata, Lorenzo (composer--Maria Elena)
Bardot, Brigitte (actress--And God Created Woman)
Bare Naked Ladies (musical group--One Week)
Bareilles, Sara (singer--Love Song)
Bari, Lynn (actress)
Baring-Gould, Sabine (priest/author/composer--Marching As To War)
Barker, Clive (author--horror--Everville)
Barker, Lex (actor--Tarzan)
Barkin, Ellen (actress--Sea of Love)
Barklely, Charles (Sir Charles) (basketball)
Barkley, Alben (politician--Truman's V.P.)
Barkley, Ivan (The Blade) (boxer)
Barlow, Kevan (football)
Barnacle, Nora (muse) (James Joyce's wife)
Barnard, Christiaan (physician--transplant)
Barnes, Billie (photographer)
Barnes, Binnie (actress)
Barnes, Clive (critic)
Barnes, Julian (critic/author--short stories)
Barnes, Randy (athlete--shot put)
Barnett, Dick (basketball)
Barnett, Vince (actor)
Barnum, Phineas Taylor (circus owner)

Baroja, Pio (author; Basque)
Barr, Nevada (author--mystery)
Barr, Roseanne (comedian/actress--She Devil)
Barr, William Pelham (politician--Bush's Attorney Gen.)
Barr, Yvonee (virologist--Epstein-Barr virus)
Barraud, Francis (painter--The Master's Voice)
Barrett, Rona (columnist--gossip)
Barrett, Syd (musician--Pink Floyd)
Barrett, Tina (singer/songwriter/actress) (band--S Club 7)
Barrie, James Matthew (author--Peter Pan, Auld Licht Idylls,
Dear Brutus/   playwright--The Admirable
Crichton, Quality Street)
Barrie, Mona (actress)
Barrow, Clyde (criminal--Bonnie Parker & Clyde)
Barrow, Ed (baseball)
Barrows, Sydney Biddle (Mayflower Madame)
(author/columnist)
Barry, Dave (author--humorist)
Barry, Gene (actor--Bat Masterson)
Barry, Len (singer--1-2-3)
Barry, Philip (playwright--Paris Bound)
Barrymore, Drew (actress)
Barrymore, Ethel (actress)
Barrymore, John (The Great Profile) (actor--Mr. Hyde, Ahab)
Barrymore, Lionel (actor--Arsene Lupin)
Barth, John (author--Giles Goat-Boy)
Barth, Karl (theologian)
Bartholdi, Frederic (sculptor--Statue of Liberty)
Bartiromo, Maria (journalist, author, editor--Fox Business
Network)
Bartlett, John (publisher/author--Bartlett's Familiar Quotations)
Bartley, Luella (fashion designer/journalist)
Bartok, Bela (composer--Miraculous Mandarin, Mikrokosmos;
Hung.)
Bartok, Eva (actress)
Barton, Clara (nurse--Red Cross)
Baruch, Bernard (author--My Own Story/financier/stock
investor/philanthropist/
         statesman/political consultant)

Baryshnikov, Mikhail (dancer--ballet)
Basie, William (Count) (musician/pianist--jazz--Swingin The Blues, One O'Clock Jump)
Basil, Toni (singer--Hey Mickey)
Baskin, Elya (actor--Air Force One)
Bass, Lance (musician--NSync)
Bass, Sam (desperado)
Basset, Brian (cartoonist--Adam)
Bassett, Angela (actress--Blood & Sand)
Bassey, Shirley (singer--Goldfinger)
Bateman, Jason (actor)
Bateman, Justine (actress)
Bates, Alan (actor--King of Hearts)
Bates, Arlo (author/poet)
Bates, Katharine Lee (songwriter--America the Beautiful)
Batista, Fulgencio (Cuban president) (overthrown by Castro)
Battier, Shane (basketball)
Baudelaire, Charles (author--Paris Spleen, Les Fleurs du Mal)
Bauer, Bruno (philosopher)
Bauer, Hank (baseball)
Baum, Lyman Frank (author--Wizard of Oz, Rinkitink in Oz, Queen Zixi of Ix)
Baum, Vicki (author--The Grand Hotel, The Grand Opera)
Bavier, Frances (actress--Andy Griffith Show)
Baxter, Anne (actress--Eve)
Baxter, Les (bandleader)
Baxter, Tom (singer; Br.)
Bayes, Nora (singer--Shine On Harvest Moon)
Bayh, Evan (politician)
Bayle, Pierrre (philosopher)
Baylor, Elgin (basketball)
Bazille, Frederic (artist--Fisherman with a Net)
Bea (Eugenie's big sister)
Beach Boys (musical group--Kokomo, California Girls, It's OK)
Beach, Adam (actor)
Beach, Amy Marcey Cheney (painter)
Beach, Michael (actor--Third Watch)
Beal, Andy (banker)
Beals, Jennifer (actress--Flash Dance)

Beame, Abe (politician)
Beamon, Bob (long jumper)
Bean, Alan (astronaut)
Bean, Leon Leonwood (business exec.) (L. L. Bean store chain founder)
Bean, Orson (actor)
Bean, Sean (actor--The Lord of the Rings)
Beard, Daniel Carter (historian/Boy Scout founder)
Beart, Emmanuelle (actress--Mission Impossible)
Beasley, Allyce (actress--Moonlighting)
Beastly Boys (musical group--Licensed to Ill)
Beatles (musical group--Honey Pie, Ask Me Why, I've Just Seen a Face, Hey Jude, She's Leaving Home, I Feel Fine, Roll Over Beethoven, Girl, If I Fell, I'm So Tired, She's a Woman, I'm a Loser, When I'm Sixty-Four) (movie--Help)
Beaton, Cecil (fashion photographer/painter/diarist/interior designer/stage and costume designer)
Beattie, Ann (author--Chilly Scenes of Winter)
Beattie, James (poet--The Minstrel)
Beatty, Ned (actor)
Beatty, Warren (actor/director--Shampoo, Bulworth, Ishtar, Reds, Bugsy Malone, McCabe and Mrs. Miller)
Beaumarchais, Pierre (playwright--Barber of Seville)
Beaumont, Francis (dramatist--The Scornful Lady) (Fletcher's collaborator)
Beck (singer--Loser)
Beck, Sanderson (English version of Isha Upanishad)
Becker, Walter (musician/vocal bassist--Steely Dan--A.J.A.)
Beckett, Samuel (author--Godot, End Game: A Play In One Act, Krapp's Last Tape, No's Knife)
Beckinsale, Kate (actress)
Beckmann, Petr (physicist)
Becquerel, Antoine Henri (physicist/nobelist)
Bede (Father of English History) (historian/theologian--Anglo Sason; Br.)
Bedelia, Bonnie (actress)
Bedingfield, Natasha (singer--pop)

Bee Gees (musical group--Odessa, How Deep Is Your Love, Stayin Alive)
Beebe, Charles William (scientist--bathysphere/author--Half Mile Down)
Beebe, Don (football)
Beecham, Thomas (Sir) (conductor--London Philharmonic)
Beecroft, John (author--Plain and Fancy Cats)
Been, Dirk (teacher/Survivor participant)
Beene, Geoffrey (designer)
Beerbohm, Max (essayist/parodist/caricaturist)
Beers, Clifford Whittingham (psychologist--mental hygiene)
Beery, Noah (actor)
Beery, Wallace (actor--Richard the Lionhearted, Viva Villa)
Beethoven, Ludwig Van (pianist/composer--Minuet in G, Les Adieux, Sinfonia Eroica, Elise,   Missa Solemnis, The Harp Quartet, Leonore Overture, Kakadu (piano trio),   Ninth (paean)) (Haydn's pupil)
Bega, Lou (lyricist--Mambo #5)
Begin, Menachem (politician; Isr.)
Begin, Monique (politician; Can.)
Behan, Brendan (playwright/satirist--Borstal Boy, The Quare Fellow)
Behar, Joy (comedian/author/actress/talk show co-host--The View)
Behn, Aphra (author/playwright/poet/translator)
Behn, Noel (author)
Bei, Liu (warrior)
Bejart, Maurice (dancer--ballet)
Bel Geddes, Norman (architect/industrial engineer)
Belafonte, Harry (singer--calypso--Matilda)
Belafonte, Shari (actress)
Beli/Heli (King; Br.) (Lud/LLud/Lludd's father)
Bell, Acton (Anne Bronte's pseudonym) (author)
Bell, Biv Devoe (musician--rap)
Bell, Catherine (golfer)
Bell, Currer (Charlotte Bronte's pseudonym) (author)
Bell, Ellis (Emily Bronte's pseudonym) (author)
Bellamann, Henry (author--King's Row)
Bellamy, Francis (author--Pledge of Allegance)

Bellamy, Ralph (actor--Sunrise at Campobello)
Belli, Melvin (attorney)
Bellinger, Eric (singer-songwriter/record producer)
Bellini, Giovanni (painter--Coronation of the Virgin) (Titian's teacher)
Bellini, Vincenzo (composer--opera--Norma, I Puritani, A Te O Cara, Casta Diva (aria))
Belloc, Hilaire (satirist--Wolsey, Cautionary Tales)
Bellow, Saul (author/nobelist--The Adventures of Augie March, Herzog, Seize the Day)
Bellows, George Wesley (painter--realism--Stag at Starkey's)
Bellows, Gil (actor)
Beltran, Robert (actor)
Belushi, Jim (actor)
Belushi, John (actor)
Bely, Andrei (poet/theorist)
Bemis, Samuel Flagg (historian/biographer--J.Q. Adams)
Ben Folds Five (musical group)
Ben, Jorge (musician/songwriter--Mas Que Nada)
Benaderet, Bea (actress)
Benatar, Pat (singer)
Benchley, Peter (author--The Deep)
Benchley, Robert (actor/critic/author--From Bed to Worse, The Sex Life of a Polyp)
Benedict, Dirk (actor)
Benes, Edvard (politician; Czech.)
Benet, Eric (singer-songwriter--R&B)
Benet, Laura (author-poet--The Hidden Valley)
Benet, Stephen Vincent (author--The Devil and Daniel Webster/poet--John Brown's Body)
Benet, William Rose (author/poet--The Dust Which is God)
Benigni, Roberto (screenwriter/director/actor--Life is Beautiful)
Bening, Annette (actress--Love Affair)
Benirschke, Rolf (football)
Benitez, Elsa (model)
Benjamin, Richrd (actor--Goodbye Columbus)
Bennet, Richard Dyer (musician)
Bennett, Enid (actress)
Bennett, Reese (actor--Loredo)

Bennett, Tony (singer--Because of You)
Benning, Annette (actress)
Benson, Amber (actress)
Benson, Edward Frederic (author--Mapp & Lucia)
Benson, Ezra Taft (Mormon leader)
Benson, Frank Weston (painter--impressionism)
Bentham, Jeremy (philosopher/economist/theoretical jurist; Br.)
Bentley, Edmund Clerihew (author--Detective Trent)
Bentley, Wes (actor--American Beauty)
Benton, Barbi (singer)
Benton, Robert (director--Kramer vs. Kramer)
Benton, Thomas Hart (muralist/painter--Cave Spring, Homestead, Self Portrait with Rita)
Benvenuti, Nino (boxer)
Beny, Roloff (photographer)
Benz, Karl (automaker)
Benzell, Mimi (singer--opera)
Berdych, Tomas (tennis)
Berenson, Marisa (actress)
Berenstain, Jan (author--Berenstain Bears)
Berenstain, Stan (author--Berenstain Bears)
Berg, Aki (hockey)
Berg, Alban (composer--opera--Wozzack, Lulu, Der Wein)
Berg, Dave (cartoonist--Mad)
Berg, Morris (Moe) (baseball/spy)
Berg, Patty (golfer)
Berganza, Teresa (singer--mezzo)
Bergen, Candice (actress)
Bergen, Edgar (actor/ventriloquist)
Bergen, Erich (actor--Jersey Boys)
Berger, Erna (singer--soprano)
Berger, Oscar (caricaturist/cartoonist)
Berger, Senta (actress)
Berger, Thomas (author--Little Big Man)
Bergman, Alan (lyricist)
Bergman, Ingmar (writer/director--The Seventh Seal, Scenes From a Marriage)

Bergman, Ingrid (actress--Ilsa in Casa Blanca, Anastasia, Joan of Arc, Indiscreet) (Pia Lindstrom's mother)
Bergner, Elisabeth (actress)
Bergonzi, Carlo (singer--tenor)
Bergson, Henri Louis (philosopher/author)
Beria, Lavrenti Pavlovich (politician; Soviet)
Berigan, Rowland Bernard (Bunny) (musician--trumpet--jazz)
Bering, Vitus (explorer)
Berkeley, Busby (born William Berkeley Enos) (choreographer/director)
Berle, Milton (comedian)
Berlin, Ellin (author) (Irving's wife)
Berlin, Irving (nee Israel Baline) (composer--All Alone, I Love a Piano, Call Me Madam, You'd Be Surprised, When I Lost You, Easter Parade, White Christmas, Mandy, Blue Skies, He's a Rag Picker, Snooky Ookums, Araby, I Got Lost in His Arms, Sadie Salome (Go Home), God Bless America, The Song is Ended, Puttin on the Ritz, There's No Business Like Show Business, Cheek to Cheek) (Ellin's husband)
Berlin, Isaiah (political theorist, philosopher, historian, scholar; Jewish)
Berliner, Emile (inventor--microphone)
Berlioz, Hector (composer--opera--Les Troyens, Symphonie Fantastique, Les Nuits d'Ete, Harold in Italy, Damnation of Faust)
Berman, Len (sportscaster)
Berman, Pandro (producer)
Berman, Shelley (comedian)
Bernanke, Ben (economist)
Bernardi, Mario (conductor)
Berndt, Walter (cartoonist--Smitty)
Berne, Eric (author--Games People Play, What Do You Say After You Say Hello)
Bernhardt, Sarah (actress)
Bernier, Sylvie (diver)
Bernini, Gian Lorenzo (sculptor)

Bernoulli, Daniel (mathematician) (Euler's student)
Bernsen, Corbin (actor--L.A. Law)
Bernstein, Aline (designer--stage)
Bernstein, Benjamin (pseudonym--Ben Blue) (actor/comedian/dancer)
Bernstein, Bonnie (journalist--sports)
Bernstein, Carl (journalist)
Bernstein, Elmer (composer)
Bernstein, Leonard (Len) (conductor/author/music lecturer/pianist/
        composer--A Boy Like That, Maria, Candide (exorcism))
Berra, Yogi (baseball)
Berry, Chuck (musician--Johnny Be Good, Almost Grown, Nadine)
Berry, Halle (actress--Boomerang)
Berry, Ken (actor)
Berry, Wendell (author)
Berryhill, Damon (author)
Bertolucci, Bernardo (director--Luna; It.)
Berton, Pierre (author)
Besey, Gary (actor--Buddy Holly Story)
Bessemer, Sir Henry (inventor--steel)
Besser, Joe (actor--Three Stooges) (replaced Shemp Howard)
Besson, Luc (director)
Best, Edna (actress--The Man Who Knew Too Much)
Best, Pete (drummer--Beatles pre Ringo)
Bettelheim, Bruno (psychologist/author--Children of the Dream)
Better Than Ezra (musical group)
Bettger, Lyle (actor)
Betti, Ugo (poet/playwright/author/judge)
Bevan, Aneurin (Nye)(politician; Welsh)
Bevan, Bev (musician--drummer--ELO)
Bevin, Ernest (politician)
Bey, Turhan (actor)
Beyle, Marie-Henri (pseudonym--Stendhal) (author)
Beyonce (a.k.a. Sasha Fierce) (singer-songwriter--End of Time/actress--The Lion   King--Nala)

Bezos, Jeff (Amazon founder)
Bhraonain, Eithne Patricia Ni (a.k.a. Enya) (musician)
Bhutto, Benazir (politician; Pak.)
Bhutto, Zulfigar Ali (politician; Pak.)
Bibb, Leslie (actress--The Skulls)
Biden, Joseph (politician)
Bidu, Sayao (diva)
Bieber, Justin (singer/sonwriter--Eenie Meenie) (Kingston collaborator)
Biehn, Michael (actor)
Biel, Jessica (actress--Seventh Heaven, The Illusionist)
Bierce, Ambrose (author--The Devil's Dictionary)
Big Boi (rapper)
Bigelow, Erastus Brigham (industrialist/inventor--power loom)
Bigelow, Jacob (physician/botanist/author--M. I. T. founder)
Bigelow, Kathryn Ann (director/producer/writer)
Biggers, Earl Derr (author--Charlie Chan)
Biggio, Craig (baseball)
Biggs, Jason (actor--American Pie)
Bikel, Theodore (actor--The Defiant Ones/folk singer/composer/activist)
Biko, Steven (founder of Black Consciousness, martyr; S. Af.)
Billy the Kid (nee William Bonney) (outlaw)
Binchy, Maeve (author--Circle of Friends)
Binet, Alfred (I. Q. Test pioneer)
Bing, Dave (basketball)
Bing, Ilse (photographer)
Bingham, Traci (actress)
Binoche, Juliette (actress--L'Heure d'Ete)
Biondi, Matt (swimmer)
Birch, Bayh (politician)
Birch, Harvey (spy)
Birch, Thora (actress--American Beauty)
Bird, Larry (basketball)
Bird, Sue (basketball)
Birdsong, Otis (basketball)
Birnbaum, Nathan (George Burn's pseudonym) (actor/comedian)
Bishop, Billy (pilot--W.W. I)

Bishop, Elizabeth (poet/author--short stories)
Bishop, Joey (nee Joseph Abraham Gottlieb) (comedian/variety-game show host/ actor--Ocean's Eleven)
Bismarck, Otto von (politician; Prussian)
Bisset, Jacqueline (actress)
Bissoondath, Neil (author)
Bittle, Jerry (cartoonist--Shirley & Son)
Bizet, Georges (composer--opera--Carmen, L'Arlesienne, Ivan IV, The Girl from Arles, The Pearl Fishers, Roma)
Bjork (singer, songwriter, actress; Iceland)
Black Sabath (musical group)
Black, Clint (singer--country--Killin Time)
Black, Hugo (justice)
Black, Jack (musician/actor--Shallow Hal)
Black, Karen (actress--Nashville)
Black, Lewis (comedian)
Black, Lucas (actor)
Black, Maher (sportscaster)
Blackbeard (nee Marshall D. Teach) (pirate)
Blackhearts (musical group) (Joan Jett's group)
Blackmore, Richard (author--Lorna Doone)
Blackwell, Ewell (baseball--pitcher)
Blades, Ruben (actor/politician/singer--salsa; Pan.)
Blaine, David (magician)
Blair, Betsy (actress)
Blair, Bonnie (speed skater)
Blair, Eric Arthur (George Orwell's pseudonym) (author)
Blair, Linda (actress--The Exorcist)
Blair, Selma (actress)
Blake, Eubie (composer--ragtime--I'm Just Wild About Harry, Memories of You)
Blake, Rebecca (singer--Amuse Me)
Blake, Robert (actor--Baretta)
Blake, William (poet--The Book of Los/mystic/painter/engraver)
Blakley, Ronee (actress)
Blanchett, Cate (actress--Elizabeth, Blue Jasmine)

Blanda, George (football)
Blane, Ralph (author--Have Yourself a Merry Little Xmas)
Blas, Gil (actor)
Blass, Bill (fashion designer)
Blavatnik, Len (businessman/investor/philanthropist)
Bledel, Alexis (actress--Gilmore Girls)
Bleeth, Yasmine (actress--Bay Watch)
Blegen, Judith (diva)
Blethyn, Brenda (actress)
Blige, Mary Jane (singer-songwriter)
Bliss, Arthur Drummond (Sir) (composer)
Blitzer, Wolf (journalist/newsman)
Blixen, Karen (pseudonym--Isak Dinesen) (Baroness) (author)
Bloch, Ernest (composer--America)
Bloch, Feliz (physicist/nobelist)
Bloch, Konrad Emil (chemist/nobelist)
Bloch, Robert (author--Psycho)
Blocker, Dan (actor--Bonanza)
Blondie (musical group--Call Me)
Bloom, Claire (actress)
Bloom, Molly (entrepreneur/speaker/author)
Bloomer, Amelia (feminist)
Blore, Edward (architect/artist; Br.)
Blore, Eric (actor--Top Hat)
Blount, Herman Poole (pseudonym--Sun Ra) (composer)
Blount, Mel (football)
Blue Rodeo (musical group--Rena)
Blue, Ben (Benjamin Bernstein's pseudonym) (actor/comedian/dancer)
Blues Brothers (musical group including Dan Akroyd & John Belushi)
Blum, Leon (statesman; Fr.)
Blume, Judy (author--Wifey)
Bly, Nellie (journalist/author--Ten Days In A Madhouse)
Bly, Robert (author/poet)
Blyleven, Bert (baseball)
Blyth, Ann (actress)
Blyton, Enid (author)
Bobbettes (musical group--Mr. Lee)

Bobick, Duane (boxer)
Boccaccio, Giovanni (author--The Eaten Heart/biographer--Dante)
Boccherini, Luigi (composer)
Bocelli, Andrea (singer--opera--Amore, Aria)
Bochco, Steven (director--L.A. Law)
Boehner, John (politician) (Ryan's predecessor)
Boeskey, Ivan (financier)
Bogarde, Dirk (actor--Darling)
Bogart, Humphrey (actor--Dr. X, High Sierra, Sahara, Key Largo, The Big Sleep, Return of Dr. X, To Have and Have Not, Petrified Forest, African Queen)
Bogdanovich, Peter (director--The Last Picture Show)
Boggs, Wade (baseball)
Bogosian, Eric (author/actor)
Bohr, Niels (atomistic/physicist--quantum theorist; Dan.)
Boitano, Brian (figure skater)
Boito, Arrigo (author/composer--opera--Nero, Mefistofele, Nerone)
Bok, Edward William (Eduard Willem Gerard Cesar Hidde Bok) (editor)
Bol, Manute (basketball)
Bolet, Jorge (pianist)
Boleyn, Anne (Anne of a Thousand Days) (Henry VIII's wife)
Bolger, Ray (actor--The Wizard of Oz)
Boll, Heinrich (author/nobelist)
Boll, Uwe (director)
Bolt, Carol (playwright)
Bolt, Usain (runner)
Bolton, Michael (singer--How Can We Be Lovers)
Bombeck, Erma (columnist/author)
Bon Jovi, Jon (singer--Born to be My Baby, These Days, Livin on a Prayer)
Bonaparte, Napoleon (General) (statesman) (Leclerc's brother in law)
Bond, Julian (politician/professor/author/activist--Civil Rights)
Bondar, Roberta (astronaut)
Bondi, Beulah (actress)
Bondone, Ambrogio (pseudonym--Giotto) (artist--murals)

Bonet, Lisa (actress)
Bonheur, Rosa (actress)
Bonner, Yelena (dissident; Soviet)
Bonney, William (Billy the Kid) (outlaw)
Bono (singer--U 2)
Bono, Sonny (singer--What Now My Love/politician)
Bontemps, Arna (author)
BookerT & the M.G.s (musical group--soul)
Boole, George (mathematician)
Boone, Aaron (baseball)
Boone, Bret (baseball)
Boone, Daniel (frontiersman/explorer--Cumberland Gap)
Boone, Debby (singer--You Light Up My Life)
Boone, Pat (singer--Thee I Love)
Boortz, Neal (author/attorney/radio host--Libertarian)
Boosler, Elayne (comedian)
Booth, Edwin (actor--Shakespeare)
Booth, Sonia (actress)
Booth, William (founder of Salvation Army)
Boothe, Powers (actor)
Borah, William Edgar (Lion) (politician; Idaho)
Borch, Gerard Ter (painter; Dutch)
Borden, Gail (surveyor/publisher/inventor--condensed milk/Borden Company)
Bordoni, Irene (singer/actress)
Boreanaz, David (actor)
Borg, Bjorn (Ice Man) (tennis)
Borges, Jorge Luis (author)
Borgia, Cesare (Duke of Valencia)
Borgia, Lucrezia (political schemer) (Pope & mistress's daughter)
Borgman, Jim (cartoonist--Zits)
Borgnine, Ernest (actor--Marty, Fatso)
Bori, Lucrezia (diva)
Boris, Robert (director--Oxford Blues)
Bork, Robert (jurist)
Borman, Frank (astronaut)
Born, Max (scientist--quantum mechanics)
Borodin, Alexander (composer--Prince Igor)

Boru, Brian (Irish King)
Bosch, Hieronymus (artist--The Garden of Earthly Delights,
The Adoration of the Magi)
Bosley, Tom (actor--Happy Days)
Boston (musical group--Amanda)
Bostridge, Ian (singer--opera)
Bostwick, Barry (actor--The Rocky Horror Picture Show)
Bosworth, Kate (actress)
Botiste (fashion designer)
Botsford, Sara (actress--E.N.G.)
Botticelli, Alessandro (Sandro) (painter--The Birth of Venice)
Boucher, Francois (artist--Nude Lying on Sofa) (Francois Le
Moyne's student)
Boulanger, Nadia (conductor)
Boulez, Pierre (conductor--N. Y. Philharmonic)
Bounarroti, Michelangelo (sculptor--Pieta)
Bourdain, Anthony (chef)
Bouton, Jim (author--Ball Four)
Boutros-Ghali, Boutros (politician)
Bova, Benjamin (author--Kinsman Saga)
Bow, Clara (The It Girl) (actress--silent movies)
Bowe, Riddick (boxer)
Bowen, Elizabeth (author--The Death of the Heart)
Bowes, Edward (Major) (radio personality)
Bowes, Walter (software-hardware manufacturer/packaging-
mailing provider)   (Arthur Pitney's
partner)
Bowie, David (singer/actor--Let's Dance) (Eno's collaborator)
Bowman, Scotty (hockey)
Boxer, Barbara (politician/Senator; Am.)
Boy George (O'Dowd) (singer)
Boyd, Billy (singer/actor--Lord of the Rings)
Boyd, Jimmy (singer)
Boyd, Liona (guitarist)
Boyd, Patti (model/photographer) (George Harrison's ex./Eric
Clapton's ex.)
Boyd, William Lawrence (actor--Hopalong Cassidy)
Boyer, Charles (actor--Pepe le Moko)
Boyer, Clete (baseball)

Boyer, Ken (baseball)
Boyle, Danny (director--Slumdog Millionaire)
Boyle, Lara Flynn (actress)
Bracken, Eddie (actor)
Bracken, Peg (author)
Bradbury, Ray (author--"R" is for Rocket)
Braddock, James (Jim) (boxer)
Bradford, Jesse (actor)
Bradford, William (Governor of Plymouth Colony/pilgrim signer of Mayflower Compact)
Bradlee, Ben (newspaper exec.)
Bradley, Ed (newsman--60 Minutes)
Bradley, Omar (General)
Bradley, William (politician)
Bradstreet, Anne (poet)
Brady, Adrien (actor)
Brady, Mathew (photographer--Civil War)
Brady, Pat (cartoonist--Rose in Rose)
Braff, Zach (actor--Scrubs)
Braga, Sonia (actress--Moon Over Parador, Dona Flor)
Bragg, Braxton (Gen.--C.S.A.)
Brahe, Tycho (nee Tyge Ottesen Brahe) (astronomer)
Brahms, Johannes (composer--Trio #1 in B)
Branagh, Kenneth (director/actor--Hamlet)
Brand, Elton (basketball)
Brand, Neville (actor--Laredo)
Brand, Stewart (author/editor--Last Whole Picture Show)
Brandeis, Louis (justice)
Brando, Marlon (actor--Viva Zapata, The Men, I Remember Mama, On the Waterfront,   Burn)
Brandt, Betsy (actress--Breaking Bad)
Brandt, Willie (politician)
Braque, Georges (painter--cubist)
Brashares, Ann (author--The Sisterhood of the Traveling Pants)
Bratkowski, Zeke (football)
Bratt, Benjamin (actor--Law and Order, Private Practice)
Braun, Eva (model) (Hitler's mistress/wife)
Braun, Karl (inventor--oscilloscope)

Braxton, Toni (singerYou're Makin' Me High)
Brazzi, Rossano (actor--South Pacific)
Brecht, Bertolt (playwright--A Man's a Man, Three Penny
Opera, Mother Courage   and Her
Children) (Weill collaborator)
Breen, Steve (cartoonist--Grand Avenue)
Brel, Jacques (composer/singer--If We Only Have Love; Belg.
)
Bremner, Ewen (actor--Black Hawk Down, Wonder Woman,
Trainsplitting)
Brennan, Eileen (actress)
Brennan, Walter (actor)
Brenneman, Amy (actress)
Brenner, Yul (actor--King and I, Anastasia)
Brent, George (actor)
Bres Ri (Bres the King) (King of Ireland)
Breton, Andre (Poet; Fr.)
Brett, George (baseball)
Brett, Ken (baseball)
Brewer, Teresa (singer)
Brewster, Paget (actress)
Brewster, William (colonist--Plymouth leader)
Breyer, Stephen (justice--Supreme Court)
Brezhnev, Leonid (politician; Rus.)
Brice, Fanny (comedienne/singer/actress--My Man, Baby
Snooks (radio))
Brickell, Edie (singer-songwriter) (Paul Simon's wife)
Brickman, Jim (songwriter/musician--piano--New Age)
Bridges, Alan (director)
Bridges, Beau (actor--Gaily, Gaily)
Bridges, Jeff (actor--Tron, Starman, Big Lebowski)
Bridges, Lloyd (actor)
Brimley, Wilford (actor)
Brimsek, Frank Charles (Mr. Zero) (hockey)
Brin, Sergey (computer scientist--Google co-founder)
Brinkley, David (newsman) (autobiog--A Memoir)
Bristow, Sydney (actress)
Britt, May (actress)

Britten, Edward Benjamin (Baron) (composer--opera--War Requiem, Turn of the Screw)
Broad, Eli (philanthropist/art collector)
Broadbent, Jim (actor--Iris)
Broder, David (journalist)
Broderick, Matthew (actor)
Brodie, John (football)
Brodie, Steve (actor)
Brodsky, Isaak (painter)
Brodsky, Joseph (poet)
Brody, Adam (actor--The O. C.)
Brody, Adrien (actor--The Pianist)
Brofeldt, Johannes (pseudonym--Juhani Alto) (author)
Brolin, James (actor--The Car)
Bronowski, Jacob (mathematician/historian/actor/inventor/author--The Ascent of Man)
Bronson, Charles (actor--Ten to Midnight)
Bronstein, Lev Davidovich (a.k.a. Trotsky) (revolutionary Marxist)
Bronte, Anne (pseudonym--Acton Bell) (author--Agnes Grey, The Tenant of Wildfell Hall)
Bronte, Charlotte (pseudonym--Currer Bell) (author--Jane Eyre, Villette, A Professor: A Tale)
Bronte, Emily (pseudonym--Ellis Bell) (author--Wuthering Heights)
Brooke, Rupert (poet)
Brookner, Anita (author--Hotel Du Lac)
Brooks, Avery (actor)
Brooks, Garth (musician/singer)
Brooks, Mel (actor/writer/director--Blazing Saddles)
Brosnan, Pierce (actor--007, Sum of all Fears, The Quest for Camelot, Golden Eye)
Broten, Neal (hockey)
Brothers, Isley (musician--The Lady)
Brown, Aaron (newscaster)
Brown, Alton (chef/actor/author/T.V. personality--Good Eats, Cutthroat Kitchen)
Brown, Bonnie Blair (actress)

Brown, Chris (singer--No Air)
Brown, Corwin (football)
Brown, Dan (author--The Lost Symbol, The Da Vinci Code)
Brown, Ed (football)
Brown, Helen Gurley (author/publisher--Cosmo)
Brown, Hubie (basketball)
Brown, James (singer--Super Bad, My Thang)
Brown, Joe E. (actor--Shut My Big Mouth)
Brown, John (actor--Digby/Digger O'Dell--Life of Riley)
Brown, Nacio Herb (composer)
Brown, Nick (Survivor participant)
Brown, Oda (psychic)
Brown, Rita Mae (author)
Brown, Samantha (Sam) (singer-songwriter)
Brown, Tina (editor--New Yorker, The Daily Beast/author--The Diana Chronicles/ founder--Talk Magazine)
Browne, Charles Farrar (pseudonym--Artemus Ward) (writer--humor)
Browne, Chris (cartoonist--Hagar the Horrible)
Browne, Dik (cartoonist--Hagar the Horrible)
Browne, Hablot Knight (pseudonym--Phiz) (illustrator--Charles Dickens)
Browne, Jackson (singer--Late for the Sky)
Browne, Roscoe Lee (actor--Black Like Me)
Browne, William (poet--A Rose As Far As Ever Saw the North)
Browning, Deep (filmmaker)
Browning, Elizabeth Barrett (poet--sonnets)
Browning, Robert (playwright/poet--Mornings at Seven, Fra Lippo Lippi, Rabbi Ben Ezra)
Browning, Tod (director--Dracula)
Broz, Josip (Tito) (politician; Yugoslavian)
Brubeck, Dave (musician/pianist)
Bruce, Elia (football)
Bruce, Lenny (comedian)
Bruce, Nigel (actor--Dr. Watson)
Bruch, Max (composer--Scottish Fantasy)
Bruckheimer, Jerry (producer)

Bruckner, Josef Anton (composer--Requiem in D Minor; Austrian)
Bruegel, Pieter (painter)
Brundage, Avery (athlete)
Brundtland, Gro Harlem (politician; Nor.)
Bruni-Sarkozy, Carla (French First Lady) (singer-songwriter/model) (Nicholas Sarkozy's wife)
Bruno, Walter (conductor)
Bry, Adelaide (psychotherapist/author--est: 60 Hours That Transorm Your Life)
Bryan, William Jennings (The Great Commoner) (politician/lawyer--Scopes Trial/ orator--Cross of Gold)
Bryant, Anita (singer)
Bryant, Paul William (Bear) (football--Bama)
Bryant, William Cullen (poet--Thanatopsis, To The Fringed Gentian)
Bryson, Peabo (singer--R & B/pop--Beauty & the Beast)
Brzezinski, Zbigniew (Zbig) (politician)
Bubbles, John W. (nee John William Sublett) (vaudevillian/dancer--rhythm-soul tap-- It Ain't Necessarily So) (Buck Washington's partner)
Buchanan, Edgar (actor)
Buchanan, Edna (author)
Buchholz, Horst (actor--The Magnificent Seven)
Buck, Pearl S. (author--Dragon Seed, Sons, The Exile, A House Divided, The Good Earth--Olan)
Buckley, William F. (commentator/author--God and Man at Yale)
Buckwald, Art (author/columnist/dramatist/journalist)
Buddha (Siddhartha Gautama) (spiritual teacher)
Budge, Don (tennis)
Buell, Don Carlos (Union General)
Bueno, Maria (tennis)
Buerge, Aaron (actor--Bachelor)
Bufett, Warren (Oracle of Omaha) (businessman/investor/philanthropist)

Bugatti, Ettore (automaker)
Bugliosi, Vincent (author--Helter Skelter) (co-author--Curt Gentry)
Bujold, Genevieve (actress--Coma)
Buketoff, Igor (conductor/arranger/teacher)
Bulfinch, Charles (architect)
Bulfinch, Thomas (author--myth)
Bull, Ole (musician--violinist)
Bullock, Sandra (actress--The Net, Practical Magic, All About Steve)
Bullock, Steve (politician)
Bulwer-Lytton, Edward (playwright/poet/politician/author--Leila)
Bunche, Ralph (Dr.) (professor/diplomat/nobelist--peace)
Bundchen, Gisele (model)
Bunin, Ivan (author/poet/nobelist; Ru.)
Bunker, Ellsworth (businessman/diplomat)
Bunting, Basil (poet; Br.)
Buntline, Ned (author--westerns)
Bunton, Emma Lee (Baby Spice) (singer)
Bunuel, Luis (director/filmmaker--surrealist cinema/consecrated auteur) (Dali's collaborator)
Burber, Martin (scholar--Judaic)
Burdette, Lew (baseball--pitcher)
Burdon, Eric (singer-songwriter/actor) (band--The Animals)
Burger, Warren (justice--Supreme Court)
Burgess, Anthony (author--A Clockwork Orange, 1985)
Burgess, Gelett (comedian)
Burghoff, Gary (actor--M.A.S.H.--Radar)
Burka, Petra (skater)
Burke, Billie (actress--Wizard of Oz)
Burke, Edmond (author/political theorist/philosopher/orator)
Burke, Joe (composer--Moon Over Miami) (Edgar Leslie's co-writer)
Burke, John (publisher--peerage)
Burnett, Betsy (news anchor)
Burnett, Carol (comedian/actress--Once Upon a Mattress)
Burnford, Sheila (author--Bel Ria/Dog of War)
Burns, Ed (actor)

Burns, George (nee Nathan Birnham) (actor--Oh, God! The Sunshine Boys/comedian/   author--Gracie: A Love Story)
Burns, Ken (filmmaker/historian--baseball/ Country Music)
Burns, Robert (poet--To A Louse, The Twa Dogs, Address to the Unco Guid/   songwriter--Auld Lang Syne, Comin Thro The Rye, Ae Fond Kiss, The Lea Rig)
Burr, Aaron (politician) (Jefferson's V.P.)
Burrell, Anne (chef)
Burress, Plaxico (football)
Burris, James Henry (lyricist--Ballin' the Jack)
Burroughs, Edgar Rice (author--At the Earth's Core)
Burroughs, Nannie Helen (educator/orator/religious leader/feminist/activist--Civil Rights)
Burstyn, Ellen (actress--Alice Doesn't Live Here Anymore)
Burton, Levar (actor)
Burton, Richard (actor--Antony and Cleopatra)
Burton, Tim (director--Ed Wood)
Busby, Thad (football)
Busby, Thomas (author--A Complete Dictionary of Music)
Buscaglia, Leo (author)
Buscemi, Steve (actor)
Busch, Adolphus (brewer--beer pasteurization)
Busch, Mae (actress)
Buschema, Sal (comic book artist--The Avengers)
Bush, Barbara (nee Pierce) (George Herbert Walker Bush's wife)
Bush, George Herbert Walker (politician)
Bush, George W. (The Decider) (politician/author--Decision Points)
Bush, Jenna (author--Ana's Story-A Journey of Hope)
Bush, John Ellis (Jeb) (politician)
Bush, Kate (singer--Oh To Be In Love)
Bush, Laura (nee Welch) (librarian--S.M.U.)
Bush, Neil (businessman/investor/philanthropist)
Bushmiller, Ernie (cartoonist--Nancy)
Bushnell, Nolan (Father of Computers) (inventor--Atari, Pong)
Busoni, Ferroccio (composer)

Buster, Prince (musician--ska)
Butala, Sharon (author)
Butler, Brett (actress--Grace Under Fire)
Butler, Robert Olen (author)
Butler, Samuel (author--Erewhon)
Butler, Yancy (actress)
Buttons, Red (nee Aaron Chwatt) (comedian)
Buzzati, Dino (author)
Buzzi, Ruth (comedienne)
Byington, Spring (actress--December Bride)
Byner, John (impressionist)
Byrd, Richard E. (Admiral) (explorer--Arctic/author--Alone)
(airplane--America)
Byrds (musical group--Turn, Turn, Turn)
Byrne, David (politician/musician--Talking Heads founder)
Byrnes, Edd (Kookie) (actor)
Byron, Ada (mathematician)
Byron, George Gordon (Lord) (poet--Lara, When We Two
Parted, Manfred, Childe Harold's   Pilgrimage/dramatist-
-Cain)

--C--

C.C.R. (Creedence Clearwater Revival) (musical group--Proud
Mary)
Caan, James (actor--Misery, The Rain People)
Caan, Scott (actor--American Outlaws, Oceans 11, Hawaii 50)
Cabell, James Branch (author--Smire)
Cabot, Bruce (actor--King Kong)
Cabot, John (explorer)
Cabrera, Orlando (boxer)
Cabrini, Mother (first U. S. Saint)
Cady, Harrison (illustrator--children's)
Caen, Herb (columnist)
Caesar, Gaius Julius (politician) (Cornelia's husband)
Caesar, Germanicus (Caligula's father)
Caesar, Sid (comedian)

Cage, John (actor--Ally McBeal)
Cage, Nicholas (actor--Raising Arizona, Con-Air)
Cagney, James (actor--G-Men)
Cahill, Thaddeus (inventor--electronic music)
Cahn, Sammy (lyricist/composer--High Hopes, Call Me Irresponsible, All the Way)
Caillat, Colbie (singer--I Do)
Cain, Dean (actor--Superman)
Cain, James Mallahan (author--Mildred Pierce, The Postman Always Rings Twice)
Caine, Michael (actor--Hannah and her Sisters, Sleuth, Alfie, Educating Rita, The Cider House Rules, Ashanti)
Calder, Alexander (sculptor--mobiles--Pinwheel and Flow)
Calderon, Erma (author--Erma)
Caldwell, Erskine (author--Aimee, God's Little Acre)
Caldwell, Janet Miriam Holland Taylor (author)
Caldwell, Sarah (conductor--opera)
Cale, John (musician--rock) (band--Velvet Underground)
Calhoun, Rory (actor)
Caligula (Germanicus Caesar's son)
Callaghan, Morley (author--That Summer in Paris)
Callahan, J. Will (lyricist--Smiles) (Roberts's partner)
Callas, Maria (diva)
Calle, Frankie (composer--Sunrise Serenade)
Calloway, Cabell (Cab) (actor/bandleader/composer--Hi De Ho)
Calloway, Thomas DeCarlo (a.k.a. CeeLo Green) (singer--rap/songwriter/record producer/T.V. personality--The Voice judge)
Callwood, June (journalist/social activist)
Calmer, Ned (journalist/author)
Calrissian, Lando (actor--Star Wars)
Calve, Emma (singer--soprano)
Calvin, John (religious leader/author--Hosea, Joel, Amos, Obadiah) (Luther contemporary)
Calvino, Italo (author--Mr. Palomar, Cosmicomics)
Cam'ron (musical group--Hey Ma)
Camacho, Hector (Macho) (boxer)

Cambage, Liz (basketball)
Cameron, James (director--Titanic, Ghosts of the Abyss, Avatar)
Cameron, John Donald (author--Omega Sub)
Cameron, Kirk (actor)
Caminiti, Ken (baseball)
Camoes, Luis de (poet; Port.)
Camp, Dalton (pundit)
Campanella, Roy (baseball)
Campbell, Glen (singer--Witchita Lineman)
Campbell, Joseph (musician)
Campbell, Michael Che (writer/actor/comedian--S.N.L.)
Campbell, Naomi (model)
Campbell, Neve (actress--Scream, Party of Five)
Campbell, Thomas (poet--Erin)
Campbell-Martin, Tisha (actress--Martin)
Campeador, el Cid (el campeador--the champion) (military leader; Sp.)
Campion, Jane (director/author--The Piano)
Camporese, Omar (tennis)
Camus, Albert (author--The Plague, Caligula L'etat de Siege, The Stranger, L'Ete)
Canaan, Trudi (author--Black Magician)
Canadas, Esther (actress)
Canby, Vincent (critic)
Candler, Asa Griggs (pharmacist/manufactured Coca Cola)
Candy, John (comedian--S.C.T.V.)
Canetti, Elias (author--The Torch in My Ear)
Caniff, Milton (cartoonist--Terry & the Pirates)
Canin, Ethan (author)
Cannon, Dyan (actress--Out To Sea, Heaven Can Wait)
Cano, Alonso (painter--Mysteries of the Virgin)
Canova, Judy (comedian/actress/singer/radio personality)
Cantor, Eddie (nee B. Edward Israel Iskowitz) (actor, comedian, singer, dancer, songwriter--   If You Knew Susie)
Cantor, Eric (politician)
Cantor, Georg (mathematician)
Cantor, Ida (Eddie's wife)

Cantor, Jim (meteorologist)
Cantrell, Blu (singer--R. & B.)
Cantrell, Lana (singer/entertainment lawyer)
Caovilla, Rene (designer--shoes)
Capek, Karel (author--RUR, The Makropoulos Secret)
Capet, Hugh (Fr. ruler--Robertians/Robertines)
Capone, Al (Scarface) (gangster)
Caponi, Donna (golfer)
Capote, Truman (author--In Cold Blood, Grass Harp) (Tru play subject)
Capp, Al (cartoonist--Fearless Fosdick, Shmoo, Stupefyin Jones, L'il Abner, Lena the   Hyena, Bald Iggle)
Cappelletti, Gino (football)
Capra, Frank (director--It Happened One Night, Meet John Doe, Arsenic and Old Lace,   Mr. Deeds Goes to Town, It's a Wonderful Life, Here Come the Groom, You Can't   Take It With You)
Capriati, Jennifer (tennis)
Capris (musical group--There's a Moon Out Tonight)
Capshaw, Kate (actress)
Cara, Irene (actress/singer--Fame, Flashdance)
Carangi, Gia (model)
Caravaggio (painter--The Sacrifice of Isaac)
Caray, Harry (sportscaster)
Caray, Harry Christopher (Chip) (sportscaster) (Skip's son)
Caray, Harry Christopher (Skip) (sportscaster) (Chip's father)
Carbo, Bernie (baseball)
Card, Orson Scott (author--sci.-fi.--Enders Game)
Cardellini, Linda (actress)
Cardin, Pierre (fashion designer)
Carell, Steve (actor--The Office)
Carew, Rod (baseball)
Carew, Thomas (poet--Celia--Cavalier group member)
Carey, Amy (actress--Dog Park)
Carey, Drew (actor/comedian)
Carey, Hugh L. (politician--N. Y. Gov.)
Carey, Mariah (singer--I Don't Wanna Cry, Love Takes Time)
Carey, Sandra (author)
Carides, Gia (actress--My Big Fat Greek Wedding)

Cariou, Len (actor--Sweeny Todd)
Carison, Oliver (author--Hearst, Lord of San Simeon)
Carle, Frankie (bandleader/pianist)
Carlisle, Belinda (singer--Go-Gos)
Carlos, Juan (El Rey) (King of Spain)
Carlton, Carl (singer--Everlasting Love)
Carmen, Eric (singer-songwriter)
Carmer, Carl Lamson (author--Stars Fell on Alabama)
Carmichael, Hoagy (composer--Lazy Bones, Stardust)
Carne, Marcel (director; Fr.)
Carnegie (Carnegey), Dale (orator/psychologist)
Carnera, Primo (Ambling Alp/Man Mountain) (boxer)
Carney, Art (actor)
Caro, Niki (director)
Caro, Robert A. (author--L. B. J.)
Carol (King of Romania)
Carolla, Adam (podcaster)
Caron, Leslie (actress--American in Paris, Is Paris Burning,
Lili, Father Goose, the L-Shaped   Room)
Carpenter, Charisma (actress)
Carpenter, John (actor--Hallowe'en)
Carpenter, Karen (singer)
Carpenter, Scott (astronaut)
Carr, Caleb (author--The Alienist, It Walks by Night) (Fell's
creator)
Carr, David (journalist)
Carr, Emily (artist)
Carr, Eric (musician--drummer) (band--Kiss)
Carr, John Dickson (author--Locked Room Mysteries)
Carr, Vikki (singer--It Must Be Him)
Carradine, Keith (actor/songwriter)
Carrera, Barbara (actress)
Carrera, Eden (actress)
Carreras, Jose Maria (singer--tenor; Sp.)
Carrere, Tia (actress)
Carrey, Drew (actor)
Carrey, Jim (actor--Count Olaf, Liar Liar, The Truman Show)
Carrington, Terri Lyne (musician--drummer)
Carroll, Charles (politician)

Carroll, Earl (producer/director/theatrical reviewer)
Carroll, Leo (actor)
Carroll, Lewis (Charles Ludwige Dodgson's pseudonym) (diarist--author--Alice in Wonderland/ Sylvie and Bruno)
Carroll, Pete (football)
Carros, Roland (aviator)
Carruth, Rae Lamar (football)
Cars (musical group--Let's Go) (band member--Ric Ocasek)
Carson, Anne (poet)
Carson, Johnny (talk show host--Carnac)
Carson, Rachel (ecologist/author--The Sea Around Us, Silent Springs)
Carte, Richard D'Oyly (producer/composer--opera)
Carter, Aaron (actor)
Carter, Amy (activist) (Jimmy & Rosalynn's daughter)
Carter, Ash (politician)
Carter, Deana (singer--country)
Carter, Helena Bonham (actress)
Carter, Howard (archaeologist)
Carter, James Earl (Jimmy) (politician/author--Why Not the Best)
Carter, Nell (singer/actress)
Carter, Ronald Levin (musician--jazz--bass)
Cartier, Pierre (jeweler)
Cartier, Pierre (musician--bass)
Cartwright, Angela (actress--Sound of Music)
Carty, Rico (baseball)
Caruso, Enrico (singer--tenor)
Carver, Brent (actor; Can.)
Carver, George Washington (inventor/botanist--peanuts)
Carver, Raymond (author)
Carvey, Dana (actor--S.N.L.)
Casals, Pablo (cellist; Sp.)
Casazza, Yolanda (dancer--ballroom) (Frank Veloz's wife)
Case, Neko (singer-songwriter--Middle Cyclone)
Cash, Johnny (singer--I Walk the Line)
Cash, June (singer)
Cash, Patrick Hart (tennis)

Cash, Rosanne (singer--Seven Year Ache)
Cashman, Wayne (hockey)
Cass, Lewis (politician)
Cass, Peggy (actress)
Cassady, Neal (author)
Cassatt, Mary (painter--portrait)
Cassidy, Iva (singer--jazz/blues)
Cassidy, Shaun (singer--Hey Deanie) (Shirley Jones's son)
Cassie, Yatie (actress)
Cassin, Rene (politician/nobelist--peace)
Casson, Alfred Joseph (artist--Group of Seven)
Castellaneta, Dan (actor)
Castle, Irene (dancer) (Vernon's wife/dance partner)
Castle, Vernon (dancer) (Irene's husband/dance partner)
Castro, Fidel (Cuban leader) (cohort--Che Guevara)
Castro, Ines de (mistress of Peter I of Portugal)
Castro, Julian (politician)
Castro, Raul (politician--Cuba)
Caswall, Edward (clergyman/hymnist--Alleluia! Alleluia!, Come Holy Ghost)
Cates, Phoebe (actress--Gremlins, Drop Dead Fred)
Cather, Willa (author--O Pioneers, My Antonia, One of Ours, A Lost Lady, Death Comes for the Archbishop)
Catilina, Lucius Sergius (politician/conspirator)
Catlin, George (artist; Native Am.)
Cato (Marcus Porcius) (the Censor) (ethicist/military leader--destroyed Carthage)
Cato, Porcius Marcus (politician)
Catt, Carrie Chapman (suffragette)
Cattrall, Kim (actress)
Cauthen, Steven (jockey)
Cavanagh, Tom (actor)
Cavaro, Paolo (filmmaker--Mondo Cane)
Cavell, Edith (nurse)
Cavett, Dick (T.V. interviewer)
Cavuto, Neil (newman--Fox News)
Caxton, William (merchant/ diplomat/author/printer)

Cayce, Edgar (The Sleeping Prophet)
(prophet/heeler/seer/author--reincarnation/afterlife)
Ceausescu, Elena (chemist; Rom.)
Cecil, David (Lord) (author--literary biographer)
Cedeno, Cesar (boxer)
Cela, Camila (author)
Celine, L. F. (Louis Ferdinand Destouches' pseudonym)
(author/pamphleteer/physician)
Celsius, Anders (astronomer/inventor--temperature scale)
Cepeda, Orlando (baseball)
Cera, Michael (actor--Superbad, Juno, Arrested Development)
Cerf, Bennett (author--At Random/publisher/T.V. personality--
What's My Line)
Cernan, Gene (astronaut)
Cervantes, Lorna D. (poet; Sp.)
Cervantes, Miguel de (author--Mum's the Word)
Cessna, Clyde (airplane manufacturer)
Cetera, Peter (singer)
Cey, Ron (Penguin) (baseball)
Cezanne, Paul (artist--Boy in a Red Vest; Fr.)
Ch,eng, Lung (pseudonym--Jackie Chan) (actor/stuntman)
Chabas, Paul Emile (apinter--September Morn)
Chabrier, Emmanuel (composer--Le Roi Malgre Lui)
Chacon, Elio (baseball)
Chafee, Linc (politician)
Chaffee, Suzy (skier)
Chagall, Marc (painter/surrealist/stainglass/muralist--I and the
Village,   Green Violinist; Fr.)
Chaiken, Ilene (author--The "L" Word)
Chaliapin, Feodor (singer--opera--basso)
Chalke, Sara (actress--Roseanne, Scrubs)
Chamberlain, Neville (politician)
Champion, Gower Carlyle (actor/theater
director/choreographer/dancer)
Champion, Marge (dancer/actress)
Chan, Jackie (nee Chan Kwong-Song's) (Lung Ch,eng's
pseudonym) (actor--Rush Hour)
Chan, Johnny (poker)
Chandler, Harry (publisher)

Chandler, Kyle (actor)
Chandler, Norman (newspaper publisher--L. A. Times)
Chandler, Otis (newspaper publisher--L. A. Times)
Chandler, Raymond (author--The Big Sleep, The Long Goodbye)
Chanel, Coco (Gabrielle) (fashion designer)
Chaney, Lon (Jr.) (actor--Son of Dracula, The Wolfman)
Chang (Siamese twin--Eng)
Channing, Carol (actress, comedian, singer, dancer, voice artist)
Channing, Stockard (actress--Six Degrees of Separation)
Channing, Tatum (actress--22 Jump Street)
Chao, Elaine (politician)
Chapin, Harry (singer--Cat's in the Cradle)
Chaplin, Charlie Spencer (Sir) (actor--Keystone Cops, Modern Times, Monsieeur Verdoux,   My Autobiography, The Gold Rush/songwriter--This Is My Song, Forever Amber) (Oona's husband)
Chaplin, Oona (nee O'Neill) (ballerina/actress--Game of Thrones) (Charlie's wife)
Chaplin, Syd (actor)
Chapman, Tracy (singer--Fast Car)
Chappell, Crystal (actress)
Charcot, Jean-Martin (neurologist)
Charisse, Cyd (nee Tula Ellice Finklea) (dancer/actress--Silk Stockings)
Charlemagne (King of the Franks) (Pepin the Short's son)
Charleson, Ian (actor--Chariots of Fire)
Charo (actress--Chico & the Man/musician) (Xavier Cugat's wife)
Charpentier, Gustave (composer--opera--Louise)
Chartier, Alain (poet)
Chase, Chevy (actor--Three Amigos, Fletch, Vacation)
Chase, Hal (baseball)
Chase, Ilka (actress) (authobiography--Past Imperfect, In Bed We Cry)
Chase, Mary Ellen (educator/scholar/author)
Chase, Salmon Portland (jurist)
Chase, Stuart (economist/author)

Chasins, Abram (pianist)
Chast, Roz (cartoonist)
Chateaubriand, Francois Rene (author--Rene)
Chaucer, Geoffrey (author--The Clerk's Tale, Canterbury Tales)
Chauchoin, Lily (Claudette Colbert's pseudonym) (actress)
Chavez, Cesar (labour leader)
Chavez, Endy de Jesus (baseball)
Chavez, Hugo (politician; Ven.)
Chayefsky, Sidney Aaron (Paddy) (playwright/author/satirist--Network)
Che (full name Che Guevara) (Fidel cohort)
Che, Michael (nee Michael Che Campbell) (writer/actor/comedian--S.N.L.)
Cheadle, Don (actor)
Chekhov, Anton (author--Loner, The Three Sisters, Ivanov, Uncle Vanya, The Cherry Orchard)
Chen, Joan (actress)
Chen, Julie (newscaster/producer/T.V. personality--The Early Show, The Talk, Big Brother)
Cheney, Elizabeth (Liz) (political commentator)
Cheney, Richard (Dick) (politician--Bush's V. P.)
Chenier, Andre (poet--guillotined)
Chennault, Claire (General--A.F.)
Cher (Goddess of Pop) (singer/actress--Mermaids, Mask, Burlesque, What Now My Love)
Cherne, Leo (sculptor/economist/author--Adjusting Your Business to War)
Cherubini, Luigi (composer--Medee)
Chesney, Francis Rawdon (explorer; Br.)
Chesney, Kenny (singer--country)
Chesterton, Gilbert Keith (G.K.) (philosopher/orator/theologian/poet/author--All I Survey, The Innocence of Father Brown)
Chevalier, Maurice (singer/actor--One Hour with You, Mimi, Gigi)
Chevrolet, Louis (automaker)
Chiang, Soong Mei-Ling (Madame Chiang Kai-shek) (First Lady of Rep. of China)

Chicago (musical group--Call on Me, 25 or 6 to 4)
Child, Lee (author--Jack Reacher)
Childress, Alvin (actor--Amos of Amos & Andy)
Childs, Julia (chef)
Chillida, Eduardo (sculptor)
Ching, Chiang/Jiang Qing (actress) (Mao's wife)
Chinmoy, Sri (spiritual leader)
Chirac, Jacques (politician; Fr.) (Mitterrand's successor)
Chisholm, Melanie (Mel C) (actress/T.V.
personality/songwriter/singer--Spice Girls)
Cho, John (actor--Sulu, Harold & Kumar)
Cho, Margaret (actress--All American Girl)
Choate, Rufus (lawyer/politician; Am.)
Chodorov, Jerome (playwright/librettist--Anniversary Waltz,
Wonderful Town)
Choe, En lai (politician--Premier of China)
Choi, Kyung-Ju (K.J.) (golfer)
Choi, Na Yeon (golfer)
Chomsky, Noam (author--linguist/media critic)
Chong, Rae Dawn (actress)
Chookasain, Lili (singer--opera--contralto)
Chopin, Francois (politician) (Nicholas's father)
Chopin, Frederic Francois (composer--nocturnes--Etude,
Polonaise, Sonata in B Minor)
Chopin, Nicholas (composer) (Francois's son)
Chopra, Deepak (author--The Path of Love, Ageless Body
Timeless Mind)
Chopra, Priyanka (actress--Quantico)
Chordettes (musical group--Mr. Sandman)
Chow, Tina (model)
Choy, Wayson (author--The Jade Peony)
Chretien, Aline (P. M.'s wife)
Chretien, Jean (politician: Canada's P. M.)
Christensen, Erika (actress/singer)
Christensen, Ute (actress)
Christian, Linda (actress)
Christiansen, Ole Kirk (toy company founder--Lego)
Christie, Agatha (author--Peril At End House, Ten Little
Indians, The Pale Horse, Evil   Under the

Sun, Sad Cypress, N or M, Death on the Nile)   (Hercules Perot creator)
Christie, Julie (actress--Away from Her, McCabe and Mrs. Miller)
Christie, Lou (singer)
Christo (artist--The Gates)
Christophe, Henri/Henry (politician; Haiti)
Chu, Asi (philosopher--Verses of Wisdom)
Chu, Steven (politician)
Chuangtse, Chuang-Tse (philosopher--Laotse follower)
Church, Eric (singer--country)
Churchill, Winston (politician/author--A Far Country, Their Finest Hour, Hinge   of Fate)
Ciano, Edda (Gian's wife) (Mussolini's daughter)
Ciano, Gian Galeazzo (politician/diplomat) (Mussolini's son-in-law, Edda's husband)
Ciara (nee Ciara Princess Hrris) (actress/dancer/singer/songwriter--Goodies)
Ciardi, John (poet--I Met a Man, As If, I Marry You, Lives of X/translater--Dante's Divine   Comedy, A Word in Your Ear)
Cibrian, Eddie (actor--Third Watch)
Cicero, Marcus Tullius (philosopher--rhetoric/essayist--Old Age)
Cilea, Francesco (composer--opera--Adriana Lecouvreur)
Cimbaue, Giovanni (painter; Florentine)
Cimino, Michael (director--Deer Hunter)
Cisneros, Sandra (author/poet)
Claiborne, Craig (food writer)
Claiborne, Liz (fashion designer)
Claiborne, Pell (politician)
Clair, Rene (director)
Claire, Ina (actress)
Clancy, Tom (author--The Sum of All Fears) (hero--Ryan)
Clanton, Ike (frontiersman; Am.) (Earp's foe)
Clapton, Eric (singer/guitarist--Slow Hand, Layla)
Clare of Assisi (Saint) (founder of Poor Clares)
Clare, Ada (Jane McElhenney's pseudonym) (actress--Bleak House)

Clark, Alvan (inventor--telescope)
Clark, Dane (actor)
Clark, Georgie Neese (politician)
Clark, Joe (politician; Can.)
Clark, Petula (singer--Downtown)
Clark, Roy (musician--country)
Clark, Terri (singer--country--Poor, Poor, Pitiful Me)
Clarke, Arthur C. (author--sci-fi--Rendezvous with Rama)
Clarke, Mae (actress--Public Enemy, The Front Page)
Clarke, Thomas Hal (justice--Supreme Court)
Clash (musical group--Should I Stay)
Classic IV (musical group--Spooky, Stormy, Traces) (lead singer--Dennis Yost)
Claudio, Arrau (pianist--Chilean)
Clavell, James (author--King Rat, Tai-pan, Shogun)
Clay, Henry (The Great Compromiser) (orator)
Clayburgh, Jill (actress)
Cleary, Beverly (author--children)
Cleese, John (actor--Fawlty Towers, Splitting Heirs, A Fish Called Wanda)
Cleghorne, Ellen (comedian)
Cleland, John (author--Fanny Hill)
Cleland, Joseph Maxwell (Max) (politician)
Clemenceau, Georges (Tiger) (politician)
Clement, Attles (politician--P.M.; Br.)
Clement, Rene (director)
Clemente, Roberto (baseball)
Clementi, Musio (composer--sonatinas)
Clemons, Clarence (musician--E Street Band)
Cleon (statesman) (opponent--Pericles)
Cleveland, Amory (critic)
Clift, Eleanor (editor--The McLaughlin Group)
Clift, Montgomery (actor--From Here to Eternity, Young Lions)
Cline, Ernest (author--Ready Player One)
Cline, Patsy (singer--Crazy)
Clinton, Dewitt (politician--Erie Canal)
Clinton, George (singer)
Clinton, Hillary (lawyer/politician/diplomat) (William's wife)
Clinton, William (politician/author--My Life) (Hillary's husband)

Clive, Robert (Major) (privateer--British East India Company)
Clooney, Amal (lawyer) (George's wife)
Clooney, George (actor--Up In the Air)
Close, Eric (actor)
Close, Glenn (actress--Fatal Attraction, Jagged Edge)
Coates, Joseph Gordon (politician; N.Z.)
Cobain, Frances Bean (Kurt Cobain & Courtney Love's daughter)
Cobain, Kurt (musician--Nirvana) (Courtney Love's husband/Frances Bean Cobain's father)
Cobb, Irvin Shrewsbury (humorist/editor/author--Judge Priest)
Cobb, Lee J. (actor--The Virginian, 12 Angry Men)
Cobb, Ty (baseball)
Coben, Harlan (author--Hold Tight)
Coburn, Donald L. (dramatist--The Gin Game)
Coburn, James (actor)
Cochran, Johnnie (lawyer--O.J. Simpson trial)
Cochran, Lance (singer)
Cochran, Thad (politician)
Cockburn, Bruce (singer)
Cocker, John Robert (Joe) (actor/composer/musician--You Are So Beautiful)
Cocteau, Jean (writer/director--Beauty & the Beast/La Belle Et La Bete)
Coe, Charlie (golfer)
Coe, David Allan (singer--country--Take This Job and Shove It)
Coe, Fred (producer)
Coe, Sebastian (runner--miler/olympian; Br.)
Coen, Ethan (writer/producer/director--Inside Llewyn Davis, Fargo, O Brother   Where Art Thou, The Ballad of Buster Scruggs) (Joel's brother)
Coen, Joel (producer/director--Fargo, Inside Llewyn Davis, O Brother Where Art Thou,   The Ballad of Buster Scruggs) (Ethan's brother)
Coetzee, John Maxwell (author/essayist/linguist/translator; Afrikaans)
Coetzer, Amanda (tennis)
Coghlan, Eamonn (runner)

Cohan, George M. (autobiographer--20 Years on Broadway)

       Cohan, George M. (lyricist/composer--Over There, Little Johnny Jones, actor--Ah Wilderness, Harrigan/director/producer/singer/dancer/playwright--Little Nellies) (autobiog.--Twenty Years on Broadway and the Years It Took to Get There) (Ethel Levy's ex-husband)

Cohen, Andy (radio/T.V. talk show host)

Cohen, Ellen Naomi (a.k.a. Cass Elliot) (singer--Mamas and Papas)

Cohen, Leonard Norman (author/poet/singer--Suzanne, Hallelujah; Can.)

Cohen, Marc (T.V. exec.)

Cohen, Myron (comedian)

Cohen, Sasha (skater)

Cohen, Sasha Noam Baron (author/comedian/actor--Ali G., Borat)

Cohen, William (politician)

Cohn, Al (musician--saxophonist--jazz)

Cohn, Ferdinand Julius (botanist)

Cohn, Harry (producer--It Happened One Night--co-founder of Columbia Pictures)

Cohn, Joel (writer/producer/director--Inside Llewyn Davis, Fargo) (Ethan's brother)

Cohn, Linda (sportscaster)

Cohn, Mindy (actress)

Cohn, Roy (lawyer--H.U.A.C.--Red Scare)

Cohon, George (entrepreneur--McDonalds)

Coker, East (author)

Colbert, Claudette (nee Lily Chauchoin) (actress--It Happened One Night)

Cole, Arthur H. (entrepreneur)

Cole, Gary (actor)

Cole, Jermaine (J.) (rapper--Born Sinner)

Cole, Kenneth (fashion designer)

Cole, Nat King (singer)

Cole, Natalie (singer/songwriter--Our Love)

Cole, Paula (singer/songwriter--Where Have All the Cowboys Gone)
Coleman, Bessie (aviator)
Coleman, Cy (composer)
Coleman, Hawkins (saxophonist)
Coleman, Ornette (saxophonist)
Coleman, Ronald (actor--Beau Geste)
Coleridge, Samuel Taylor (poet--Rime of the Ancient Mariner, To A Young Ass) (Elia's   friend)
Colet, Louise (poet) (Gustave Flaubert's mistress)
Colette, Sidonie (author--Cheri, Gigi, The Other One)
Collette, Toni (actress)
Collier, Lesley (dancer--ballet)
Collin, Carla (actress)
Collin, Phil (singer) (band--Genesis)
Collins, Eileen (astronaut)
Collins, Jackie (author--Lucky)
Collins, Joan (actress--Batman (The Siren))
Collins, Michael (revolutionary--I.R.A.)
Collins, Wilke (author--Moonstone)
Collins, William Earl (Bootsy) (songwriter/bassist/singer--jazz--Funk)
Collinsworth, Cris (football)
Collyer, Bud (T. V. game show host--Beat the Clock, To Tell the Truth)
Colm, Feore (actor)
Colmes, Alan (radio/T.V. personality/political commentator)
Color Me Badd (musical group)
Colter, Jessi (singer--I'm Not Lisa)
Columbo, Russ (bandleader/crooner)
Colzie, Neal (football)
Comaneci, Nadia (gymnast)
Combs, Earle (baseball)
Combs, Sean (a.k.a. P. Diddy) (singer)
Comden, Betty (playwright/performer/lyricist) (Adolph Green's partner)
Comets (Bill Halley & The Comets) (musical group--Rock Around the Clock)
Comfort, Alex (author--A Good Age)

Commodores (musical group--Too Hot Ta Trot)
Como, Perry (singer--And I Love You So, Hot Diggity, Tia
Maria, Juke Box Baby, It's   Impossible, Chi
Baba, Chi Baba, Bibbidi-Bobbidi-Boo)
Compton, Ann (newsperson)
Compton-Burnett, Ivy (author)
Conan, Neal (radio journalist/producer/N.P.R. host--Talk of the
Nation)
Conboy, Sara (labor leader)
Condon, Eddie (musician--jazz)
Cone, David (baseball)
Conford, Ellen (author--Dreams of Victory)
Confucius (nee K'Ung Fu Tse) (thinker/politician/educator)
Congwen, Shen (author)
Conlan, Shane (football)
Conley, Darby (cartoonist--Get Fuzzy)
Conn, Billy (boxer)
Conn, Edith (Didi) (actress--Grease, Benson)
Connell, Evan S. (author)
Connelly, Marc (actor/writer/director)
Connery, Sean (actor--007, Robin & Marian, Hunt for Red
October)
Connick, Harry (Jr.) (singer--She)
Connolly, Maureen Catherine (Little Mo) (tennis)
Connor, Mike (actor--Mannix)
Conrad, Joseph (author--A Set of Six, Heart of Darkness,
Typhoon--Lena)
Conrad, Robert (actor--The D.A.)
Conrad, William (actor--Cannon)
Conran, Shirley (author--Lace)
Conroy, Pat (author--The Great Santini)
Conscience, Hendrick (author--The Lion of Flanders)
Constable, John (painter--landscapes)
Constantine the Great (Roman Emperor)
Conti, Bill (composer)
Conway, Kelly Anne (politician)
Conway, Tim (comedian/actor)
Cooder, Rys (musician--quitar)
Coogan, Jackie (actor--Addam's Family)

Cook Jr., Elisha (actor--Maltese Falcon)
Cook, Robin (author--Coma)
Cook, Tim (C.E.O.--Apple) (Steve Job's successor)
Cooke, Alistair (T.V. host--Omnibus)
Cooke, Jay (financier)
Cooke, Sam (singer--You Send Me, Cupid, Twistin' the Night Away)
Cool & the Gang (musical group)
Cool, Tre (drummer--Green Day)
Coolbrith, Ina (poet)
Coolidge, Rita (singer)
Coolio (musician--rap--Gangsta's Paradise)
Coombs, Ernie (actor--Mr. Dressup
Cooney, Joan Ganz (author/creator--Sesame Street)
Cooper, Alice (singer--rock)
Cooper, Cecil (baseball)
Cooper, Dan B. (bankrobber--escaped by jumping from plane)
Cooper, Gary (actor--A Farewell to Arms, Gehrig, Lilac Time, Mr. Deeds, Meet John Doe)
Cooper, Gladys (actress--My Fair Lady)
Cooper, Gordon (Gordo) (astronaut)
Cooper, James Fenimore (author--Bumppo, The Deerslayer, The Pilot: A Tale of the Sea)
Coors, Adolf (brewer)
Coote, Robert (actor--Othello, My Fair Lady)
Coots, John Fred (songwriter--Love Letters in the Sand)
Copernicus, Nicholas (astronomer)
Copland, Aaron (composer--Rodeo, Fanfare for the Common Man, El Salon Mexico)
Copley, John Singleton (painter)
Copley, Teri (actress)
Coppard, Alfred Edgar (author--Adam & Eve and Pinch Me)
Copperfield, Agnes (David Copperfield's second wife)
Copperfield, David (magician)
Copperfield, Dora (nee Spenlow) (David Copperfield's first wife)
Coppola, Francis Ford (director)
Coppola, Sofia (director--Lost in Translation)
Cora, Joey (baseball)

Corbett, James John (Gentleman Jim) (boxer)
Corby, Ellen (actress)
Corcoran, Noreen (actress--Bachelor Father)
Corday Marie Charlotte (revolutionary) (killed Marat)
Corea, Armando Anthony (Chick) (musician--jazz--Crystal Silence)
Corelli, Arcangelo (composer, violinist--sonatas)
Corelli, Franco (singer--tenor)
Corey, Irwin (Prof.) (comedian)
Corey, Jeff (actor/director)
Corey, Wendell (actor/politician)
Cori, Carl F. (biochemist/pharmacologist)
Cori, Gerty (biochemist)
Corio, Ann (burlesque)
Corneille, Pierre (dramatist--tragedian--Le Cid)
Cornelia (Julius Caesar's wife)
Cornell, Ezra (businessman--founder of Western Union Telegraph/university founder)
Cornell, Katharine (actress--Juliet)
Cornish, Audie (journalist--N.P.R.)
Cornwall, David John Moore (pseudonym--John Le Carre) (author)
Cornwall, Patricia (author)
Cornwallis, Edward (military officer) (Tarleton shipmate)
Coronado, Francisco (explorer--Seven Cities of Gold)
Corot, Jean-Baptiste Camille (painter--landscape/portrait/realism--Orphee, Ville d'Avray, Le Repos, The Burning of Sodom, The Bridge of Narni, La Danse des Nymphes)
Cort, Bud (nee Walter Edward Cox) (ctor--Harold & Maude)
Cortes, Hernan (conquistador)
Cortese, Deena (actress--Jersey Shore)
Cosby, Bill (actor/comedian)
Cosell, Howard (author--I Never Played the Game)
Cosgrave, Liam (politician; Ir.)
Costa, Michael (conductor/composer--oratorio--Eli)
Costas, Bob (broadcaster)
Costello, Elvis (singer/songwriter--My Aim is True)
Costello, Lou (actor/comedian--Here Come the Co-eds)

Costner, Kevin (actor--Wyatt Earp, Ness, Tin Cup)
Cotillard, Marion (actress--La Vie En Rose (Piaf))
Cotton, Joseph (actor--Citizen Kane)
Coty, Rene (politician; Fr.)
Coufax, Sandy (baseball)
Cougar, John (singer--Hurt So Good)
Coughlan, Marisa (actress)
Coulter, Ann (author--Godless the Church of Liberalism, Slander, In Trump We Trust)
Couperin, Francois (composer--Tic-Toc-Choc)
Coupland, Douglas (author--Girlfriend in a Coma)
Couples, Fred (golfer)
Couric, Katie (T. V. personality)
Court, Don (a.k.a. Ken Murray) (actor/comedian/author/T.V. personality)
Cousins, Kirk (football)
Cousteau, Jacques Ives (explorer--sea)
Cousy, Bob (basketball)
Coveleski, Stan (baseball)
Coverly, Dave (cartoonist--Speed Bump)
Cowan, Lee (newsperson)
Cowan, Wes (anthropologist/auctioneer/antique appraiser--History Detectives)
Coward, Noel (playwright--Future Indefinite, Blithe Spirit, To Step Aside/composer/lyricist/singer--Nina/director/actor)
Cowell, Simon (T.V. producer/entrepreneur/T.V. personality--X Factor, American Idol)
Cowl, Jane (writer/director/actress--Juliet)
Cowper, William (author--War's a Game, The Task/hymnodist)
Cox, Courtenay (actress--Friends)
Cox, James M. (politician--Harding opponent)
Cox, Ronny (actor--St. Elsewhere)
Coyle, Kathleen (author--Liv)
Crabbe, Buster (actor--Tarzan, Buck Rogers)
Crabtree, Lotta (actress/comedian)
Craig, John D. (author--Danger if My Business)
Craig, Yvonne (actress--Batgirl)
Crain, Jeanne (actress)

Cram, Stephen (Steve) (miler)
Cramer, Floyd (singer--country--On the Rebound)
Cramer, Jim (hedge fund manager/author/television personality--Mad Money)
Crandall, Del (baseball)
Crane, Hart (poet--The Bridge)
Crane, Les (T.V. talk show host)
Crane, Stephen (Stephcrane) (newspaperman/author--Red Badge of Courage)
Craner, Thomas (Archbishop of Canterbury)
Cranston, Alan (politician)
Cranston, Bryan (actor)
Cranston, Lamont (actor--The Shadow)
Cranston, Toller (skater)
Crates of Mallos (poet; Gr.)
Cravalho, Auli-i (musician/singer/actress--Moana)
Craven, Wes (director--Scream, Swamp Thing)
Crawford, Broderick (actor--All the King's Men)
Crawford, Christina (author--Mommie Dearest)
Crawford, Cindy (model)
Crawford, Sam (baseball)
Crazy Horse (Native leader--Oglalas)
Creasey, John (author--Detective Gideon)
Creedence Clearwater Revival (musical group--Up Around the Bend, Born on the Bayou, Suzie Q, Bad Moon Rising, Who'll Stop the Rain, Proud Mary)
Creighton, Abrams (General)
Crenna, Richard (actor--Body Heat, The Flamingo Kid, The Real McCoys, Rambo)
Crenshaw, Ben (golfer)
Crews, Terry (football/bodybuilder/activist/comedian/actor/T.V. personality-- America's Got Talent)
Crichton, Michael (author--Jurassic Park, Congo, Andromeda Strain, The Terminal Man)
Crick, Francis H. C. (biologist--D.N.A.)
Crier, Catherine Jean (author--A Deadly Game, The Case Against the Lawyers/journalist/ T.V. host--C.N.N.)
Crile, George Washington (surgeon)

Criss, Darren (actor--Glee)
Criss, Peter (drummer--Kiss)
Crist, Charlie (politician)
Crist, Judith (critic)
Cristela, Alonzo (comedian)
Critters (musical group--Mr. Dieingly Sad)
Croce, Benedetto (philosopher)
Croce, Jim (singer--Operator, Time in a Bottle, I Got A Name, Haven't Got Time for Pain,   Bad, Bad Leroy Brown, You Don't Mess Around with Jim)
Cromwell, Oliver (General Ironside) (politician)
Cromwell, Thomas (Earl of Essex) (lawyer statesman--Henry VIII)
Cronenberg, David (filmmaker; Can.)
Cronin, Archibald Joseph (author--The Citadel, Hatter's Castle)
Cronyn, Hume (actor--A Letter for Evie) (Jessica Tandy's husband)
Crosby, Bing (actor--Holiday Inn/singer--Amore, So Do I, Top O The Morning)
Crosby, David (musician)
Crosby, Harry Lillis (Bing) (actor/singer-Waikiki Wedding)
Crosby, Norm (comedian)
Cross, Amanda (author--mystery)
Cross, Ben (actor--Chariots of Fire)
Cross, Irv (sportscaster)
Cross, Marcia (actress--Desperate Housewives)
Crosse, Rupert (actor--The Reivers)
Crothers, Benjamin (Scatman) (actor/songwriter/composer/singer/comedian/musician)
Crouse, Russel (playwright--Call Me Madame, A Beautiful Mind)
Crow, Sheryl (musician--rock--All I Wanna Do, Soak Up the Sun)
Crowe, Cameron (writer/director--Fast Times at Ridgemont High, Jerry Maguire,   Almost Famous)
Crowe, Russell (actor--The Insider, Gladiator)
Cruise, Suri (Tom Cruise/Katie Holmes's daughter)

Cruise, Tom (actor--War of the Worlds, Cocktail) (Katie Holmes ex./Suri's father)
Crumb, Robert (cartoonist--Keep on Trucking)
Cruz, Celia (singer--salsa)
Cruz, Penelope (actress)
Cruz, Teo (boxer)
Cryer, Jon (actor)
Cuddy, Jim (singer--Blue Rodeo)
Cugat, Xavier (bandleader) (Charo's husband)
Cukor, George (director--The Ardmore Story, Born Yesterday, A Bill of Divorcement, A Star is Born)
Culbertson, Ely (bridge expert)
Culkin, Kieran (actor)
Culkin, Macaulay) (actor--Home Alone)
Culkin, Rory (actor)
Cullen, Countee (poet)
Cullen, Sean (comedian)
Culpepper, Daunte (bowler)
Cult Jam (musical group lead by Lisa Lisa--Lost in Emotion)
Cumia, Anthony (radio show host) (Gregg Hughes (Opie) co-host)
Cumming, Alan (actor--The Good Wife)
Cummings, Edward Estlin (e.e.) (poet/painter/essayist/playwright/author--Eimi)
Cunningham, Merce (choreographer)
Cuny, Alain (actor)
Cuoco, Kaley (actress--Big Bang Theory)
Cuomo, Andrew (politician)
Cuomo, Mario (politician)
Curci, Amelita Galli (singer--soprano)
Cure (musical group--There Is No If)
Cure (musical group--There Is No If, Friday I'm in Love)
Curie, Eve (author/journalist/pianist)
Curie, Irene Joliot (scientist; Fr.) (Pierre & Marie's daughter)
Curie, Marie (scientist; Fr.) (Irene's mother)
Curie, Pierre (scientist; Fr.) (Irene's father)
Curl, Rodney (Rod) (golfer)
Currie, Robert (poet)
Currier, Nathaniel (lithographer--Currier & Ives)

Curry, Ann (newswoman)
Curry, Seth (basketball)
Curry, Timothy James (Tim) (actor/author--Abel's Island)
Curtis, Helene (beautician/salon product manufacturer)
Curtis, Jamie Lee (actress--Hallowe'en) (Janet Leigh's daughter)
Curtis, Tony (actor/singer--Mr. Cory)
Curtiss, Glenn (inventor--seaplane)
Cusack, Joan (actress--Working Girl, In and Out)
Cusack, John (actor--Say Anything, Eight Man Out)
Cushing, Caleb (diplomat)
Cussler, Clive (author--Sahara)
Custis, Mary (publisher/editor) (Robert E. Lee's wife)
Cuthbert, Elisha (actress--24)
Cuyp, Aelbert (artist--landscapes)
Cyaxares (King of Medea)
Cyrus, Billy Ray (singer/actor)
Cyrus, Miley (actress--Hannah Montana)
Czolgsz, Leon (anarchist/assassin)
Czowski, Peter (interviewer)

--D--

d'Abo, Olivia (actress--The Wonder Years)
D'Agnolo, Donato (architect)
D'Amato, Alfonse (politician)
D'Amboise, Jacques (dancer--ballet)
D'Angelo, Beverly (actress--Coal Miner's Daughter)
D'Annunzio, Gabriele (author/poet/playwright--Francesca Da Rimini/journalist)   (Eleonora Duce's partner)
D'Arc, Jean (Jeanne) (Joan of Arc) (revolutionary)
d'Este, Isabella (politician--Mantua ruler)
D'Orsay, Fifi (actress)
d'Urfe, Honore (author)
Da Gama, Vasco (explorer) (ship--St. Gabriel)
Da Silva, Eduardo (soccer)

da Vinci, Leonardo (artist--Vitruvian Man, Adoration of the Magi)
Dache, Lilly (designer--hats)
Dafoe, Willem (actor--Green Goblin, Daybreakers, John Wick)
Daggett, Tim (author--Dare to Dream, Gymnastics)
Daguerre, Louis (photographer)
Dahl, Arlene (actress--Diamond Queen)
Dahl, Roald (author--Willie Wonka, James and the Giant Peach, Fantastic Mr. Fox,   The Witches, Matilda, The BFG)
Dahl, Vincenzo (author--The Gremlins, The Witches)
Dai, Bao (politician/emporer--Viet.)
Dailey, Dan (artist/designer)
Daimler, Gottlieb (automaker)
Daisy Mae (Abe's mother)
Dajani, Nadia (actress)
Dal, Shannon (singer--rock star)
Dalai Lama (The Great Precious Conqueror) (religious leader)
Dale, Clamma (singer--soprano)
Dale, Cynthia (actress)
Dale, Jennifer (actress)
Dalen, Nils Gustaf (inventor--Swed.)
Daley, Richard (politician--mayor of Chicago)
Dalhart, Vernon (singer--country)
Dali, Salvadore (painter--Atomic Leda/Leda Atomica, Swans Reflecting Elephants, Burning   Giraffe, Christ of St. John of the Cross, The Hallucinagenic Toreador, Nostalgic Echo,   Basket of Bread or Bread, Rather Death than Shame, Dreamscape, Helena   Rubinstein, Persistence of Memory/sculptor/graphic artist/designer) (autobio--   Diary of a Genius)
Dalman, Christian (philosopher)
Dalton, John (chemist--atomic theory)
Dalton, Timothy (actor--James Bond)
Daltrey, Roger (musician--The Who)
Daly, Carson (T.V. host--M.T.V.)
Daly, John (T. V. host--What's My Line)
Daly, Tim (actor--Wings)
Daly, Tyne (actress)

Damato, Jason (politician; N. Y.)
Damian (St.) (patriarch of Alexandria)
Damien, Father (nee Joseph de Veuster) (missionary--lepers of Molokai)
Damon, Matt (actor--Mr. Ripley, The Martian)
Damone, Vic (singer--I Have But One Heart)
Damones (musical group--I Wanna Be Sedated)
Dampier, Erick (basketball)
Dana, Charles Anderson (newspaper editor)
Dana, Richard Henry (author--Seaman's Friend, Two Years Before the Mast; Am.)
Dandridge, Dorothy (actress--Carmen Jones)
Danes, Claire (actress--Homeland)
Daniel, Beth (golfer)
Daniels, Bebe Phyllis (actress--world's youngest Shakespearean-Rio Rita; Am.)
Daniels, Jeff (actor)
Daniels, Lee (director--The Butler)
Dannay, Frederic (pseudonym--Ellery Queen) (author--mystery)
Danner, Blythe (actress/ Gwyneth Paltrow's mother)
Danny & the Juniors (musical group--At the Hop)
Dano, Linda (actress)
Dano, Paul (actor--There Will Be Blood)
Danson, Ted (actor--Becker)
Dante, Alighiere (poet--La Vita Nuova, De Vulgare Eloquentia) (Brunetto Latini's student   and guardian)
Dantley, Adrian (basketball)
Danton, Georges (French revolutionist) (Marat's colleague)
Danton, Raymond Caplan (actor--The Legs Diamond)
Danza, Tony (actor/boxer)
Dara, Enzo (singer--opera--basso)
Darby, Kim (actress)
Darin, Bobby (singer--Mack the Knife, Splish Splash, Dream Lover)
Dark, Alvin Ralph (Swamp Fox/Blackie) (baseball)
Darling, Ron (baseball)
Darnell, Linda (actress--Forever Amber)
Darren, James (singer/actor--Gidget)

Darrow, Ann (actress--King Kong)
Darrow, Clarence (lawyer--Scopes Trial--Leopold & Loeb)
Darwin, Charles Robert (naturalist)
Dash, Stacey (actress--Clueless)
Dassler, Adolf (Adi) (inventor--Adidas founder)
Daudet, Alphonse (author)
Daumier, Honore (painter)
Davenport, Marcia (author/music critic)
Davenport, Nigel (actor)
Davi, Robert (singer/actor--License to Kill)
David, Gerard (painter--Flight into Egypt)
David, Hal (lyricist) (Burt Bacharach's partner)
Davidson, Sara (author--Loose Change)
Davies, Dave (musician--guitar/singer-songwriter--The Kinks)
Davies, Laura (golfer)
Davies, Ray (musician--guitar/singer-songwriter--The Kinks)
Davies, Robertson (author--Deptford Trilogy)
Davis, Adelle (author--nutrition)
Davis, Alana (singer)
Davis, Angela Yvonne (author/activist)
Davis, Bette (actress--New Voyager, The Scapegoat)
Davis, Brad (actor--Blood Ties)
Davis, Clive (record producer--Arista Records)
Davis, Elmer (author/news reporter)
Davis, Ernie (football)
Davis, Essie (actress--Matrix)
Davis, Geena (actress--Sara, The Long Kiss Goodnight, The
Scapegoat)
Davis, Gray (politician; Calif.--recalled)
Davis, Jefferson (General--Confederates, C.S.A.)
Davis, Jim (cartoonist--Garfield)
Davis, Kristin (actress)
Davis, Lanny (lawyer)
Davis, Mac (singer/songwriter/actor)
Davis, Miles (musician--jazz--Nonet band)
Davis, Ozzie, Ossie (actor--Jungle Fever, Dinosaur, I'm Not
Rappaport, Dr. Doolittle,   The Hill, Evening Shade)
(Ruby Dee's husband)
Davis, Paige (T. V. personality--Trading Spaces)

Davis, Paul (singer--I Go Crazy)
Davis, Sammy (dancer/actor--Ocean's Eleven/singer--The Candy Man)   (autobiography--Yes I Can)
Davis, Skeeter (singer--The End of the World)
Davis, Spencer (musician--I'm A Man)
Davis, Terrell (Ralo) (singer--Can't Lie)
Davutoglu, Ahmet (academic/politician/Turkish chief)
Dawber, Pam (actress)
Dawes, Charles (politician)
Dawson, Ernest (poet--Terre Promise, A Requiem, Benedictio Domini)
Dawson, Len (football)
Dawson, Rosario (actress)
Day, Clarence (author/essayist--Life with Father)
Day, Doris (nee Doris von Kappelhoff) (actress--Pillow Talk, Midnight Lace/singer--Again,   Tea For Two)
Day, Edith (actress--Irene)
Day, Hap (hockey)
Day, Laraine (actress)
Day, Otis (musician--The Knights)
Dayan, Moshe (politician; Isr.)
Daye, Stephen (printer)
Dayne, Ron (football)
Dayne, Taylor (singer--pop)
de Anza, Juan Bautista (explorer--founder of San Francisco)
de Armas, Ana (actress--Knives Out)
De Backer, Wouter Andre (Wally) (Gotye) (musician/songwriter/singer--Somebody   I Used to Know)
de Balboa, Vasco Nunez (explorer)
De Balzac, Honore M. (playwright/author--Le Pere Goriot, La Cousine Bette)
de Beauvoir, Simone (feminist)
de Beranger, Pierre Jean (poet)
de Bourbon, Louis (Prince de Conte)
de Brunhoff, Cecile (author--Babar)
de Camoes, Luis (poet; Port.)
de Camp, Rosemary (actress)

de Carlo, Yvonne (actress--Munsters)
de Cavalieri, Emilio (composer)
de Cervantes, Miguel (author--Don Quixote)
de Champlain, Samuel (explorer)
de Chateaubriand, Francois-Rene (author--Rene)
De Cusa, Nicholas (philosopher)
de Estleman, Loren (author--crime)
De Falla, Manuel (composer--La Vida Breve, El Amor Brujo)
de Fermat, Pierre (probability theorist)
de Ferran, Gil (race car driver)
De Gaulle, Charles (politician/author--The Army of the Future)
De Generes, Ellen (actress/comedienne/author--My Point and I Do Have One)
de Groot, Huig (jurist)
de Havilland, Olivia (actress) (Joan Fontaine's sister)
de Kooning, Elaine (painter--portraits)
De Kooning, Willem (painter; Am.)
de L'Epee, Abee (sign language pioneer)
de la Cruz, Sor Juana Ines (poet)
de la Fontaine, Jean (poet/fabulist)
De La Fressange, Ines (model/fashion designer)
De La Garza, Alana (actress--Law and Order)
de la Halle, Adam (composer)
de la Hoya, Oscar (boxer)
De la Mare, Walter ([poet--The Listeners, Nod)
de la Ramee, Marie Louise (pseudonym--Ouida) (author--A Dog of Flanders)
de la Renta, Oscar (fashion designer)
de la Roche, Mazo (author)
de la Salle, Sieur (explorer)
de la Tour, Georges (painter--The Fortune Tellers)
de Lange, Ilse (singer)
de Larrocha, Alicia (pianist)
de Laurentiis, Aurelio (director/actor--Vino)
de Laurentiis, Dino (actor/producer)
De Laurentiis, Giada (chef)
de Lavoisier, Antoine-Laurent (Father of Modern Chemistry) (chemist)

de Lesseps, Ferdinand-Marie, Vicomte de (engineer--Suez Canal)
de Lisle, Leconte (poet)
de Lisle, Rouget (composer--La Marseillaise)
de Lucia, Paco (guitarist--Sp.)
De Matteo, Drea (actress--Desperate Housewives, Sopranos)
De Maupassant, Guy (author--short story)
de Medici, Catherine (Reine) (noblewoman)
de Medici, Giovanni di Bicci (banker)
de Medici, Lorenzo (statesman/art patron)
De Mille, Agnes (choreographer--Carousel, Rodeo, Fall River Legend)
De Mille, Cecil (director--The King of Kings, The Sign of the Cross)
De Mille, Nelson (author--thrillers)
de Montaigne, Michel (author--essays)
De Nerval, Gerard (author--Aurelia)
De Niro, Robert (actor--Ronin, The King of Comedy, A Bronx Tale, Casino, The Fan   /director--The Good Shepherd)
de Palma, Brian (screenwriter/director--Carrie, Dressed to Kill, Scarface, Carlito's Way)
de Pineda, Alonso Alvarez (explorer)
De Putti, Lya (actress--silent films)
de Queiroz, Jose Maria Eca (author)
de Ravin, Emilie (actess)
de Ribera, Jusepe (a.k.a. Lo Spagnoletto) (painter)
de Ronsard, Pierre (Prince of Poets) (poet--odes)
de Rossi, Portia (actress--Ally McBeal)
de Sade, Donatien Alphoso Francois (author--Justin)
de Sade, Marquis (soldier/author--Justine and Juliet)
de Saint-Exupery, Antoine-Marie (pilot--W.W. II/author--The Little Prince; Fr.)
De Salvo, Anne (actress--My Favorite Year)
De Santis, Ron (politician)
de Secondat, Charles Louis (Baron of Montesquieu) (philosopher)
De Sica, Vittorio (director/actor--The Bicycle Thief)
de Soto, Hernando (explorer)

De Soto, Rosana (actress)
de Stael, Louise Germaine (Madame--Baroness) (author--Delphine)
de Sucre, Antonio Jose (politician--first Bolivian president)
de Tirtoff, Romaine (pseudonym--Russ Erte) (fashion designer/illustrator)
de Torquemada, Tomas (friar--Inquisitor)
de Trillo, Pero (architect)
De Valera, Eamon (politician--former leader of Ireland)
de Vega, Lope (author--5 Plays)
de Vivar, Rodrigo Diaz (El Cid) (military leader; Sp.)
de Waart, Edo (maestro)
De Wilde, Brandon (actor)
Dean, Abner (nee Abner Epstein) (cartoonist) (Jacob Epstein's nephew)
Dean, James (actor--Rebel Without a Cause)
Dean, Loren (actor--Space Cowboys)
Dean, Morton (author/newsman)
Deane, Silas (politician--recruited Lafayette)
Deaver, Michael (politician)
Debs, Eugene (union leader--socialist)
Debussy, Achille-Claude (composer--opus--La Mer, L'isle Joyeuse, Clair de Lune)
Dee, Frances (actress)
Dee, Joey (and the Starlighters) (musical group)
Dee, Kiki (nee Pauline Matthews) (singer)
Dee, Kool Moe (musician--rap)
Dee, Ruby (actress--Jungle Fever)
Dee, Sandra (singer/actress--Gidget, The Dunwich Horror, A Summer Place)
Deems, Taylor (musicologist/composer/music critic)
Deen, Paula (actress/T.V. personality/author--cooking--It Ain't All About Cooking,   Paula's Home Cooking)
Deep Purple (musical group--Smoke Over the Water)
Def Leppard (musical group--Hysteria)
Def, Mos (actor/musician--rap--The Ecstatic)
Defoe, Daniel (author--A Journal of the Plague Year, An Essay Upon Projects)

Degas, Edgar/ Hilaire-Germain-Edgar (artist--pastels--human figure in motion--Race Horses,   L'Absinthe, Cotton Broker's Office, Prima Ballerina, The Ballet Class, Ballet
     Rehearsal The Dance Class, The Dancing Class; Fr.)
Degun, Zhu (Chu Teh-Chun/Zhu De) (politician--Chinese Communist Party)
Deighton, Len (author--The Ipcress File, Funeral in Berlin, The Berlin Game)
Dekker, Thomas (dramatist/pamphleteer--The Bellman of London)
Del Ajar, Emile (author--Momo)
Del Pollaiuolo, Antonio (painter/sculptor/engraver/goldsmith) (Lorenzo Medici's protégé)
Del Rey, Lana (singer--Born to Die)
Del Rey, Lester (author--sci-fi)
Del Rio, Dolores (actress/singer--Ramona)
Del Sarto, Andrea (painter)
Del Toro, Benicio (actor)
Del Toro, Guillermo (director)
Delaney, Dana (actress)
Delaney, Kim (actress)
Delaney, Shelagh (playwright--A Taste of Honey)
Delano, Sara (F.D.R.'s mother)
Delany, Sam Ron (author--sci-fi)
Delaria, Lea (actress/comedienne)
Delaunay, Sonia (painter)
Delaware, Alex (detective)
DeLay, Tom (politician)
Delfonics (musical group--Lala Means I Love You)
Delibes, Leo (composer--opera--Lakme)
Delillo, Don (author--White Noise)
Dell, Floyd (author--avant-garde)
Della Casa, Lisa (singer--soprano)
Dellums, Ron (politician)
Delon, Alain (actor; Fr.)
Delong, George Washington (explorer--Arctic)
Delpy, Julie (actress--The Air I Breathe)
Delray, Lester (author--sci-fi)
DeLuise, Dom (actor/comedian/director/producer--Fatso)

Demarest, William (actor)
Dementieva, Elena (tennis)
Demento, Dr. (D.J.) (nee Barret Eugene Hansen) (Barry)
(radio broadcaster)
Demich, Irina (actress)
Demme, Jonathan (Ted) (director/screenwriter/producer--
Philadelphia, Silence of the Lambs)
Democritus (Laughing philosopher/Chosen of the People)
(philosopher--cheerfulness/   scientist--
atomic theory)
Demornay, Rebecca (actress--Risky Business)
Demosthenes (statesman/orator)
Dempsey, William Harrison (Jack) (Manassa Mauler) (boxer)
(Luis Angel Firpo's opponent)
Demy, Jacques (director)
Dench, Judi (actress--The Best Exotic Marigold Hotel)
Deneuve, Catherine (actress--Repulsion, Indochine)
Denholm, Elliott (actor)
Deniro, Robert (producer/actor--Ronin)
Denisof, Alexis (actress)
Denning, Kat (actress--The Forty-Year Old Virgin)
Dennis, Sandy (actress--Any Wednesday, Who's Afraid of
Virginia Woolf)
Dent, Russell Earl (Bucky) (baseball)
Denton, Sandra (Pepa) (actress/musician--hip-hop--Whatta
Man) (Salt-N-Pepa)
Denver, John (singer--Annie's Song, Aerie)
Deodato, Eumir (musician/producer--Also Sprach Zarathustra)
Depardieu, Gerard (actor--Danton, The Man in the Iron Mask)
Depeche Mode (musical group)
Depew, Chauncey (orator)
Depp, Johnny (actor--Edward Scissorhands, Sleepy Hollow,
Mr Esco, Don Juan de Marco,   Dark
Shadows, Tonto)
Derain, Andre (painter)
Dere, Mehmet (painter)
Derek, Bo (actress--Tarzan, Ten, Orca)
Derek, John (actor/director)

Dern, Bruce (actor--Monster, The Hateful Eight, Family Plot, After Dark My Sweet)
Dern, Laura (actress--I Am Sam, Jurassic Park, Blue Velvet, Big Little Lies, Citizen Ruth)
Dershowitz, Alan (lawyer/author--Chutzpah)
Des Barres, Pamela (author--Rock Bottom, Take Another Little Piece of My Heart)
Des Pres, Tristan (composer/producer; Flemish)
Des'ree (singer--You Gotta Be)
Descartes, Rene M. (philosopher/mathematician/author; Fr.)
Desert, Alex (actress)
Desica, Vittorio (director--The Bicycle Thief)
Desoto, Hernando (explorer; Sp.)
Desspiau, Charles (sculptor)
Detmar, Ty (football)
Detoire, Rick (cartoonist--One Big Happy)
Devereux, Robert (Earl of Essex)
Devereux, Stella Penelope (Lady Rich) (noblewoman) (Robert's sister, Charles Bount   (Lord Rich/Earl of Devonshire's wife)
Devers, Gail (runner)
Devine, Andy (actor)
DeVito, Danny (actor--Taxi)
Devo (musical group--Whip It)
Dewar, James (chemist/physicist/inventor--thermos)
Dewar, John (entrepreneur--Scotch Whiskey)
Dewar, Tommy (entrepreneur--Scotch Whiskey)
Dewey, Melvil (librarian--Dewey Decimal System; Am.)
Dewey, Thomas Edmund (politician; Am.)
Dewhurst, Colleen Roco (Queen of Broadway) (actress)
Dexter, Colin (author--mystery--Morse)
Dexter, Gordon (saxophonist)
Dey, Susan (actress--Blue River)
di Buoninsegna, Duccio (painter)
Di Rupo, Elio (politician; Bel.)
Di Terlizzi, Tony (author--The Spiderwick Chronicles)
Diamond Rio (musical group)
Diamond, I.A.L. (screenwriter)
Diamond, Jack (Legs/Gentleman Jack) (gangster--bootlegger)

Diamond, Neil (singer--Cherry Cherry, I Am I Said, Shilo)
Diamond, Selma (actress)
Diamonds (musical group--Little Darlin)
Diaz, Cameron (actress--My Best Friend's Wedding, Gangs of New York, In Her Shoes)
Diaz, Edith (actress)
Diaz, Porfirio (politician; Mex.)
Diaz, Rodrigo (El Cid) (military leader)
Dick, Philip Kindred (author--sci-fi/paranormal)
Dickens, Charles (Boz) (author--Hard Times, The Mystery of Edwin Drood, Martin Chuzzlewit, Sketches by Boz, Barnaby Rudge, Betsey Prig, A Tale of Two Cities)
Dickenson, Vic (musician--jazz)
Dickey, James (author--Into the Stone, Deliverance)
Dickinson, Amy (columnist--advice)
Dickinson, Angie (actress)
Dickinson, Emily (poet--For Every Bird a Nest)
Dickson, Carter (nee John Dickson Carr) (author)
Diddley, Bo (singer-songwriter--I'm a Man)
Diddy, P. (nee Sean Combs) (actor/music producer/singer--rap)
Diderot, Denis (philosopher/encyclopedist; Fr.)
Didion, Joan (author--Play It As It Lay)
Dido (singer/songwriter--Thank You)
Dido, Elissa (Queen of Carthage)
Didrikson, Babe (golfer)
Diem, Ngo Dinh (politician; Vietnam)
Diesel, Vin (actor--A Man Apart)
Dieskau, Dietrich Fischer (Lieder) (singer--baritone)
Dietrich, Dena (actress)
Dietrich, Marlene (nee Maria Magdalena von Losch) (actress--Just a Gigolo)
DiFranco, Ani (singer)
Diggs, Taye (actor)
Dilfer, Trent (football)
Dillon, Matt (actor--Wayward Pines)
Dillon, Melinda (actress--A Christmas Story)
Dimaggio, Dom (baseball)
Dimaggio, Joe (Joltin Joe) (baseball)

Dinesen, Isak (Karen Blixen's pseudonym) (author--Out of Africa, Babette's Feast,   Winter's Tales)
Ding Gedicht, Rilke (poet)
Dino, Desi & Billy (musical group--Dean Martin, Desi Arnaz, Billy Hinsche)
Dio, Cassius (author)
Diogenes (philosopher--founder of Cynic Philosophy)
DioGuardi, Kara (singer/songwriter/music producer/T.V. personality--American Idol)
Dion (singer--Dion and the Belmonts--Ruby Baby, The Wanderer, Where or When,   It's All Coming Back to Me Now)
Dion, Celine (singer--Titanic, My Heart Will Go On, It's All Coming Back to Me Now)   (Rene Angelil's wife)
Dionne, Annette (quintuplet)
Dionne, Cecile (quintuplet)
Dionne, Emilie (quintuplet)
Dionne, Farris (producer/actress/singer-songwriter--I Know)
Dionne, Marie (quintuplet)
Dionne, Yvonne (quintuplet)
Dior, Christian (fashion designer--New Look)
DiPietro, Guido (Fra Giovanni Angelico's pseudonym) (painter)
Diplo (nee Thomas Wesley Pentz) (songwriter/record producer/D.J.)
Dirac, Paul Adrian (physicist/nobelist; Br.)
Dire Straits (musical group--Sultans of Swing)
Disch, Thomas M. (author--sci. fi.)
Disney, Walter Elias (entrepreneur/cartoonist)
DiSpirito, Rocco (chef/author--Now Eat This!)
Disraeli, Benjamin (politician; Br.)
Disraeli, Isaac (author--Curiosities of Literature)
Divac, Vlade (basketball)
Dix, Dorothy (Dorothea) Lynde (reformer/columnist--advice)
Dix, Otto (painter--expressionist; Ger.)
Dixon, Ivan (actor)
Dixon, Jeane (astrologer)
Djokovic, Novak (tennis)
Dobbs, Kildare (broadcaster/author)

Dobbs, Lou (newsman)
Dobrev, Nina (actress--The Vampire Diaries)
Dobson, Kevin (actor--Kojak)
Doctorow, Edgar Lawrence (E.L.) (author--Billy Bathgate, Ragtime, Loon Lake)
Dodd, Chris (politician)
Dodd, Ed (cartoonist--Mark Trail)
Dodd, Frank Howard (publisher) (Moses's son/Edward Mead's partner)
Dodd, Jimmie (actor/songwriter--Mickey Mouse Club)
Dodd, Moses Woodruff (publisher) (Frank's father/John S. Taylor's partner)
Dodgson, Charles Ludwidge (pseudonym Lewis Carroll) (author--Alice in Wonderland)
Doeg, John Godfray Hope (tennis)
Doenitz, Karl (admiral--W.W.II; Ger.)
Doerr, Anthony (author--All the Light We Cannot See)
Doerr, Bobby (baseball)
Dogg, Nate (nee Nathaniel Dwayne Hale) (singer--rap)
Doherty, Shannen (actress)
Dohnanyi, Erno (composer/musician--pianist)
Dokan, Ota (Edo/Tokyo founder)
Dokic, Jelena (tennis)
Dolan, Charles (founder of HBO)
Dolan, Timothy (Archbishop--New York)
Dole, Robert (politician) (Lott's predecessor)
Dolenz, Ami (actress)
Dolenz, Mickey (singer--The Monkeys)
Dolin, Anton (Sir) (dancer)
Domenici, Peter (politician)
Domingo, Dia (politician; Brazil)
Domingo, Placido (singer--opera)
Domino, Antoine (Fats) (singer)
Domosthenes (orator)
Donahue, Elinor (actress--Get A Life, Father Knows Best)
Donahue, Phil (talk show host)
Donaldson, Sam (newsman)
Donat, Richard (actor--Blackfly)

Donat, Robert (actor--Goodbye Mr. Chips, The Ghost Goes West)
Donati, Danilo (designer--costumes)
Donati, Giulio (football)
Donen, Stanley (director--Funny Face)
Donitz, Karl (Admiral)
Donizetti, Gaetano (composer--La Fille du Regiment, Regnava Nel Selenzio, Rita, L'elisir D'amore, Anna Bolena)
Donlevy, Brian (actor--Beau Geste)
Donne, John (poet--metaphysical--Death Be Not Proud, Go and Catch a Falling Star, Meditation XVII, Devotions, Death's Duel)
Donovan (singer/songwriter--Mellow Yellow)
Donovan, Elisa (actress--Clueless)
Donovan, William Joseph (Wild Bill) (lawyer, intelligence officer, diplomat--O.S.S.)
Doobie Brothers (musical group--Takin It to the Streets, What A Fool Believes)
Dooley, Vince (football)
Doolittle, Hilda (poet--imagist)
Doors (musical group--L.A. Woman)
Dorat, Jean (poet)
Dorati, Antal (conductor)
Dore, Gustave (illustrator--Dante's Divine Comedy)
Dorff, Stephen (actor)
Doria, Andrea (doctor/Director of Research)
Doria, Andrea (Liberator of Genoa) (Father of Peace) (politician/Admiral)
Dormer, Natalie (actress--Game of Thrones)
Dorr, Thomas W. (revolutionary--rebel leader of 1842)
Dors, Diana (Blonde Bombshell) (actress)
Dorsey, Jimmy (composer--Maria Elena, Besamo Mucho, Not Mine, So Rare)
Dorsey, Tommy (orchestra leader/musician--trumpet/trombone--Our Love)
Dos Passos, John (author--U.S.A. Trilogy)

Dostoevsky, Fyodor (Feodor(e)) Mikhailovich (author--The Possessed, Idiot, Crime and Punishment)
Doubleday, Abner (sports--invented baseball)
Douglas, Kirk (actor)
Douglas, Lloyd C. (author--opus)
Douglas, Michael (actor--Fatal Attraction)
Douglas, Stephen Arnold (politician/orator)
Douglas-Home, Alec (politician; Br.)
Dourdan, Gary (actor)
Dourif, Brad (actor--One Flew Over the Cuckoo's Nest)
Dove, Rita (poet--On The Bus with Rosa Parks)
Dow, Charles Henry (founder of Dow Jones Market)
Dowd, Maureen (columnist--N.Y. Times)
Down, Angela (actress)
Downes, Olin (critic--music)
Downey Jr., Robert (actor--Chaplin)
Downey, Morton (talk show host/screenwriter/autobiographer/diarist)
Downey, Roma (actress)
Downie, Gord (musician/poet)
Dowson, Ernest (poet)
Doyle, Arthur Conan (Sir) (author--Sir Nigel, The White Company, A Study in Scarlet, Micah Clarke, The Valley of Fear, A Case of Identity, The Lost World)
Dr. Dre (nee Andre Romelle Young) (singer--rap)
Dr. John (singer--Right Place, Wrong Time)
Dr. Ruth (Westheimer) (media personality/therapist/author--Sex for Dummies)
Dragon, Daryl (musician--Captain of Captain and Tennille)
Drake (singer--rap--Views)
Drake, Stan (cartoonist)
Draper, Paul (singer/songwriter/record producer/musician) (band--Mansun)
Dreiser, Theodore (author--American Tragedy, Sister Carrie, Jennie Gerhardt)
Drescher, Fran (actress--The Nanny, Happily Divorced)
Dressler, Marie (nee Leila Koerber) (actress)
Drexler, Clyde (basketball)

Dreyfos, Alfred (soldier--1890 French, wrongly convicted)
Dreyfuss, Richard (actor)
Driver, Adam Douglas (actor--Girls, BlackkKlansman)
Driver, Minnie (actress)
Dru Hill (musical group--R & B)
Dru, Joanne (actress--Red River, Wagon Master, The Pride of St. Louis)
Drucker, Mort (cartoonist--Mad)
Drudge, Matt (talk host--Internet)
Drury, Allen Stuart (author--Advise and Consent)
Drusilla, Livia (Empress) (Augustus Caesar's wife/Tiberius's mother)
Dryden, John (poet--restoration--Annus Mirabilis, Absalom and Achitophel, The Rival Ladies)
Dryden, Ken (hockey)
Duarte, Juan (polititcian) (Maria Eva's husband)
Duarte, Maria Eva (Evita/Little Eva) (actress/First Lady of Argentina) (Juan's wife)
Dubner, Stephen (radio host/journalist/author--Freakonomics)
DuBois, William Edward Burghardt (W.E.B.) (activist--NAACP founder/author--The Souls   of Black Folk)
Dubos, Rene (environmentalist/microbiologist/author--Think Globally, Act Locally)
Ducasse, Alain (chef; Fr.)
Duccio (di Buoninsegna) (painter)
Duce, Eleonora (actress) (Gabriele D'Annunzio's partner)
Duchamp, Marcel (artist--dada--Mona Lisa--antiart--nudes)
Duchamps, Gaston (pseudonym--Francois Villon) (poet)
Duchin, Eddy (musician--piano/band leader) (Peter's father)
Duchin, Peter (musician--piano/band leader) (Eddy's son)
Duckworth, Kendrick Lamar (singer--rap--King Kunta)
Duckworth, Ladda Tammy (politician)
Ducommun, Elie (journalist/peace activist)
Dudek, Louis (poet/editor)
Dudevant, Aurore (pseudonym--George Sand) (author)
Duffy, Carol Ann (poet)
Dufresne, Wylie (chef/T.V.personality--Top Chef)
Dufy, Raoul (artist)
Dukas, Paul (composer--LaPeri)

Duke, Annie (poker)
Duke, Doris (heiress/socialite/horticulturalist/art collector/philanthropist)
Duke, Patty (actress--The Miracle Worker)
Dullea, Keir (actor--1001 A Space Odyssey, David and Lisa)
Dulles, Allen (lawyer/diplomat/C.I.A. director)
Dumas, Alexandre (Pere) (author--La Dame Aux Camelias/Lady of Camelias, Acte,
        The Black Tulip)
DuMaurier, Daphane (artist/author--Jamaica Inn, Rebecca)
Dumm, Edwina (cartoonist--Alec the Great)
Dumont, Margaret (actress--Marx Brothers films)
Dunaway, Faye (actress--Mommie Dearest)
Duncan, Arne (politician)
Duncan, Isadora (dancer)
Duncan, Renault Renaldo (actor)
Duncan, Sandy (actress)
Dundee, Angelo (boxing)
Dunham, Jeff (ventriloquist)
Dunham, Lena (filmmaker/actress--Girls)
Dunn, Nora (actress/comedian--S.N.L.)
Dunne, Dominick (author--An Inconvenient Woman)
Dunne, Finey Peter (writer/humorist)
Dunne, Irene (actress--Awful Truth, A Guy Names Joe)
Dunst, Kirsten (actress--Marie Antoinette, Spider-Man)
Dupin, Amandine (Amandine Aurore Lucie Dupin Dudevant) (pseudonym--George Sand) (author)
duPlessis, Louise (composer; S. Afr.)
Dupre, Jules (painter--Barbizon School)
Dupuis, Roy (actor)
Duran Duran (musical group--Rio)
Duran, Jose (Hands of Steel) (boxer)
Duran, Roberto (Hands of Stone) (boxer)
Durance, Erica (actress--Smallville)
Durant, Ariel (pseudonym--Ida (Ada) Kaufman) (author--The Story of Civilization) (Will's wife)
Durant, Kevin (basketball)
Durant, Will (author--The Story of Civilization) (Ariel's husband)

Durbin, Deanna (actress)
Duren, Ryne (baseball)
Durer, Albrecht (engraver/artist--Ger.)
Durkheim, Emile (socialist)
Duroc, Geraud Christophe Michel (Gen.--Napoleonic)
Durocher, Leo (The Lip) (baseball)
Durrell, Lawrence (author--Tunc)
Durst, Fred (musician--Limp Bizkit)
Duryea, Dan (actor)
Duse, Eleonora (actress; It.)
Dushku, Eliza (actress--Tru Calling, Buffy the Vampire Slayer)
Dutton, Charles S. (actor--Roc)
Duval, Claude (highwayman)
Duval, David (golfer)
Duvalier, Jean-Claude (politician--exiled)
Duvall, Clea (writer/producer/director/actress--21 Grams)
Duvall, Robert (actor--Tender Mercies)
Duvall, Shelley (actress)
Duvant, Ariel (historian)
Duveen, Joseph (art connoisseur)
DuVernay, Ava (director--Selma)
Dvorak, Anton(in) Leopold (composer--Nine Symphonies, New World Symphony, Slovonic Dances; Bohem.)
Dwyer, Jim (reporter)
Dykstra, Len (baseball)
Dylan, Bob (singer/songwriter--Knockin on Heaven's Door, Nettie Moore, If Not For You, It Ain't Me Babe)
Dyson, Frank Watson (astronomer)
Dyson, Michael Eric (author)
Dzhugashvili, Iosif V. (Stalin's pseudonym) (politician)

--E--

E Street Band (musical group--Little Steven's band/Bruce Springstein's band)

E. Sheila (nee Sheilae Cecilia Escovedo)
(percussionist/singer/actress/author) (Prince's band)
E.L.P. (Emerson, Lake and Palmer) (musical group--Brain
Salad Surgery)
E.LO. (Electric Light Orchestra) (musical group--El Dorado,
Evil Woman, Calling America,   Rock 'n Roll is King,
Do Ya, Out of the Blue, Hold on Tight, Xanadu, Telephone
Line)   (drummer--Bev Bevan)
E.M.F. (musical group--Unbelievable)
Eadie, Betty (author--Embraced by the Light)
Eads, George (actor--C.S.I.)
Eads, James Buchanan (inventor/architect--St. Louis Bridge)
Eagan, Daisy (actress)
Eager, Edgar (author--Half Magic)
Eagles (musical group--Lyin Eyes, Hotel California)
Eaker, Ira (General--W.W.II)
Eames, Charles (designer--furniture)
Eames, Emma (singer--opera--soprano)
Earhart, Amelia (aviator) (George Putnam's wife)
Earl of Avon (United Kingdom peerage title) (Sir Robert
Anthony Eden--first Earl)
Earl of Clarendon (Edward Hyde's title) (historian)
Earle, Pliny (inventor--carding machine)
Earle, Ralph (artist--portrait--primitive)
Earle, Robert (T.V. game show host)
Earle, Steve (singer--Guitar Town)
Early, Jubal (lawyer/politician--C.S.A.)
Earp, Morgan (lawman) (Virgil & Wyatt's brother)
Earp, Virgil (lawman) (Virgil & Wyatt's brother)
Earp, Wyatt (lawman) (Clanton's foe, Virgil and Morgan's
brother)
Eason, Tony (football--quarterback)
Eastman, Max (author/poet)
Easton, Sheena (singer--U Got the Look, For Your Eyes Only)
Eastwood, Clint (actor--The Eiger Sanction, Joe Kidd, J.
Edgar, Two Mules for Sister Sara)
Eaton, John Henry (politician--Jackson's S. Of War)
Eaton, Mary (actress--The Coconuts)
Eaton, Theophilus (merchant; Br.)

Eazy E (musician--rap)
Eban, Abba (Aubrey) (politician--Israeli/author--My People,
Voice of Israel, Personal   Witness: Israel
Through My Eyes)
Ebb, Fred (lyricist--Cabaret)
Eber, Jose (hair stylist)
Eberle, Abastenia St. Leger (sculptor)
Eberle, Ray (singer)
Ebersal, Dick (T.V. exec. producer--S.N.L.)
Ebert, Friedrich (politician; Ger.)
Ebert, Roger (movie critic/author--Your Movie Sucks, Video
Companion, Movie Yearbook,   The Great Movies,
Awake in the Dark, I Hated, Hated, Hated This Movie)
              (Siskel's/Roeper's partner)
Ebon, Martin (author--Psychic Warfare)
Ebsen, Buddy (actor)
Eck, Johann (theologian--Luther opposition)
Eckert, William (baseball)
Eckhart, Aaron (actor)
Eckhart, Meister (mystic; Ger.)
Ecko, Marc (fashion designer)
Eco, Umberto (author--Foucault's Pendulum, The Name of the
Rose, Baudolino, The   Island of the Day
Before)
Edberg, Stefan (tennis)
Ed-Din, Nasr (Shah; Persia)
Eddy, Duane (actor/musician--Rebel Rouser)
Eddy, Mary Baker (Christian Science founder/author--No and
Yes)
Eddy, Nelson (actor/singer--Stout Hearted Man, Naughty
Marietta)
Edeet, Ravel (author--10,000 Lovers)
Edel, Leon (author, biographer--Henry James, James Joyce)
Edel, Uli (director)
Edelstein, Lisa (actress)
Eden, John (of Winston--Sir) (Churchill's successor)
Eden, Robert Anthony (Sir) (first Earl of Avon) (politician)
Eder, Linda (singer--Jekyll and Hyde's Someone Like You)
Eder, Richard (critic)

Ederle, Gertrude (swimmer)
Edison, Thomas Alva (inventor--stock ticker, fluoroscope/G.E. founder)
Edmonds, Walter Dumaux (author--Drums Along the Mohawk)
Edmund II (Ironside) (King of England)
Edred (conqueror--Northumberland)
Edsels (musical group--Rama Lama Ding Dong)
Edson Arantes do Nascimento, Pele (soccer)
Edugyan, Esi (author--Half Blood Blues)
Edwards, Anne (biographer--celebrities)
Edwards, Anthony (actor)
Edwards, Blake (director--Victor-Victoria, A Fine Mess)
Edwards, Elizabeth (attorney/health care activist/author--Saving Graces)
Edwards, Herm (football)
Edwards, John (politician) (John Kerry's running mate)
Edwards, Ralph (television/radio host--This is Your Life)
Edy, Joseph (ice cream maker)
Efron, Zac (actor--High School Musical, Neighbors, Baywatch)
Egan, Eddie (actor--French Connection)
Egan, Edward (Cardinal)
Egan, Jennifer (author--A Visit From the Goon Squad, Manhattan Beach)
Egan, Raymond (songwriter--Sleepy Time Gal)
Egan, Richard (actor--Pollyanna, A Summer Place)
Egan, Walter (singer--Magnet & Steel)
Egan, William A. (first gov. of Alaska)
Egbert/Echberht (King of Wessex) (Alfred the Great's grandfather)
Eggar, Samantha (actress--Dr. Doolittle, Walk Don't Run, The Collector)
Egoyan, Atom (director--Ararat)
Ehle, Jennifer (actress--Pride and Prejudice, Zero Dark Thirty)
Ehrenburg, Ilya (author)
Eiffel, Gustave (engineer--Eiffel Tower)
Eigen, Manfred (chemist)
Eilers, Sally (actress)
Einstein, Albert (physicist--Ger.-Am.) (Elsa's husband)
Einstein, Elsa (Albert's wife)

Eisele, Donn Fulton (astronaut)
Eisen, Rich (newscaster)
Eisenberg, Jesse (playwright/actor--Social Network)
Eisenberg, Ned (actor)
Eisenhower, Dwight David (politician) (Mamie's husband)
Eisenhower, Mamie (nee Doud) (Dwight David Eisenhower's wife)
Eisenstein, Sergei (director/theorist--montage)
Eisley, Anthony (actor--Hawaiian Eye)
Eisner, Michael (businessman/C.E.O. Wald Disney Company) (Card Walker & Raymond Watson's successor/Robert Iger's predecessor)
Eisner, Will (cartoonist--The Spirit)
Ekberg, Anita (actress--La Dolce Vita)
Ekland, Britt (actress)
El Cid (military leader) (horse--Babieca)
El Greco (architect/sculptor/painter--The Disrobing of Christ, View of Toledo)
Elam, Jack (oater--Rio Lobo)
Elam, Jason (football)
Elba, Idrissa (Idris) (musician/producer/actor--Nelson Mandella)
Elder, Lee (golfer)
Eldredge, Todd (figure skater; Am.)
Eldrich, Louise (author--The Round House)
Electric Light Orchestra (musical group-Do Ya)
Elena of Montenegro (Queen; It,) (Victor Emmanuel III's consort)
Eleniak, Erika (actress)
el-Fayed, Dodi (producer)
Elfman, Danny (musician--Beetlejuice, The Simpsons)
Elfman, Jenna (actress--Darma & Greg)
Elg, Taina (dancer/actress--Les Girls)
Elgar, Edward William (Sir) (composer--Pomp and Circumstance, Enigma Variations, King Olaf, The Dream of Gerontius)
Elgort, Ansel (singer/actor--The Fault In Our Stars)
Eli (Priest of Shiloh)
Eli (Yale U. musical group--Whiffenpoof Song, Boola Boola)

Elia (Charles Lamb's pseudonym) (author/essayist--Popular
Fallacies, Tales from Shakespeare,   A Chapter of
Ears, Dream Children, The Praise of the Chimney Sweepers,
New   Year's Eve, Roast Pig)
Eliade, Mircea (author--Bengal Nights)
Eliav, Arie/Aryeh (Lova) (politician; Isr.)
Elie, Mario (basketball)
Elion, Gertrude (biochemist/pharmacologist/inventor--leukemia
drug)
Eliot, Charles William (academic--Harvard president)
Eliot, George (Mary Anne Evan's pseudonym) (author--
    Silas Marner, Daniel Deronda, Spanish   Gypsy,
    Adam Bede, Scenes of Clerical Life, Romola, A Mill on
    the Floss)
Eliot, T.S. (Thomas Stearns) (essayist/playwright/poet--Mr.
Apollinax, Four Quartets,   Gerontion, The Rock, The
Cocktail Party, The Hollow Men, East Coker, Sweeney
                Erect, A Cooking Egg, Macavity; The Mystery
Cat, The Naming of Cats, Sweeney   Among
the Nightingales, Jellicle Cats, Dante--book essay)
Elise, Christine (actress--E.R.)
Elise, Kimberly (actress--Close to Home)
Elizabeth, Shannon (actress--American Pie)
Elkin, Stanley (author--The Magic Kingdom)
Eller, Carl (football)
Ellerbee, Linda (author--And So It Goes/T.V. host--Nick News)
Elliman, Yvonne (singer--If I Can't Have You)
Ellington, Edward Kennedy (Duke) (musician--Satin Doll,
Mood Indigo)
Elliot, Cass (nee Ellen Naomi Cohen) (singer--Mamas and
Papas)
Elliott, Alison (actress--Spitfire Grill)
Elliott, Chris (actor) (Robert's son)
Elliott, David James (actor)
Elliott, Missy (singer--Work It, Dat's What I'm Talkin Bout)
Elliott, Robert (actor/comedian--Bob & Ray (Goulding) Show--
radio)
Elliott, Sam (author)
Ellis, Bret Easton (author--American Psycho, Less Than Zero)

Ellis, Dock (baseball)
Ellis, Havelock (psychologist--sex)
Ellis, Herb (guitarist--jazz)
Ellis, Perry Edwin (fashion designer)
Ellison, Harlan (author)
Ellison, Ralph Waldo (educator/author--Invisible Man)
Elman, Mischa (violinist) (Leopold Auer's student)
Elman, Ziggy (musician--trumpeter)
Elmore, Leonard (author--Get Shorty)
Elon, Amos (essayist/author--The Israelis: Founders and Sons)
Els, Ernie (Big Easy) (golf)
Elston, Howard (baseball)
Elway, John (football)
Elwes, Cary (actor--Princess Bride, Robin Hood)
Ely, Eugene (aviator)
Ely, Jack (singer--The Kingmen)
Ely, Joe (singer--country)
Ely, Ron (Ronald Pierce's pseudonym) (actor--Tarzan/host--Miss America)
Emanuel, Rahm Israel (politician--Chicago mayor)
Embry, Ethan (a.k.a. Ethan Randall) (actor)
Emerson, Ralph Waldo (Sage of Concorde) (poet--Ode to Beauty, Each and All/essayist--Nature)
Emerson, Roy (tennis)
Eminem (Marshal Bruce Mather's pseudonym) (a.k.a. M & M, Slim Shady) (singer--   Lose Yourself, Love the Way You Lie)
Emme (nee Melissa Miller) (model)
Emmerich, Roland (director--Independence Day)
Emmet, Robert (patriot; Ir.)
Emmett, Daniel Decatur (songwriter--Dixie)
En Lai, Zhou (politician; Chin.)
Ena (Alfonso's queen)
Enberg, Dick (sportscaster)
Encina/Enzina (Father of Spanish Drama) (poet/playwright/composer)
Ende, Michael (author--The Never Ending Story, Momo)
Endo, Harry (actor--Hawaii 5 0)

Enesco, Georges (violinist/composer--Oedipus, Romanian Rhapsody)
Eng (Siamese twin--Chang)
Engel, Georgia (actress--M.T.M.)
Engel, Howard (author--Benny Cooperman Mysteries)
Engel, Lehman (composer/conductor)
Engel, Marion (author--Bear)
Engels, Fredrick (author/revolutionist) (Karl Marx's collaborator)
Engle, Paul (poet--The Word of Love)
Enke, Karin (speed skater)
Enlai, Zhou (politician)
Enna, August (composer--The Princess On the Pea)
Ennis, Del (baseball)
Ennius, Quintus (Father of Latin/Roman poetry) (author/poet)
Eno, Brian (singer/composer--The Lovely Bones, Small Craft on a Milk Sea, A Year with Swollen Appendices, Another Green World, Lux, The Microsoft Sound, Music for Airports) (Bowie collaborator)
Enos (first chimp in space)
Enriquez, Rene (actor)
Ensler, Eve (playwright/monologist--The Vagina Monologue)
Ensor, David (reporter--national security--C.N.N.)
Ensor, James Sydney (artist--expressionist--Spooky, Carnival Sur La Plage (Carnival on the Beach), The Entry of Christ into Brussels; Bel.)
Enya (nee Eithne Patricia Ni Bhroanain) (musician--new age--Day Without Rain, Paint the Sky with Stars, Only Time, The Memory of Trees, May It Be, Watermark, The Winter Came, Orinoco Flow, Dark Sky Island, Amarantine, Shepherd Moons)
Enzi, Mike (politician)
Epee, Charles (Abbe) (teacher--sign language)
Ephron, Delia (author--Hanging Up, You've Got Mail) (co-writer--Nora Ephron)
Ephron, Nora (producer/director/screenwriter--Sleepless in Seattle, Heartburn, I Feel Bad About My Neck, You've Got Mail, Lucky Guy) (co-writer--Delia Ephron)

Epictetus (philosopher--stoicism)
Epps, Jack (screenwriter--Top Gun)
Epps, Omar (actor--House, Mod Squad, Higher Learning, In Too Deep)
Epstein, Abner (pseudonym--Abner Dean) (cartoonist) (Jacob Epstein's nephew)
Epstein, Brian (music manager--Beatles)
Epstein, Jacob (sculptor) (Abner Dean's uncle)
Epstein, Michael (virologist--Epstein-Barr virus)
Epstein, Theo (baseball)
Erasmus, Desiderius (author--The Praise of Folly; Dan.)
Erastus, Thomas (theologian)
Erbe, Kathryn (actress--Law & Order, Oz)
Erdman, Paul Emil (author--The Silver Bears)
Erdos, Paul (mathmatician)
Erede, Alberto (conductor)
Erhard, Werner (seminar leader--E.S.T.)
Eric II (The Memorable) (Denmark king)
Ericson/Erikson, Lief (explorer; Iceland)
Erikson, Erik (psychoanalyst)
Erinna (poet) (Sappho's contemporary)
Erne, Frank (boxer) (Joe Gans opponent)
Ernst, Joni (politician)
Ernst, Max (painter--dada--The Antelope, The Great Forest, The Hat Makes the Man,   The Murdering Airplane: Ger.)
Erra-Pater (astrologer)
Errol, Leon (actor/comedian)
Erskine, John (author)
Erte, Russ (Romaine de Tirtoff's pseudonym) (designer--Folies Bergere/illustrator--   Harper's Bazaar/artist--Symphony in Black)
Ertugrul (Ottoman leader O) (Osman's father)
Ertz, Susan (Mrs. Ronald McCrindle's pseudonym) (author--Madame Claire)
Ervin, Sam (politician)
Erwin, Stu (actor)
Esai, Bob (actor--La Bamba)
Esar, Evan (comic dictionary compiler)

Escher, Maurits C. (artist--graphic)
Escherich, Theodor (pediatrician/bacteriologist--ecoli)
Escobar, Pablo (gangster)
Escoffier, Auguste (chef/author)
Eshkol, Levi (politician; Isr.) (Golda Meir's predecessor)
Esiason, Norman Julius (Boomer) (football)
Esme (Salinger girl)
Espy, Willard (author)
Espy, William Gray (actor)
Este (Italian noble family)
Estefan, Gloria (singer)
Estes, Bob (golfer)
Estes, Clara Pinkola (author--Woman Who Runs with Wolves)
Estes, Eleanor (author--children--The Moffats)
Estes, John Adam (Sleepy John) (songwriter/singer/musician--
guitar--Blues)
Estes, Pete (General Motors C. E. O.)
Estes, Richard (painter--photorealist)
Estes, Rob (actor--Melrose Place)
Estes, Shawn (baseball)
Estes, Simon (singer--opera)
Estes, Will (actor--Blue Bloods)
Estevez, Emilio (actor--Repo Man, The Mighty Ducks)
Estevez, Ramon (Ray) (actor/director)
Estrada, Erik (actor--Chips)
Estrada, Joseph (politician; Philippine)
Ethelred the Unready (King of England)
Etheridge, Melissa (singer--I Need to Wake Up)
Etrog, Sorel (sculptor)
Etten, Nicholas Raymond (Nick) (baseball)
Eubanks, Kevin Tyrone (musician--
guitar/composer/bandleader/music director--
        The Tonight Show)
Euclid (mathematician/author--Elements)
Euler, Leonhard (mathematician--calculus/author--Introduction
to the Analysis of the   Infinite; Swiss)
(Bernoulli's teacher)
Euripedes (tragedy author--Medea, Ion, Electra)
Euwe, Max (chess master)

Evangelista, Linda (model)
Evans, Arthur (Sir) (archeologist--Knossos, Crete)
Evans, Bergen (T.V. host)
Evans, Bill (musician--pianist--jazz)
Evans, Chris (actor--Captain America)
Evans, Dale (actress/singer--country)
Evans, Dwight (baseball)
Evans, Edith (Dame) (actress)
Evans, Greg (cartoonist--Luann)
Evans, Janet (swimmer)
Evans, Mary (Mary Evans-Eliot) (pseudonym--George Eliot) (author)
Evans, Matthew Rhys (actor--The Americans)
Evans, Maurice (actor)
Evans, Medgar (author/activist)
Evans, Peter (author--Ari)
Evans, Redd (lyricist)
Evans, Ron (astronaut)
Evans, Rowland (journalist) (Novak's partner)
Evans, Walker (photographer)
Evans-Eliot, Mary Anne (also Marian) (pseudonym--George Eliot) (author; Br.)
Evatt, Herbert Vere (Dr.) (judge/author/politician)
Everage, Edna (Dame) (actress)
Everett, Rupert (actor--An Ideal Husband)
Everhart, Angie (actress)
Everly Brothers (Don & Phil) (musical group--So Sad)
Everly, Ike (musician--guitarist)
Evers, Johnny (Crab) (baseball)
Evers, Medgar Wiley (martyr--civil rights)
Evers, Walter Arthur (Hoot) (baseball)
Evert, Chris (tennis)
Ewbank, Weeb (football)
Ewell, Richard Stoddery (Gen.) (Lee subordinate)
Ewell, Tom (actor--The Seven Year Itch)
Ewen, David (author--autobiographer--Gershwin)
Exon, James (politician)

Fabi, Teo (race car driver)
Fabian (nee Fabiano Anthony Forte) (singer/actor)
Fabio (model)
Fabray, Nanette (actress--Harper Valley P.T.A.)
Face, Elroy (baseball)
Fafard, Joe (sculptor--cows)
Fagan, Donald (musician--Steely Dan--A.J.A.)
Fagan, Eleanora (pseudonym--Billie Holiday)
(singer/songwriter--jazz)
Fagin (cartoonist--Drabble)
Fahey, Jeff (actor)
Fair, A.A. (Erle Stanley Gardner's pseudonym) (author--
Donald Lam)
Fairbanks Sr., Douglas (actor--Zorro)
Faisal (politician--Saudi king)
Falana, Lola (singer/actress--The Liberation of L. B. Jones)
Falco, Edie (actress--Nurse Jackie)
Falk, Peter (actor--Happy New Year, The In-laws)
Fallaci, Oriana (journalist, author, political interviewer--egoist)
Fanning, Dakota (actress--Man on Fire)
Fanning, Elle (actress)
Faraday, Michael (scientist-electromagnetism--ions)
Fargo, Donna (singer/songwriter/musician--quitar)
Farina, Mimi (singer)
Faris, Anna (actress--Scary Movies)
Farley, Chris (actor--S.N.L.)
Farley, James (politician)
Farley, Mike (singer/songwriter--Farmer in the Dell)
Farmer, Art (musician--jazz)
Farmer, Fannie (author--cookbooks)
Farmer, James (activist--CORE (Congress of Racial Equality)
Farouk (Egyptian king)
Farr, Diane (actress--Numbers)
Farr, Felicia (actress)
Farr, Jamie (actor--MASH)

Farr, Tommy (boxer) (defeated by Joe Louis)
Farragut, David Glasgow (Admiral--first in U. S. Navy)
Farrar, Frederic (cleric/ teacher/ author/ singer--The First Sweet Christmas)
Farrar, Geraldine (singer)
Farrar, John C. (editor/author/publisher)
Farrar, Margaret (journalist/editor--crossword puzzles)
Farrell, Charles (actor)
Farrell, Eileen (diva; Am.)
Farrell, James Thomas (author--Studs, Bernard Clare)
Farrell, Mike (actor/director)
Farrow, Mia (actress--See No Evil, Hannah and Her Sisters) (Ronan's mother/ Previn's wife)
Farrow, Ronan (activist/lawyer/journalist--MSNBC) (Mia's son)
Farrow, Tisa (actress)
Fassbinder, Rainer Werner (director--Ali: Fear Eats the Soul)
Fast, Howard (author--Spartacus)
Fatima (Mohammed's daughter)
Fatsis, Stefan (author--Word Freak--competitive Scrabble)
Faubus, Orval (politician)
Faulkner, William (author--These Thirteen, As I Lay Dying, A Rose for Emily, The Bear)
Faure, Elie (art historian)
Faure, Gabriel Urbain (teacher/pianist/organist/composer--Penelope, Messe de Requiem)   (Ravel's teacher)
Fausta, Flavia Maxima (Roman Empress) (Constantine the Great's wife)
Favre, Brett (football)
Favre, Jean Baptiste Castor (author)
Fawcett, Farrah (actress)
Fawkes, Guy (Guido) (fighter--Gunpowder Plot)
Faxon, Brad (golfer)
Fayad, Dody (businessman/producer--Chariots of Fire)
Faye, Alice (actress/singer--Hollywood Cavalcade)
Faye, Julia (actress)
Federer, Roger (tennis)
Fehr, Donald (baseball) (Weiner's predecessor)
Feiffer, Jules (cartoonist)

Feingold, Russ (politician)
Feinstein, Dianne (politician)
Feldman, Corey (actor--Stand By Me)
Feldshuh, Tovah (actress)
Feller, Bob (Bullet Bob/Rapid Robert) (baseball)
Fellini, Federico (filmmaker--Roma, La Strada)
Felson, Eddie (Fast Eddie) (pool)
Felt, William Mark (Deep Throat) (F.B.I. agent)
Fender, Leo (designer--guitars)
Fenn, George Manville (author)
Fenn, Sherilyn (actress--Twin Peaks)
Ferber, Edna (author--Ice Palace, Cimarron, So Big)
Fermat, Pierre de (probability theorist)
Fermi, Enrico (physicist)
Fernandez, Sid (baseball)
Ferrara, Abel (director)
Ferrari, Enzo (automaker)
Ferraro, Geraldine (attorney/politician)
Ferrell, Will (actor--Elf)
Ferrer, Jose (actor--Cyrano de Bergerac)
Ferrer, Mel (actor--Lili)
Ferri, Ciro (painter)
Ferrigno, Lou (actor--Incredible Hulk)
Ferris, Gerry (engineer)
Fey, Tina (actress--S.N.L.--Liz Lemon/author--
Bossypants/writer--Mean Girls)
Fiasco, Lupe (singer--rap)
Fibonacci, Leonardo (mathematician)
Field, Eugene (poet)
Field, Marshall (investment banker, publisher, philanthropist--
Marshall Field's Stores)
Field, Rachel (author--A Road Might Lead You Anywhere)
Field, Sally (actress--Sybil)
Field, Syd (screenwriter)
Fielder, Cecil (baseball)
Fielding, Helen (author--Bridget Jones Diary)
Fielding, Henry (author--Tom Jones, Amelia)
Fields, Debbi (founder--Mrs. Fields Bakeries)
Fields, Totie (comedian)

Fields, William Claude (pseudonym--Mahatma Kane Jeeves) (actor/author--The Bank   Dick)
Fiennes, Joseph (actor--Shakespeare in Love)
Fiennes, Ralph (actor--Harry Potter)
Fieri, Guy (chef/T.V. personality--Food Network)
Fiestas (musical group--So Fine)
Filadelfeia, Nea (singer; Ger.)
Filene, Edward (business exec.--Boston clothing store)
Finch, Peter (actor; Br.)
Finch, Spade (actor)
Findley, Edwina (actress)
Fine, Larry (actor/comedian--Three Stooges)
Fingers, Rollie (baseball)
Finklea, Tula (Cyd Charisse's pseudonym) (actress)
Finkleman, Danny (radio DJ)
Finn, Neil (singer/songwriter--One All)
Finney, Albert (actor--Under the Volcano)
Finney, Charles G. (religious leader)
Finney, Jack (author--Time and Again)
Fiorentino, Linda (actress)
Fiorito, Joe (author--The Closer We Are To Dying)
Firpo, Luis Angel (boxer) (Jack Dempsey's opponent)
Firth, Colin (actor)
Firth, Peter (actor; Br.)
Fischer, Bobby (chess master/author--My 60 Memorable Games)
Fischer-Dieskau, Dietrich (singer--lieder)
Fishburne, Laurence (actor--C.S.I.)
Fisher, Anna Lee (chemist/astronaut)
Fisher, Avery (entrepreneur--hi-fi)
Fisher, Bud (co-cartoonist with Al Smith--Mutt & Jeff)
Fisher, Carrie (actress--Debbie Reynolds's daughter)
Fisher, Eileen (fashion designer)
Fisher, Hammond (Ham) (cartoonist--Joe Palooka)
Fisher, Isla (actress)
Fiske, Minnie Maddern (nee Marie Augusta Davey) (actress)
Fiske, Robert (attorney--White Water)
Fitch, Ezra (businessman--Abercrombie & Fitch)
Fitch, John (inventor--steamboat)

Fitz, John Francis (Honey) (politician) (Rose Kennedy's father)
Fitzgerald, Edward (poet--translated poems of Omar Khayyam)
Fitzgerald, Ella (singer--A Tisket, A Tasket, How High the Moon)
Fitzgerald, Francis Scott (author--The Last Tycoon)
Fitzgerald, Roy (a.k.a. Rock Hudson) (actor--Pretty Maids All In a Row)
Fitzgerald, Zelda (author--Save Me the Waltz) (F. Scott's wife)
Fitzwater, Marlen (politician)
Fixx, James (runner)
Flagello, Ezie (singer--basso)
Flagg, Ernest (architect--Corcoran Gallery)
Flagg, Fannie (author--Fried Green Tomatoes)
Flagg, James Montgomery (artist--Uncle Sam poster)
Flagler, Henry (railroad builder)
Flaherty, James (politician)
Flaherty, Robert J. (producer/director--Man of Aran, Moana, Nanook of the North)
Flair, Ric (wrestler)
Flatow, Ira (uthor/journalist/T.V. personality/radio host--Science Friday)
Flatt, Lester (singer--bluegrass) (Earl Scrugg's partner)
Flaubert, Gustave (author--realism) (Louise Colet's lover)
Flavius (historian; Roman)
Flay, Bobby (chef)
Fleck, Bela (musician--banjo--Fleck and the Fleckstones--jazz)
Fleetwood Mac (musical group--Sara)
Fleetwood, Mick (drummer--Fleetwood Mac)
Fleetwoods (musical group--Mr. Blue)
Fleischer, Ari (politician/memoirist--Taking Heat)
Fleischer, Nat (Mr. Boxing) (boxer)
Fleming, Ian (author--James Bond, Casino Royale, Dr. No)
Fleming, Peggy (skater)
Fleming, Renee (singer--soprano)
Fleming, Rhonda (actress)
Fleming, Victor (director)
Fletcher, John (dramatist--The Scornful Lady) (Beaumont's collaborator)

Flood, Curt (baseball)
Florio, James (politician)
Floyd, Charles (Pretty Boy) (criminal)
Floyd, Raymond (golfer)
Flying Dutchman girl (Senta)
Flying Finn--Nurmi, Paavo (track & field)
Flynn, Errol (actor--Captain Blood/author--My Wicked, Wicked Ways, The Prince and   the Pauper)
Fo, Dario (actor/playwright/comedian/singer--satire)
Foch, Ferdinand (author/soldier/Field Marshall--France/Allied Supreme Commander)
Foch, Nina (actress--Spartacus, An American in Paris)
Foer, Jonathan Safran (author)
Foerster, Josef/Joseph Bohuslav (composer--opera--Eva)
Fogazzaro, Antonio (author--Leila)
Fogerty, John (singer--Creedance Clearwater Revival)
Fokine, Mikhail (also Michel) (dancer; Ru.)
Foley, Dave (actor)
Foley, John Henry (sculptor)
Foley, Rae (author)
Foley, Scott (actor--Scandal)
Follett, Ken (author--World Without End)
Follows, Megan (actor)
Folsom, Allan (author--The Day After Tomorrow)
Fonda, Henry (actor)
Fonda, Jane (actress--Julia, Barbarella, Cat Ballou, Klute)
Fonda, Peter (actor--Ulee's Gold)
Fontaine, Joan (actress--Suspicion, Jane Eyre) (Olivia de Havilland's sister)
Fontanne, Lynn (actress) (Alfred Lunt's wife)
Fonteyn, Margot (dancer--ballet) (Nureyev's partner)
Foo Fighters (musical group) (drummer--David Grohl)
Foote, Horton (playwright--The Trip to Bountiful, The Young Man from Atlanta, Tender Mercies)
Foote, Shelby Dade (historian/author--Civil War)
Foran, Charles (author--Butterfly Lovers)
Forbes-Robertson, Johnstone (actor/theater manager)
Ford, Eileen (model agent)
Ford, Ernie (Tennessee Ernie) (singer--Sixteen Tons)

Ford, Ford Maddox (author--The Last Post)
Ford, Gerald (politician) (Leslie Lynch King's son)
Ford, Glenn (actor)
Ford, Harrison (actor--Air Force One)
Ford, John (director--My Darling Clementine, The Quiet Man)
Ford, John (playwright)
Ford, Len (football)
Ford, Lita (singer--The Runaways)
Forester, Cecil Scott (author--The African Queen)
Forman, Milos (director--One Flew Over the Cuckoo's Nest, Amadeus; Czech.)
Forrest, Frederic (actor)
Forster, Edward Morgan (author--Room with a View, A Passage to India)
Forsyth, Frederick (author--The Odessa File, The Dogs of War)
Forsythe, John (actor--Bachelor Father, Charlie's Angels)
Fortas, Abe (justice)
Forte, Fabiano Anthony (Fabian) (singer/actor)
Forzano, Giovacchino (composer--opera--Gianni Schicci)
Foss, Lukas (conductor/pianist/composer--Time Cycle, Echoi)
Fosse, Bob (director--All That Jazz, Cabaret, Little Me, Dancin, Pippin) (Gwen Verdon's husband)
Fossey, Dian (author--Gorillas in the Mist)
Foster, Harold (Hal) (cartoonist--Prince Valiant)
Foster, Jodie (actress--Nell)
Foster, Stephen (Father of American Music) (songwriter--Oh! Susanna, Old Dog Tray, De Camptown Races, Katy/Katie Bell, Nelly Bly)
Foucault, Leon (physicist--earth rotation pendulum, gyroscope, eddy currents, speed of light measurement
Fountain, Pete (musician)
Four Knights (musical group)
Four Lads (musical group)
Four Seasons (musical group--Marlena)
Four Tops (musical group--Aint No Woman)
Fouts, Dan (football)

Fowke, Edith (author/folklorist)
Fowler, Clara Ann (pseudonym--Patti Page) (singer)
Fowler, Gene (author--Barrymore biographer)
Fowles, John (author--The Magus)
Fox, James (actor--A Passage to India)
Fox, Jorja (actress--C. S. I.)
Fox, Michael J. (actor--Teen Wolf)
Fox, Nellie (baseball)
Foxworthy, Jeff (comedian)
Foxx, Inez (singer--Mockingbird)
Foy, Eddie (actor--vaudeville performer/dancer)
Foyt, A. J. (Anthony Joseph) (racecar driver)
Fracci, Carla (dancer--ballet)
Fragonard, Alexandre-Evariste (painter/sculptor) (Jean-Honore's son)
Fragonard, Jean-Honore (painter/ printmaker) (Alexandre-Evariste's father)
Frampton, Peter (singer/musician--guitarist)
France, Anatole (Jacques Anatole Thibault's pseudonym) (journalist/poet/author--Thais)
Francesca, Piero Della (artist)
Franchi, Sergio (singer)
Franchot, Tone (actor)
Francis Scott Fitzgerald (author--Tender is the Night)
Francis, Arlene (actress)
Francis, Arthur (Ira Gershwin's pseudonym) (lyricist)
Francis, Dick (author--Dead Cert)
Francis, Emile (The Cat) (hockey)
Franck, Cesar (composer)
Franco, Francisco (dictator; Sp.)
Francona, Terrence Jon (Tito) (baseball)
Frank, Anne (author)
Frank, Barney (politician)
Franken, Al (politician)
Franken, Rose (author--Claudia)
Frankfurter, Felix (justice)
Franklin, Aretha (singer--Ain't No Way)
Franklin, Bonnie (actress)
Franklin, Erma (singer--gospel--Piece of My Heart)

Franz, Dennis (actor)
Franz, Marc Robert (musician; Ger.)
Fraser, Brendan (actor--Encino Man)
Fraser, Douglas (union leader--U.A.W.)
Fraser, James Earle (sculptor)
Fraser, Neale (tennis)
Fraser, Sylvia (author--My Father's House)
Frawley, William (actor--I Love Lucy)
Frazier, Charles (author--Cold Mountain)
Frazier, Ian (author--On The Rez)
Frazier, Walt (Clyde) (basketball)
Freberg, Stan (satirist)
Freed, Albert James (Alan) (radio DJ)
Freeh, Louis (F. B. I. director)
Freeman, Douglas Southall (author--R. E. Lee, Lee's
Lieutenants)
Freeman, Mona (actress)
Freeman, Morgan (actor--Lean on Me, The Bucket List)
Freeman, Robert Thomas (Bobby) (record producer/singer-
sogwriter--Do You Wanna Dance)
Frehley, Ace (musician--quitarist--Kiss)
Frei, Eduardo (politician; Chili)
French, Dan (comedian)
French, Perry (poet--Abdul Abulbul Amir)
Fresnel, Augustin-Jean (inventor--lighthouse lens)
Freud, Anna (psychoanalyst--children)
Freud, Sigmund (psychoanalyst/author--Totem and Taboo,
Medusa's Head) (contemporaries--   Adler & Jung)
Frey, Glenn (musician--rock --The Heat Is On) (band--The
Eagles)
Frey, James (author--A Million Little Pieces)
Fricker, Brenda (actress--My Left Foot)
Fridtjof, Nansen (explorer; Nor.)
Friedan, Betty (author/feminist)
Friel, Brian (playwright; Ir.)
Friesen, Eric (T. V. personality)
Friml, Rudolf (composer--The Firefly, Only A Rose)
Frings, Ketti (playwright--Look Homeward Angel)
Frisch, Otto (physicist--Manhattan Project)

Frobe, Gert (actor--Goldfinger)
Frome, Ethan (actor)
Frome, Milton (actor--comedy)
Fromm, Erich (psychoanalyst, social philosopher--World
Perspective Series, The Art of Loving)
Frost, David (Sir) (talk show host)
Frost, Robert Lee (poet--Mending Wall, A Boy's Will, In a Vale,
North   of Boston, In the Clearing)
(muse--Erato)
Frum, Barbara (newscaster--C. B. C.)
Fry, Christopher (playwright)
Frye, David (comic impressionist)
Frye, Northrop (critic)
Fuchs, Vivian (Sir) (Bunny) (explorer/geologist)
Fuentes, Carlos (author--Gringo Viejo; Mex.)
Fuentes, Daisy (T.V. host--M.T.V.)
Fugard Athol (directo/author/actor/playwright--A Lesson from
Aloes)
Fujimori, Alberto (politician; Peru)
Fukuda, Takeo (politician; Japan)
Fulbright, James William (politician)
Fuller, Buckminster (architect)
Fullerton, Fiona (actress)
Fulton, Eileen (actress)
Fumanchu (physician) (patient--Rohmer)
Funseth, James Rodney (Rod) (golfer)
Furman, Roy (investment banker/entertainment industry
analyst)
Fu-Tse, Kung (philosopher)

--G--

G, Kenny (Gorelick) (musician--saxophone)
Gabel, Martin (actor--The Thief)
Gable, Clark (actor--Gone with the Wind, Red Dust)
Gabor, Eva (actress)

Gabor, Jolie (entrepreneur/jeweler/memoirist) (Magda, Zsa Zsa, Eva's mother)
Gabor, Magdolna (Magda) (actress/socialite) (George Sanders's wife)
Gabor, Zsa Zsa (actress) (George Sanders's wife)
Gaboriau, Emile (author--Lecoq)
Gabrieli, Giovanni (composer/organist)
Gabrilowitsch, Ossip (pianist)
Gade, Jacob (musician--violin/composer--Jalousie)
Gadot, Gal (model/actress--Wonder Woman)
Gadsden, James (politician--Mexico purchase)
Gagarin, Yuri (cosmonaut) (spacecraft--Vostok I)
Gage, Nicholas (author) (memoir--Eleni)
Gage, Thomas (General) (Colonial America Governor)
Gahn, Johan Gottlieb (chemist)
Gailey, Fred (actor--Miracle on 34th St.)
Gaiman, Neil (author)
Gaines, Ernest J. (author--The Autobiography of Miss Jane Pitman)
Gaines, Rowdy (swimmer)
Gainsborough, Thomas (draughtsman/printer/painter--portrait/landscape)
Gal, Uziel (Uzi) (gun designer)
Galarraga, Armando (baseball)
Galba (ruler of Rome/Nero-Galba-Otho)
Galbraith, John Kenneth (Ken) (author--The Affluent Society)
Gale, Zona (author/playwright)
Galeazzo, Gian Ciano (politician/diplomat) (Mussolini's son-in-law, Edda's husband)
Galen (physician; Gr.)
Galento, Tony (boxer)
Galilei, Galileo (astronomer/physicist/engineer/philosopher/mathematician/author--   Two New Sciences)
Gallagher, Ed (comedian) (Al Shean's partner)
Gallagher, Megan (actress)
Gallant, Mavis (author)
Gallaudet, Thomas Hopkins (Rev.) (Dr.) (educator--American Sign Language)

Gallico, Paul (author--The Snowgoose: A Story of Dunkirk)
Galli-Curci, Amelita (singer--soprano)
Gallo, Ernest (winemaker)
Gallo, Julio (winemaker)
Galsworthy, John (author--The Forsythe Saga, A Man of Devon, To Let)
Gam, Rita (actress)
Gandhi, Indira (politician; India) (Nehru's daughter)
Gandhi, Jawaharlal (politician; India)
Gandhi, Mahatma (politician)
Gandhi, Rajiv (politician) (successor--Rao)
Gandhi, Sonia (politician; India)
Ganger, Rolf (Viking chieftain)
Gann, Ernest K. (author--The High and the Mighty)
Gannett, Lewis (author--The Living One)
Gans, Joe (boxer) (Frank Erne's opponent)
Garand, John C. (inventor--M 1 rifle)
Garber, Jan (bandleader/songwriter--Baby Face)
Garber, Terri (actress)
Garbo, Greta (actress--Queen Christina, Camille, Love)
Garcia, Andy (actor)
Garcia, Jerry (musician--guitarist--Grateful Dead)
Garcia, Nina (journalist/critic/T. V. personality--fashion--Project Runway)
Garciaparra, Nomar (baseball)
Garden, Mary (singer--opera--soprano)
Gardner, Ava (singer/actress--Knights of the Round Table, The Great Escape, The Barefoot Contessa, The Killers)
Gardner, Erle Stanley (pseudonym--A.A. Fair) (author--Perry Mason, The Case of the Velvet   Claws, The D.A. Calls It Murder)
Gardner, Herb (playwright--A Thousand Clowns)
Gardner, Rea (cartoonist)
Garfield, James Abram (politician)
Garfunkel, Art (singer/musician--Cecilia)
Gargan, Edward (actor)
Gargan, William (actor--I Wake Up Screaming)
Garibaldi, Giuseppe (Gen.) (politician)
Garland, Hannibal Hamlin (author--A Son of a Middle Border)

Garland, Judy (nee Gumm) (actress/singer--The Wizard of Oz)
Garn, Jake (astronaut/politician)
Garneau, Marc (astronaut; Can.)
Garner, Erroll (composer/musician--pianist--jazz--Misty)
Garner, James (actor--Maverick)
Garner, Jennifer (actress--Alias)
Garner, John Nance (politician)
Garnum, Dustin (singer/dancer/actor)
Garofalo, Janeane (comedian/actress/author/activist)
Garr, Ralph (baseball)
Garr, Teri (actress--Tootsie, Dumb and Dumber)
Garrett, Brad (actor--Everybody Loves Raymond)
Garrett, Leif (singer)
Garrett, Pat (lawman) (Billy the Kid's killer)
Garroway, Dave (radio host)
Garson, Greer (actress--Mrs. Miniver, Goodbye Mr. Chips)
Garson, Kanin (author)
Garten, Ina (chef/author/host--Barefoot Contessa)
Garth, Jennie (actress)
Gary, Romain (pseudonym--Emile Ajar) (author--Momo)
Gaskell, Elizabeth (author/biographer--Charlotte Bronte)
Gasol, Pau (basketball)
Gasset, Jose Ortega y (philosopher/author/essayist; Sp.)
Gasteyer, Ana (actress--S.N.L.)
Gaudi, Antoni (architect; Sp.)
Gauguin, Paul (artist--Tahitian Woman on the Beach)
Gauss, Carl Freidrich (mathematician)
Gautama, Siddhartha (Buddha) (spiritual teacher)
Gay, John (poet/dramatist--The Beggar's Opera, Alms and the Man)
Gaye, Marvin (Prince of Soul) (singer--Can I Get a Witness, Sexual Healing, Let's Get It On,   Mercy, Mercy Me, What's Going On)
Gaye, Nona (actress--Ali)
Gaylord, Mitch (gymnast)
Gaynor, Gloria (singer--I Will Survive)
Gaynor, Janet (actress)
Gaynor, Mitzi (actress)

Gazzara, Ben (actor)
Gedge, Pauline (author--Child of the Morning)
Gedicht, Rilke Ding (poet)
Gedrick, Tom (actor--Boomtown)
Geer, Will (actor--The Waltons)
Geffen, David (media mogul)
Gehrig, Lou (Iron Horse) (baseball #4)
Gehry, Frank (architect)
Geiger, Hans (inventor)
Geisel, Theodore Seuss (Dr. Seuss) (author--children's)
Geist, William Russell (Willie) (T.V. personality)
Geldof, Bob (actor/musician--rock--founder of Live Aid)
Gellar, Sarah Michelle (actress)
Gellee, Claude (a.k.a. Claude Lorrain)
(etcher/painter/printmaker/art theorist)
Geller, Uri (mentalist--spoonbender)
Gell-Mann, Murray (physicist/Nobelist)
Gemayel, Amin (politician; Leb.)
Gemison, Mae (astronaut)
Genet, Jean (author--Our Lady of the Flowers/playwright--The
Screens, The Maids,   The Balcony)
Gennaro, Peter (choreographer--Annie)
Genova, Lisa (author--Still Alice)
Gentry, Curt (author-Helter Skelter) (co-author--Vincent
Bugliosi)
George VI (Bertie) (King of England)
George, Boy (singer)
George, Dan (Chief) (Native American leader)
George, Lloyd (politician--Lenin contemporary)
Gephardt, Richard (Dick) (politician) (Pelosi's predecessor)
Gerard, Gil (actor)
Gerardo (singer--rap--Rico Suave, We Want the Funk)
Gere, Richard (actor--King David, Sommersby, Bee Season,
Dr. T, Nights in Rodanthe,   The Jackal, Days of
Heaven, American Gigolo, Arbitrage, Primal Fear)
Germain, Russ (T. V. personality--C. B. C.)
Gernreich, Rudi (designer)
Gerritsen, Tess (author)
Gerry, Elbridge Thomas (diplomat)

Gershon, Gina (actess)
Gershwin, George (composer--Soon, It's A New World, Rosalie, Embraceable You, Swanee,   Funny Face, The Man I Love, Porgy and Bess, American in Paris, Slap That   Bass, La La Lucille, So Am I, Our Nell, Looking for a Boy, I(ve) Got Rhythm,   (Piano) Concerto in F Major, Liza, Girl Crazy, Rhapsody in Blue, Oh Lady   Be Good, The Goldwyn Follies, Of Thee I Sing)
Gershwin, Ira (pseudonym--Arthur Francis) (lyricist--It's A New World)
Gertis, Marina (actress)
Gertz, Jami (actress--Twister)
Gervin, George (Ice Man) (baseball)
Gesell, Arnold (Dr.) (nrthopedic surgeon) (co-authors Ilg & Ames)
Gesner, Abraham Pineo (physician/geologist/inventor--kerosene)
Getty, Estelle (actress)
Getty, J. Paul (philanthropist; Am.)
Getz, Stan (musician--sax--jazz)
Giamatti, Paul (actor--Sideways)
Gibb, Andrew Roy (Andy) (singer--Shadow Dancing)
Gibbon, Edward (author-- history)
Gibbons, Leeza (T. V. personality)
Gibbs, Barry (musician--Bee Gees)
Gibbs, Joe (football)
Gibbs, Marla (actress--The Jeffersons, 227)
Gibbs, Maurice (musician--Bee Gees)
Gibbs, Robin (musician--Bee Gees)
Gibbs, Terri (singer--country)
Gibran, Kahlil (author--The Prophet)
Gibson, Althea (tennis)
Gibson, Debbie (singer/songwriter/record producer/actress)
Gibson, Mel (actor--Bret Maverick)
Gibson, Michael Tyrese (producer/singer/songwriter/model/writer/actor--2 Fast 2 Furious)

Gide, Andre (author--The Immoralist, Strait Is the Gate, If It Die, The Counterfeiters)
Gielgud, John (Sir) (actor--King Lear)
Gifford, Frank (football) (Kathie Lee's husband)
Gifford, Kathie Lee (actress/singer/T.V. personality) (Frank Gifford's wife)
Gilbert, Sara (actress/T.V. personality--The Talk)
Gilbert, William C. (Sir) (songwriter--libretto--The Yeoman of the Guard)
Gilberto, Astrud (singer--Bossa-Nova)
Gilchrist, Ellen (author)
Gilden, Bert (K.B.) (author--Hurry Sundown)
Gilden, Katya (K.B.) (author--Hurry Sundown)
Gilels, Emil (pianist)
Gillen, Aidan (actor--Game of Thrones)
Gilliam, Stu (actor/comedian)
Gilliam, Terry (screenwriter/animator/producer/director--Fisher Kings)
Gillibrand, Kirsten (politician)
Gilmore, Artis (basketball)
Gilpin, Peri (actress--Frasier)
Gilroy, Tony (director--Michael Clayton)
Gimpel, Erica (actress)
Gingold, Hermione (actress--Gigi)
Gingrich, Newton (Newt) (politician)
Ginsberg, Allen (poet--Howl, Plutonian Ode)
Ginsburg, Ruth Bader (Supreme Court justice)
Giordano, Umberto (composer--Fedora)
Giotto (Ambrogio Bondone's pseudonym) (artist—murals, frescoes--Florence Cathedral   Bell Tower, Scrovegni Chapel)
Giroux, Robert (editor/publisher)
Gish, Annabeth (actress)
Gish, Dorothy (actress)
Gish, Lillian (actress)
Giuliani, Rudy (politician--N. Y. City)
Gladstone, William Ewart (politician)
Glaser, Paul Michael (director/actor--Starsky and Hutch)
Glasgow, Ellen (author)

Glashow, Sheldon (physicist/Nobelist)
Glaspell, Susan (playwright/actress/director/author--Norma Ashe/journalist)
Glass, Ira (radio host--This American Life)
Glass, Philip (composer)
Glazer, Ilana (actress--Broad City)
Gleason, Jackie (musician/comedian/actor--The Great One, Gigot) (bio.--How Sweet It Is)
Gleason, James Austin (actor)
Glenn, John (astronaut)
Glenn, Scott (actor)
Gless, Sharon (actress--Rosie)
Glinka, Mikhail Ivanovich (composer--opera--Ivan Susanin, A Life for the Tsar)
Glover, Danny (actor)
Glover, Savion (dancer--tap)
Gluck, Alma (actress/singer--soprano)
Gluck, Christopher (composer--opera--Alceste, Orfeo Ed Euridice, Paride ed Elena)
Glyn, Elinor (author)
Gnu, Gary (actor)
Gobat, Charles Albert (politician/peace nobelist; Sw.)
Gobel, George (Lonesome George) (comedian/actor)
Godard, Jean-Luc (director--Passion)
Goddard, Robert Hutchings (professor/scientist--rocketry)
Godden, Rumer (author--In The House of Brede)
Godel, Kurt (mathematician)
Godunov, Boris (politician--tsar of Russia)
Godwin, Gail (author)
Godwin, William (author--The Adventures of Caleb Williams)
Goethe, Johann (poet--Faust, The Sorcerer's Apprentice)
Goff, Norris (pseudonym--Abner) (actor--Lum's partner)
Go-Go's (musical group--We Got the Beat, Vacation)
Gogol, Nikolai (author--Taras Bulba, Dead Souls, The Overcoat, The Government Inspector,   Nos)
Gold, Tracey (actress--Growing Pains)
Goldberg, Adam (actor)
Goldberg, Rube (cartoonist--Inventions)

Goldberg, Whoopi (actress/comedienne--Lion King's Shenzie, Sister Act)
Golden, Arthur (author--Memoirs of a Geisha)
Goldin, Nan (photographer)
Golding, William (author--Lord of the Flies)
Goldman, Emma (anarchist)
Goldoni, Carlo (playwright; It.)
Goldoni, Leila (actress)
Goldsberry, Renee Elise (actress--Hamilton)
Goldsboro, Bobby (singer--See the Funny Little Clown)
Goldsmith, Oliver (author--The Vicar of Wakefield, She Stoops to Conquer)
Goldwyn, Samuel (producer/studio exec.)
Golgi, Camillo (medicine/nobelist)
Golonka, Arlene (actress)
Gompers, Samuel (labor leader--founder of A. F. L.) (Meany's predecessor)
Gonzales, Alberto (politician)
Gonzalez, Elian (boy found floating on tube near Miami from Cuba)
Gonzalez, Gio (baseball)
Goodall, Jane (author--In the Shadow of Man)
Goode, Wilson (politician--Philly mayor)
Goodell, Roger (football)
Gooden, Dwight (Dr. K.) (baseball)
Gooding, Cuba (actor)
Gooding, Omar (actor)
Goodman, Dody (actress)
Goodman, Ellen (columnist)
Goodman, John (actor)
Goodman, Len (T.V. personality--Dancing with the Stars)
Goodman, Paul (playwright/poet/psychotherapist/author--Growing Up Absurd)
Goodwin, Doris Kearns (author--biographer--L.B.J.)
Goolagong, Evonne (tennis)
Gorbachev, Mikhail (politician; Ru.)
Gorbachev, Raisa (wife of Mikhail; Ru.)
Gorcey, Leo (actor--Bowrey Boys, Mr. Buggs Steps Out)
Gordimer, Nadine (author)

Gordon, Adam Lindsay (poet)
Gordon, Bruce (actor--Nitti)
Gordon, Jeff (race car driver)
Gordon, Noele (actress--musicals--Gypsy; Br.)
Gordon, Ruth (actress)
Gore, Al (politician/author--Earth in the Balance)
Goren, Charles Henry (author/bridge expert--Contract Bridge in a Nutshell) (Helen Sobel Smith's   partner)

Gorham, Jabez (silversmith)
Gorki, Maxim (Aleksei Peshkov's pseudonym) (author)
Gorky, Arshile (model/painter)
Gorme, Eydie (singer--Blame it on the Bosa Nova, Eydie Sings the Blues, Eso Es El Amor)
Gorshin, Frank (actor--Riddler)
Gorsuch, Neil McGill (Supreme Court justice) (Antonin Scalia's successor)
Gorton, Slade (politician--senator)
Gosco, Elyse (author--Can You Wave Byebye Baby?)
Gosling, Ryan (actor--First Man)
Gossett, Lou (actor)
Gothe, Jurgen (radio DJ/T. V. personality--Disc Drive--C. B. C.)
Gotti, Irv (record exec.)
Gotti, John (crime boss)
Gottlieb, Joseph Abraham (a.k.a Joey Bishop) (comedian/talk-game show host/actor--   Ocean's Eleven)
Gotye (nee Wouter Andre De Backer (Wally)) (musician/songwriter/singer--Somebody   That I Used to Know)
Goudge, Elizabeth (author)
Gould, Chester (cartoonist-- Dick Tracy)
Gould, Elliott (actor--Spys)
Gould, Glen (composer/musician--pianist)
Gould, Jason (Jay) (railroad developer--Erie R.R.)
Gould, Lois (author)
Gould, Stephen Jay (biologist/author--The Panda's Thumb)
Goulding, Ellie (singer)

Goulding, Ray (actor/comedian--Bob (Elliott) & Ray Show--radio)
Gounod, Charles Francois (composer--Faust, Philemon Et Baucis)
Gowdy, Curt (sportscaster
Goy, Luba (comedian)
Goya, Francisco Jose de Lucientes (artist--Duchess of Alba, Naked Maja, Satan Devouring His Children, Witches Flight)
Grabar, Igor (painter)
Grable, Betty (actress)
Gracchus, Caius (reformer)
Grace, Bud (cartoonist--Ernie)
Grady, James (author--Six Days of the Condor)
Graf, Steffi (tennis)
Graff, Ilene (actress--Mr. Belvedere)
Grafton, Sue (author--"N" is for Noose; Am.)
Graham, Alex (cartoonist--Fred Basset)
Graham, Bette Nesmith (inventor--liquid paper)
Graham, Heather (author--Drop Dead Gorgeous, Runaway)
Graham, Martha (dancer/choreographer)
Graham, Otto (football)
Graham, Stedman (educator/author) (Oprah's beau)
Grahame, Kenneth (author--The Wind in the Willows, Toads Adventure)
Grainger, Percy (composer)
Gramm, Phil (politician)
Grammaticus, Saxo (historian)
Grande, Ariana (Ari) (singer)
Grandy, Fred (actor--Love Boat/ politician--Iowa congressman)
Granet, Francois Marius (painter)
Granger, Farley (actor)
Grant, Amy (singer--Every Heartbeat)
Grant, Cary (nee Archibald Leach) (actor--Notorious, Once Upon a Honeymoon, Indiscreet, Awful Truth, Father Goose, Suspicion, Only Angels, In Name Only)
Grant, Eddy (singer--reggae)
Grant, George (author--Lament for a Nation)

Grant, Gogi (singer--The Wayward Wind)
Grant, Hiram (politician--U. S. President)
Grant, Hugh (actor--Nine Months, Notting Hill, Four Weddings and a Funeral, Love Actually)
Grant, Lee (actress--Shampoo)
Granville, Bonita (actress)
Grass, Gunter (author)
Grassle, Karen (actress--Little House on the Prairie)
Grasso, Ella (politician; Conn.)
Grateful Dead (musical group--Without a Net)
Gratian (Roman Emperor)
Gratien, Gelinas (actor/director)
Grau, Shirley Ann (author)
Grauman, Sid (Grauman's Chinese Theater founder)
Graves, Alfred Percival (author--Songs of Killarney)
Graves, Robert (author--I, Claudius)
Gray, Asa (botanist/author--Gray's Manual of Botany)
Gray, Elisha (inventor)
Gray, Erin (actress)
Gray, Gilda (actress)
Gray, Henry (physician/author--anatomy)
Gray, Macy (singer/songwriter/record producer/actress)
Gray, Thomas (poet--elegist/odes)
Graynor, Ari (actress)
Greasy, Neale (football)
Greb, Harry (boxer)
Greco, Jose (dancer--Manolete)
Greeley, Horace (editor--N. Y. Tribune)
Green Day (musical group)
Green, Abel (journalist--Variety)
Green, Adolph (playwright/performer/lyricist) (Betty Comden's partner)
Green, Al (singer--Sha-La-La, Love and Happiness, I'm Still In Love With You, Let's Get Together)
Green, CeeLo (nee Thomas DeCarlo Calloway) (songwriter/singer--rap/record producer/ record producer/T.V. personality--The Voice judge)
Green, Eva (actress--Penny Dreadful, Casino Royale, Dumbo)
Green, Hetty (financier)

Green, Hubert (golfer)
Green, Seth (actor--Austin Powers, The Italian Job, Robot Chicken)
Green, Tammie (golfer)
Greenberg, Hank (Hammerin Hank) (baseball)
Greene, Ann Catherine (author--Our Man in Havana)
Greene, Charles Edward (Mean Joe) (football)
Greene, Gael (food critic)
Greene, Graham (actor)
Greene, Graham (author--The Quiet American, England Made Me, The End of the Affair,   The Power and the Glory, The Ministry of Fear, The Third Man, The Potty Shed,   Brighton Rock)
Greene, Lorne (actor--Bonanza/singer--Ringo)
Greene, Nathaniel (Gen.--American Rev.)
Greenfield, Meg (columnist)
Greenspan, Alan (politician--Chairman of Federal Reserve/author--The Age of Turbulence)
Greenstreet, Syd (actor--Casablanca)
Greenwich, Ellie (songwriter)
Greer, Germaine (author--The Female Eunich)
Greer, Sonny (musician--drummer--Duke Ellington's Band
Gregg, Clark (nee Robert Clark Gregg) (actor--The Avengers)
Gregg, Forrest (football)
Gregory, Andre (actor--My Dinner with Andre)
Greiner, Dan (inventor/entrepreneur/T.V. personality--Shark Tank)
Grey, Jennifer (actress)
Grey, Joel (actor/singer)
Grey, Lita (actress) (Chaplin's wife)
Grey, Nan (actress)
Grey, Zane (dentist/author--westerns--Riders of the Purple Sage, West of the Pecos, Nevada)
Gridley, Charles Vernon (Navy officer)
Grieg, Edvard Hagerup (composer--Peer Gynt, Anitra's Dance, Ases Death,   Piano Concerto in A Minor; Norwegian)
Grier, David Alan (actor)
Grier, Pam (actress--Jackie Brown)

Grier, Rosey (football)
Griffey, Ken (baseball)
Griffin, Archie (boxer)
Griffin, Merv (T.V. hot/actor/musician/media mogul)
Griffith, Andy (actor--Matlock)
Griffith, David Wark (director)
Griffith, Emile (boxer)
Griffith, Melanie (actress)
Griffith, Nanci (singer--country)
Griffiths, Rachel (actress)
Grimaldi, Rainier (Prince of Monaco)
Grimes, Burleigh (baseball)
Grimes, Gary (actor--Summer of 42)
Grimes, Martha (author--The Horse You Came In On)
Grimm Brothers (authors--folklore/fairytales--Pied Piper of
Hamelin)
Grimm, Jacob (Grimm Brother)
Grimm, Wilhelm (Grimm Brother)
Grint, Rupert Alexander (actor--Harry Potter)
Gris, Juan (artist--cubism)
Grisham, John (author--Pelican Brief, The Runaway Jury, The
Firm, A Time to Kill)
Grissom, Gil (actor--C.S.I.)
Grissom, Gus (astronaut)
Grist, Reri (singer--soprano)
Groening, Matt (cartoonist/satirist--The Simpsons, Life in Hell)
Grofe, Ferde (composer--Grand Canyon)
Grogan, Steve (football)
Groh, David (actor--Rhoda)
Grohl, David (musician--drummer--Foo Fighters)
Gromyko, Andrei (politician; Ru.)
Groom, Winston (author--Forrest Gump)
Gros, Antoine-Jean (Baron) (painter--the Battle of Eylau--
Napoleonic)
Gros, Peter (naturalist--Animal Kingdom)
Gross, Arye (actor)
Gross, Milt (cartoonist)
Grossman, Rex (football)
Grove, Robert Moses (Lefty) (baseball)

Groza, Lou (The Toe) (football)
Gruffudd, Loan (actor)
Grunberg, Louis (composer)
Gruning, Ilka (actress--Casablanca)
Guafeng, Hua (politician--Deng Xiaoping's predecessor)
Guare, John (playwright--Six Degrees of Separation, The House of Blue Leaves, Free Man of Color)
Guarnieri, Andrea (violin maker)
Gucci, Aldo (designer)
Guccioni, Bob (publisher/magazine founder--Omni)
Guerra, Saverio (actor)
Guerrero, Pedro (baseball)
Guess Who (musical group--These Eyes)
Guest, Egdar (poet)
Guevara, Che (byname of Ernesto Guevara de la Serna) (theorist/author--Guerilla Warfare; Cuban)
Guggenheim, Peggy (art collector)
Guidry, Ron (Gator) (baseball)
Guillaume, Robert (actor--Benson)
Guinier, Lani (legal scholar/author--Lift Every Voice)
Guinness, Alec (Sir) (actor--Obi Wan Kenobi, The Scapegoat)
Guisewite, Cathy (cartoonist--Cathy)
Guiteau, Charles Julius (lawyer--Pres. Garfield's assassin)
Guitry, Alexandre-Pierre (Sacha) (playwright/actor/director/screenwriter)
Guizot, Francois Pierre (historian/orator/statesman)
Gulager, Clu (actor)
Gulbis, Natalie (golfer)
Gumbel, Greg (sportscaster)
Gunn, Anna (actress--Breaking Bad)
Gunn, Ben (actor--Treasure Island)
Gunn, Tim (fashion designer)
Guns & Roses (guitarist--Slash)
Gunther, John (journalist, author--Inside books)
Guofeng, Hua (politician; Chin.)
Gupta, Sanjay (medical correspondent/neurosurgeon)
Gurdin, Natasha (Natalie Wood's pseudonym) (actress)
Gurney, Ivor (poet)

Gustav, Adolf (King of Sweden)
Guterson, David (author--Snow Falling on Cedars)
Guthrie, Arlo (singer-songwriter)
Guthrie, Janet (racecar driver)
Guthrie, Tyrone (William) (Sir) (producer--theater; Br.)
Guttenberg, Steve (actor--Bedroom Window, No Soap Radio)
Guy, Jasmine (actress)
Guyot, Arnold (geologist)
Gwenn, Edmund (actor--The Trouble with Harry)
Gwyn, Nell (actress)
Gwynn, Tony (#19) (baseball)
Gwynne, Fred (actor--The Munsters)
Gyllenhaal, Jake (actor--Brokeback Mountain)
Gyllenhaal, Maggie (actress)

--H--

Haar, Bernard Ter (poet)
Haas, Ernst (photographer)
Haas, George William (Mule) (baseball)
Haas, Jay (golfer)
Haas, John Lukas (actor--Witness, Jobs)
Haas, Tommy (tennis)
Haba, Alois (composer)
Haber, Fritz (chemist)
Hack, Stan (baseball)
Hackett, Buddy (actor/comedian)
Hackman, Gene (actor--French Connection's Popeye Doyle, Hoosiers)
Haden, Sterling (actor)
Hader, William Thomas (Bill) (actor--Trainwreck, Barry/producer/writer/   comedian-- S.N.L.)
Hadl, John Willard (football)
Hadrian (Roman Emperor) (Trajan's successor)
Hagan, Kay (politician)
Hagel, Charles (Chuck) (politician) (Panetta's successor)

Hagel, Georg Wilhelm (philosopher--German Idealism/Absolute Idealism)
Hagen, Earle (composer--Harlem Nocturne)
Hagen, Jean (actress--Adam's Rib)
Hagen, Uta (actress/author--Respect for Acting)
Hagen, Walter (golfer)
Haggard, H. Rider (Sir) (author--She)
Haggard, Merle (singer--country--Swinging Doors)
Hagin, Joe (politician)
Hagin, Tim (politician)
Hagler, Marvin (boxer)
Hagman, Larry (actor)
Hague, Michael (author--Aesop's Fables)
Hahn, Emily (author--Look Who's Talking)
Hahn, Otto (chemist)
Haig, Alexander (politician--Regan's Sect. Of State)
Hailey, Arthur (author--Airport, Hotel)
Haim, Corey (actor--The Lost Boys)
Haircut One Hundred (musical group)
Hakim, Omar (musician--drummer--jazz)
Hal, David (lyricist--Alfie)
Halaby, Lisa Najceb (Queen Noor Noo of Jordon) (author--Leap of Faith)
Halas, George (Papa Bear) (football--coach)
Hale, Alan (actor--Gilligan's Island)
Hale, Edward Everett (author--The Man Without A Country (Philip Nolan))
Hale, John Rigby (Sir) (speaker; Br.)
Hale, Nathan (Capt.) (patriot--Am. Rev. War)
Hale, Sarah Josepha (author--Mary Had a Little Lamb)
Halevy, Fromental (composer--La Juive)
Haley, Alex (author--Roots)
Haley, Jack (actor--The Wizard of Oz--Tin Man)
Hall & Oates (musical group--She's Gone, Rich Girl, Sara Smile)
Hall, Arsenio (comedian/actor--Coming to America)
Hall, Brad (actor--S.N.L.) (co-founder of Practical Theater Company)
Hall, Carla (chef/T.V. personality--The Chew)

Hall, Charles Francis (explorer; Am.)
Hall, Daryl (musician--Hall & Oates--Rich Girl, She's Gone)
Hall, Edd (announcer--Tonight Show/Leno)
Hall, Gus (American Communist leader)
Hall, Irma (actress--Ladykillers)
Hall, Jonte (Too Tall) (basketball--Harlem Globetrotters)
Hall, Juanita (actress)
Hall, Richard Melville (Moby) (singer/songwriter)
Hall, Tom T. (singer--I Love)
Halley, Bill (& the Comets) (singer--Rock Around the Clock)
Halley, Edmond (astronomer)
Halliburton, Erle (oil businessman)
Halliwell, Geri (musician--Spice Girl)
Hallstrom, Lasse (director--My Life as a Dog)
Hals, Frans (painter--The Merry Toper, Archers of St. George,
Laughing Cavalier, Gypsy Girl,   Descartes)
Halsey, William F. (Bull) (Admiral)
Hamel, Ken (author)
Hamel, Veronica (actress)
Hamer, Rusty (actor--Make Room for Daddy)
Hamill, Dorothy (ice skater)
Hamill, Mark (actor--Luke Skywalker)
Hamilton, Alexander (politician)
Hamilton, Edith (mythologist)
Hamilton, George (actor--Love at First Bite)
Hamilton, Linda (actress)
Hamlin, Hannibal (politician)
Hamlisch, Marvin (composer--Try A Little Tenderness)
Hamm, Jon (actor--Mad Men)
Hamm, Mia (soccer; Am.) (autobiography--Go for the Goal)
Hamm, Paul (gymnast/Olympian)
Hammarskjold, Dag (politician--U. N.)
Hammer, Armand (oil exec./entrepeneur/art collector; Am.)
Hammer, MC (rapper/actor--U Can't Touch This)
Hammerstein, Oscar (lyricist--South Pacific, King and I, Kiss
me Kate, Edelweiss)   (composer--Richard
Rodgers)
Hammett, Samuel Dashiell (author--mystery--Sam Spade,
Hard Boiled, Big Knockover,   The Glass

Key, The Thin Man, The Dain Curse, The Maltese Falcon)
(dog--Asta)
Hammond, Darrell (actor/impersonator--Al Gore)
Hammond, Innes (author)
Hampton, Lionel (musician--vibes)
Hampton, Wade (Gen.) (politician)
Hamson, Knut (author--Pan)
Hancock, Herbie (pianist--jazz)
Hand, Billings Learned (judge/jurist/author--Spirit of Liberty)
Handel, George Frederick/Frideric (composer--Nero, Acis and Galatea, Chandos Anthems, Water Music, La Resurrezione, Ero e Leandro, Music for the Royal Fireworks, Messiah, Atalanta, Largo (Xerxes), Israel in Egypt, Oratorio, Zadok; the Priest, Orestes, Serse, Aci Galatea e Polifermo)
Handford, Martin (author/illustrator--Where's Waldo, Where's Wally)
Handler, Chelsea (comedian/actress/writer/producer/T.V. talk show personality)
Handler, Daniel (a.k.a. Lemony Snicket) (author--children's)
Handy, William Christopher (Father of the Blues) (composer--The Memphis Blues)
Haney, Chris (inventor--Trivial Pursuit)
Hanks, Tom (actor--The Burbs, That Thing You Do, Apollo 13, Big)
Hanley, James (author--The Furys)
Hanna, William (Bill) (director/producer/voice actor/cartoonist--Tom & Jerry)
Hannah, Daryl (actress--Kill Bill)
Hannibal (invader--defeated Scipio--Punic Wars)
Hannity, Sean (talk show host)
Hanover, Bret (harness racer)
Hansen, Barret (Barry) (Dr. Demento) (radio broadcaster)
Hansen, Gunnar (actor)
Hansen, Liane/Liani (journalist/radio personality--N.P.R. host)
Hanson (musical group--Mmm Bop)
Hanson, Howard (composer--Merry Mount)
Hanson, John (politician--Pres. of Cont. Congress)
Hansson, Ola (poet)

Hara, Mary (actress)
Harald V (King; Nor.) (Olav V's son)
Harbach, Otto (lyricist--No, No, Nanette)
Hard, Darlene (tennis)
Hardin, Ty (baseball)
Harding, Ann (actress)
Harding, Daniel (football)
Harding, Tonya (figure skater)
Hardwick, William (Billy) (bowler)
Hardwicke, Cedric Webster (Sir) (actor; Br.)
Hardy, Oliver (comedian/actor--Great Guns)
Hardy, Thomas (author/poet--Tess of the d'Ubervilles, Jude the Obscure, Lifes Little Ironies, Egdon Heath, Return of the Native, Under the Greenwood Tree, The Dynasts)
Hare, David (playwright--Plenty)
Hari, Mata (spy)
Harian, John Marshall (Supreme Court Justice)
Haring, Keith (artist)
Harlow, Jean (actress--Bombshell, Red Dust)
Harmon, Angie (actress)
Harmon, Mark (actor)
Harmon, Merle (sportscaster)
Harmon, Tom (Old 98) (football)
Harney, Ofra (musician--cellist)
Harper, Frances Ellen Watkins (poet--Bury Me in a Free Land)
Harper, Glynn Compton (author--A Perfect Peace)
Harper, Tess (actress--Tender Mercies)
Harper, Valerie (actress)
Harrah, Toby (baseball--coach)
Harriman, Pamela (diplomat)
Harriman, William Averell (Ave) (businessman/diplomat)
Harrington, John (author, inventor--flush toilet)
Harris, Ciara Princess (Ciara) (actress/dancer/singer/songwriter--Goodies)
Harris, Ed (actor--Apollo 13, Westworld)
Harris, Emmy Lou (singer--country)
Harris, Joel Chandler (journalist/author--Uncle Remus)
Harris, Lou (pollster)

Harris, Neil Patrick (actor)
Harris, Phil (singer/songwriter/actor/comedian/musician--jazz)
Harris, Roy (composer)
Harris, Steven (actor--The Practice)
Harris, Youree Dell (a.k.a. Miss Cleo) (shaman/psychic)
Harrison, George (singer/songwriter- Let It Roll/author--I Me Mine)
Harrison, Reginald Carey (Rex) (actor)
Harrison, William Henry (Old Tippecanoe) (politician)
Harry, Debbie (singer--Kookoo)
Hart, Bret (wrestler)
Hart, Charles Joseph (Joe) (football)
Hart, Doris (tennis)
Hart, Johnny (cartoonist--B.C., Wizard of Id)
Hart, Lorenz (lyricist--Blue Moon, Pal Joey, Isn't It Romantic, The Lady is a Tramp, Soon)   (Rodger's collaborator)
Hart, Melissa Joan (actress--Teenage Witch, Melissa and Joey)
Hart, Moss (playwright--Act One/game show host--Answer Yes of No)
Harte, Bret (author--Ah Sin's creator, The Lost Galleon, The Luck of Roaring Camp, Plain   Language from Truthful James, The Outcasts of Poker Flats, Under the Redwoods,   Heathen Chinee)
Hartke, Rupert Vance (politician)
Hartley, Fred A. (politician--Taft-Hartley Act)
Hartman, Lisa (singer/actress)
Hartman, Phil (actor/comedian)
Hartmann, Ilka (photographer)
Harvey, Laurence (nee Larushka Mischa Skikne) (actor)
Hasek, Dominik (hockey)
Hasek, Jaroslav (author; Czech)
Hassam, Childe (painter)
Hasselbeck, Matt (football)
Hasso, Signe (actress)
Hastert, Dennis (politician) (Pelosi's predecessor)
Hastings, Alcee (politician)
Hatch, Orrin (politician--senator--Utah)

Hatcher, Teri (actress)
Hathaway, Anne (actress--Princess Diaries, The Intern)
Hathaway, Anne (Shakespeare's wife)
Hatlo, Jimmy (cartoonist--They'll Do It Every Time, Little Iodine)
Hauer, Rutger (actor--Blade Runner)
Hauptmann, Gerhart (playwright)
Havel, Vaclav (politician/playwright--A Private View; Checz.)
Havelock, Ellis (psychologist)
Havens, Richie (singer)
Haver, June (actress--The Dolly Sisters)
Havers, Nigel (actor)
Hawes, Esme (author--biographer)
Hawes, Harriet (archaeologist)
Hawk, Tony (skateboarder)
Hawke, Bob (politician; Australia)
Hawke, Ethan (actor--Alive, Training Day, Before Sunrise)
Hawking, Stephen (mathematician)
Hawkins, Coleman (saxophonist)
Hawkins, Osie (singer--baritone)
Hawkins, Sally (actress)
Hawkins, Sophie B. (singer/songwriter)
Hawks, Howard (producer/director--Red River, Big Sleep)
Hawley, Willis C. (politician) (Smoot's colleague)
Hawn, Goldie (actress--The Banger Sisters) (Bill Hudson's wife)
Hawthorne, Nathaniel (author--House of theSeven Gables, Marble Faun, Fanshawe: A Tale, The Blithedale Romance)
Hawthorne, Nigel (actor)
Hay, George (founder of Grand Ole Opry)
Hay, Ian (playwright)
Hayakawa, Sessue (actor)
Hayden, Tom (radical--S.D.S.)
Haydn, Franz Joseph (Papa) (composer--The Creation, Trio, Largo Quartet) (Beethoven's teacher)
Hayek, Salma (actress--Frida, Grown Ups)
Hayes, Elvin (Big "E") (basketball)

Hayes, George Francis (Gabby) (actor)
Hayes, Helen (actress--Time Remembered)
Hayes, Isaac (musician/singer--soul/actor--South Park)
Hayes, Linc (actor--Mod Squad)
Hayes, Peter Lind (singer/songwriter/actor)
Hayes, Rutherford (politician--White House Easter egg hunt)
Hayes, Sean (actor--Jack of Will & Grace)
Haynes, Roy (musician--jazz)
Hays, Robert (actor--Airplane)
Hays, William Harrison (Will) (politician/film censor) (Mary Hays McCauly's husband)
Hayward, Leland (producer, agent)
Hayward, Susan (actress)
Haywood, William (Big Bill) (I.W.W. founder)
Hayworth, Rita (actress--Salome, Gilda)
Head, Edith (costume designer)
Headey, Lena (actress--Game of Thrones)
Headley, Glenne (actress--Mr. Holland's Opus)
Healy, Mary (singer)
Healy, Ted (nee Ernest Lea Nash) (vaudevillian/creator--Three Stooges)
Heaney, Seamus (poet; Ir.)
Heard, John (actor--C.H.U.D., Home Alone, Pelican Brief)
Hearn, George (actor--La Cage aux Folles)
Hearn, Patrick (actor--A Little History of Crime)
Hearn, Patrick Lafcadio (Koizumi Yakumo) (author--collection of Japanese legends and ghost stories)
Hearns, Thomas (Little Hitman) (boxer)
Hearst, Patricia (Patty) (S.L.A. member--Tania)
Hearst, Phoebe Apperson (suffragette/philanthropist/educator--P.T.A.)
Hearst, William Randolph (Lord of San Simeon) (newspaper publisher/inspired Citizen Kane)
Heart (musical group--Never, Alone)
Heath, Ted (politician)
Heatherton, Davenie Johanna (Joey) (actress/dancer/singer)
Heaton, Charlie (actor--Stranger Things)
Hebb, Bobby (singer--Sunny)

Hebert, Anne (author--Kamouraska)
Heche, Anne (actress--Wag the Dog, Psycho)
Hecht, Ben (author)
Heckart, Eileen (author)
Heckerling, Amy (filmwriter/director)
Heder, Jon (actor--Napoleon Dynamite)
Hedin, Sven (geographer/topographer/explorer/illustrator/author--travel)
Hedren, Tippi (actress--Marnie)
Hees, George (politician; Can.)
Heflin, Howell (politician--Alabama senator)
Heflin, Van (actor--Battle Cry)
Hefner, Hugh M. (magazine founder/publisher--Playboy/actor--The Girl Next Door)
Hefti, Neal (composer/singer--Lil Darlin)
Hegel, Georg Wilhelm (philosopher--metaphysicist/logic)
Heidegger, Martin (philosopher--being; Ger.)
Heiden, Eric (speed skater)
Heifetz, Jascha (musician--violinist) (Auer's student)
Heigl, Katherine (actress--27 Dresses, Suits)
Hein, Mel (football)
Heine, Heinrich (poet--Die Lorelei, Atta Troll, Romanzero)
Heinlein, Robert A. (author--The Moon is a Harsh Mistress)
Heiss, Carol (skater)
Held, Anna (singer/actress) (Florenz Ziegfeld's wife)
Helgenberger, Marg (actress)
Helliwell, Geri (singer--Spice Girl)
Hellman, Lillian (playwright--The Little Foxes, Toys in the Attic)
Helms, Shane (wrestler)
Helmsley, Leona (business exec.--hotelier)
Heloise (scholar) (Peter Abelard's lover)
Hemingway, Ernest Miller (author--In Our Time, A Farewell to Arms, Across the River and Into the Trees, The Killers, The Sun Also Rises)
Hemingway, Mariel (actress)
Hemsley, Sherman (actor--The Jeffersons, Amen)
Hemsworth, Chris (actor--Thor)
Hemsworth, Liam (actor--Hunger Games)
Henderson, Rickie (baseball)

Hendrix, Jimi (musician--guitarist--Hey Joe)
Hendryx, Nona (singer--pop)
Henie, Sonja (skater/actress--Iceland)
Henley, Beth (playwright--Crimes of the Heart)
Henley, Don (singer/songwriter)
Henley, William Ernest (poet--In Victus)
Henman, Tim (tennis)
Henner, Marilu (actress)
Henning, Doug (magician)
Henreid, Paul (actor--Casablanca)
Henri, Robert (teacher/painter)
Henry I (King of England) (William the Conqueror's son)
Henry II (King of England) (Eleanor Aquitaine's husband)
Henry VIII (King of England) (Thomas Abel/Abell's foe)
Henry, O. (William Sydney Porter's pseudonym) (author--short stories/ironic--The Ransom   of Red Chief, Gift of the Magi)
Hensch, Philip Showalter (physician--Mayo Clinic)
Henson, John (actor/comedian/host--Talk Soup)
Hentoff, Nat (journalist--critic)
Henty, George Alfred (author--Young Bugler)
Henze, Hans Werner (composer--Ondine)
Hepburn, Audrey (nee Edda Hepburn) (actress--Charade, Gigi)
Hepburn, Katherine (actress--Sabrina, Lion in Winter, Rooster Cogburn)
Heppner, Ben (singer--tenor)
Heracvlitus (philosopher; Ionian)
Herber, Arnie (Flash) (football)
Herbert, Don (television personality--Mr. Wizard)
Herbert, Lom (actor--Pink Panther)
Herbert, Victor (composer--Babes in Toyland, Mlle Modiste)
Herlie, Eileen (actress)
Herlihy, Tim (writer/producer/actor)
Herman, Jerry (composer/lyricist--Hello Dolly)
Herman, Woddy (musician--jazz)
Herndon, Ty (singer--country)
Herrick, Robert (poet--Hesperides, Cherry-Ripe)

Herriot, James (veterinarian/author--All Things Great and Small)
Herschel, William (Sir) (astronomer--discovered Uranis)
Hersey, Barbara (actress)
Hersey, John Richard (author/journalist--Hiroshima, Into the Valley)
Hersh, Seymour (journalist)
Hershfield, Harry (Jewish Will Rogers) (author/radio personality/cartoonist--Abie, The Agent)
Hershiser, Orel (baseball)
Herzfeld, John (actor/director/producer/screenwriter--Daddy)
Herzog, Emile (author--biographer)
Herzog, Werner (director/screenwriter/producer--Aguirre, The Wrath of God)
Hesiod (poet--epic--Theogony)
Hess, Erika (skier)
Hess, Leon (oil tycoon--N. Y. Jets owner)
Hess, Myra (Dame) (pianist)
Hess, Walter Rudolf (psychologist)
Hesse, Hermann (poet/author--Rosshalde/painter--Siddhartha, The Glass Bead Game, Steppenwolf, Demian, Narcissus and Goldmund, Demian; Ger.)
Hesse, Victor (physicist/nobelist)
Heston, Charlton (actor/author--An Actor's Life, El Cid, Ben Hur, Soylent Green)
Hewett, Edgar Lee (archeologist)
Hewitt, Abram (inventor--mercury vapor lamp)
Hewitt, Jennifer Love (actress)
Hewitt, Lleyton (tennis)
Hewlett, William (Bill) (engineer/co-founder of Hewlett-Packard computers)
Heyer, Georgette (author--romance)
Heyerdahl, Thor (explorer/author--Aku Aku) (craft--Rai)
Heyward, DuBose (author--Porgy)
Heywood, Broun (journalist)
Hi Five (musical group--I Like the Way)
Hiaasen, Carl (journalist)
Hiatt, John (singer--Slow Turning)
Hiawatha (Indian leader; Am.) (grandmother--Nokomis)

Hickman, Dwayne (actor--Dobie Gillis)
Hidalgo, Miguel (revolutionary; Mex.)
Higham, Charles (author--Bette)
Hiken, Nat (writer/lyricist/composer--created Sgt. Ernie
Bilko/Phil Silvers Show)
Hilderbrand, Elin (author)
Hilfiger, Tommy (fashion designer)
Hill, Anita (lawyer/sex harrassment litigant)
Hill, Carla (politician)
Hill, Dan (singer)
Hill, Dule (actor--West Wing, Psych)
Hill, Erica (journalist/co-host--Weekend Today)
Hill, Faith (singer)
Hill, Graham (racecar driver)
Hill, Jonah (actor--Moneyball)
Hill, Lauryn Noelle (singer/songwriter)
Hill, Mildred J. (composer--Happy Birthday)
Hiller, Wendy (actress)
Hillerman, Tony (author) (detective--Jim Chee)
Hilligoss, Candace (actress)
Hilton, Conrad (hotelier)
Hilton, James (author--Lost Horizon, Good-Bye Mr. Chips)
Hilton, Kathy (nee Kathleen Elizabeth Avanzino)
(actress/socialite/fashion designer/
        philanthropist) (Richard's wife, Paris & Nicky's mother)
Hilton, Nicky (socialite/fashion designer) (Richard & Kathy's
daughter, Paris's sister)
Hilton, Paris (singer/actress/model/fashion designer/media
personality)
Hilton, Richard (businessman--real estate)
Himmler, Heinric (politician--Nazi)
Hind, Lorenz (lyricist--My Funny Valentine)
Hindemith, Paul (composer/musician--viola)
Hines, Cheryl (actress--Curb Your Enthusiasm)
Hines, Earl Fatha (musician; Am.)
Hines, Gregory (dancer)
Hines, Jerome (singer--basso)
Hingis, Martina (tennis)
Hingle, Martin Patterson (Pat) (actor--Batman)

Hinley, Beth (playwright--Crimes of the Heart)
Hinsche, Billy (singer--Dino, Desi & Billy)
Hinton, Susan Eloise (author--Tex)
Hirohito, Showa (Emporer of Japan) (Tsugu Akihito's father)
Hirsch, Elroy (Crazy Legs) (football)
Hirsch, Emile (actor--Into the Wild)
Hirsch, Judd (actor--Taxi)
Hirschfeld, Albert (artist--hides "Nina" in his artwork))
Hirt, Al (Jumbo) (trumpeter/bandleader--jazz--Java, Honey in the Horn, Sugar Lips)
His, Chu (philosopher)
Hiss, Alger (spy)
Hitchcock, Alfred (actor/writer/producer/director--Psycho, The 39 Steps, Marnie, Lifeboat,   Rebecca, Rope, Saboteur, To Catch a Thief)
Hitchcock, Alma (Alfred's wife)
Hite, Shere D. (author--sex--Women and Love, Sexual Honesty by Women for Women)
Hitler, Adolph (politician--Nazi Party leader) (Eva Braun's partner)
Ho, Don (singer--Women and Love, Tiny Bubbles--The Aliis, Pearly Shells, Live at the   Polyesian Palace)
Hoad, Lew (tennis)
Hoag, Tami (author)
Hoare, Samuel (1st Viscount Templeton)
Hoban, James (architect--White House)
Hobbema, Meindert (painter)
Hobby, Oveta Cult (journalist/attorney/politician--Sect. of U. S. Dept. of Health/   director--Women's Army Corps)
Hobson, Laura (author)
Hoch, Hannah (painter)
Hoch, Scott (golfer)
Hodge, Patricia (actress--Betrayal)
Hodges, Gil (baseball)
Hodgins, Jack (author--The Macken Charm)
Hoest, Bunny (cartoonist--the Lockhorns)
Hoff, Benjamin (author--The Tao of Pooh)
Hoff, Syd (cartoonist--Danny and the Dinosaur)

Hoffa, Jimmy (labor leader)
Hoffenberg, Steve (publisher)
Hoffer, Eric (philosopher--moral and social)
Hoffman, Abbie (radical activist)
Hoffman, Dustin (actor--Tootsie, All The President's Men, Lenny)
Hoffman, Ernst Theodor Amadeus (E.T.A.) (composer/author/jurist/caricaturist)
Hoffman, Gabrielle Mary (Gaby) (actress--Transparent, Girls, Sleepless in Seattle, Now and Then)
Hoffman, Philip Seymour (director/actor--Capote)
Hoffman, William (playwright--As Is)
Hofstadter, Douglas (scientist--cognition--sense of I/author--Godel, Escher, Bach/G.E.B.)
Hogan, Ben (golfer)
Hogarth, William (painter--The Rake's Progress/printmaker/etcher)
Hoge, Merril (sportscaster)
Hogen, Paul (actor)
Hogg, Ima (philanthropist)
Hogg, James (The Ettrick Shepherd) (author/poet--The Queen's Wake)
Holbein, Hans (painter--Erasmus)
Holbrook, Hal (actor--Twain)
Holden, Amanda (actress)
Holden, William (actor)
Holder, Eric (politician) (Lynch's predecessor)
Holiday, Billie (nee Eleanora Fagan) (Lady Day) (singer/songwriter--jazz--   He's
Funny That Way, Don't Explain)
Holland, Cecelia (author--historical)
Hollander, Nicole (cartoonist--Sylvia)
Hollander, Xaviera (author--Happy Hooker)
Holliday, Polly (actress--Flo)
Hollies (musical group--Bus Stop)
Holliman, Earl (actor)
Hollis, Stacy (golfer)
Holloway, Josh (actor)
Holly, Charles Hardin (Buddy) (musician/singer/songwriter)

Holm, Celeste (actress)
Holm, Eleanor (swimmer)
Holm, Ian (actor; Br.)
Holman, Bill (cartoonist--Smokey Stover)
Holman, Nat (basketball)
Holmes, Katie (actress--Dawson's Creek)
Holmes, Larry (boxer)
Holst, Gustav Theodore (composer--The Planets, The Perfect
Fool, The Hymn of Jesus)
Holt, Jack (actor--westerns)
Holt, John (Sir) (Chief Justice; Br.)
Holt, Lester (newsman)
Holt, Tim (actor)
Holt, Victoria (author--gothic romance)
Holtby, Winifred (feminist/author; Br.)
Holyfield, Evander (boxer)
Homel, David (author/translater; Can.)
Homer (author--Epos)
Homer, Winslow (artist--The Life LineThe Gulf Stream,
Launching the Boat, Maine Coast)
Homolka, Oscar (actor)
Honegger, Arthur (composer--A Christmas Cantata)
Honour, Joseph (author--Nostromo)
Hood, Hugh (author)
Hooke, Robert (author--Micrographia)
Hooper, Tobe (director)
Hooper, William DeWolf (actor--Casey at the
Bat/singer/comedian)
Hootie and the Blowfish (musical group)
Hooton, Ernest Albert (anthropologist)
Hoover, Herbert (politician) (dog--King Tut)
Hoover, Lou Henry (Herbert's wife)
Hope, Dolores (Bob's wife)
Hope, Leslie Townes (Bob) (comedian/actor--I'll Take
Sweden) (Dolores's husband)
Hopkins, Anthony (actor--Hannibal Lector in Silence of the
Lambs, Thor)
Hopkins, Gerard Manley (poet)
Hopkins, Harry Lloyd (social worker/political advisor--W.P.A.)

Hopkins, Telma (actress--Family Matters)
Hopman, Harry (tennis)
Hoppe, William Frederick (carom billiards)
Hopper, Dennis (actor--Easy Rider)
Hopper, Edward (printmaker/painter--oils--realism)
Hopper, Grace (inventor--Cobol computer language)
Horace (author--odes--Ars Poetica, Dulce Et Decorum Est Pro Patria Mori)
Horne, Lena (singer--Stormy Weather, Deed I Do, One For My Baby)
Horne, Marilyn (singer--mezzo-soprano)
Horney, Karen (psychoanalyst)
Horse, Michael (actor--Tonto)
Horst, Mel (photographer--Amish)
Hoskins, Bob (actor--Smee)
Hospital, Janette Turner (author)
Hostovsky, Egon (author)
Houdini (Eric Weiss's stage name) (magician)
Housman, Alfred Edward (author--A Shropshire Lad, To An Athlete Dying Young)
Houston, Sam (politician--Texas governor/fought Mexicans)
Houston, Whitney (singer--Arista Records--Greatest Love of All, I Have Nothing)
Howard, Curly (actor/comedian--Three Stooges)
Howard, Elston (baseball)
Howard, Esme (diplomat)
Howard, Henry (Earl of Surrey) (poet; Br.)
Howard, Leslie (actor--Scarlet Pimpernel; Br.)
Howard, Moe (actor/comedian--Three Stooges)
Howard, Ron (actor/director--Ed. T. V.)
Howard, Shemp (actor/comedian--Three Stooges)
Howard, Tim (hockey--goalie)
Howatch, Susan (author--Sins of the Father)
Howe, Elias (inventor)
Howe, Gordie (hockey)
Howe, Julia Ward (suffragette/author/poet--Battle Hymn of the Republic)
Howe, Tina (playwright)
Howe, William (General)

Howells, William Dean (author--Their Wedding Journey)
Howes, Sally Ann (actress)
Hoyle, Edmond (author--card games--A Short Treatise on the Game of Whist)
Hoyt, Waite (baseball)
Hoyt, Wilhelm (baseball)
Hruska, Roman Lee (politician)
Hsi, Chu (philosopher)
Hua, Huang (politician; Chin.) (Mao's successor/Dang's predecessor)
Hubbard, Cal (football)
Hubbard, L. Ron (scientologist/author--Dianetics)
Hubbell, Carl (baseball)
Hubble, Edwin (inventor--telescope)
Hubedr, Hans (composer; Swiss)
Huber, Anke (tennis)
Hudgens, Vanessa (singer/actress--High School Musical)
Hudson, Bill (musician--guitarist) (Goldie Hawn's husband)
Hudson, Henry (explorer) (ship--Half Moon)
Hudson, Rock (nee Roy Fitzgerald) (actor--Pretty Maids All In a Row, Darling Lili)
Hudson, William Henry (author--Green Mansions)
Huffington, Arianna (author)
Huffman, Robert Booker Tio (Booker T.) (wrestler/promoter/color commentator)
Hughes, Charles Evans (politician; Am.)
Hughes, Gregg (Opie) (radio show host) (Anthony Cumia's co-host)
Hughes, Langston (poet--I Too)
Hughes, Sarah (figure skater)
Hughes, Ted (poet)
Hughes, Tresa (actress)
Hugo, Victor (author/poet--Le Roi s'amuse, Toute La Lyre, L'Annee Terrible/dramatist--Hernani)
Hulce, Thomas (actor--Amadeus)
Hull, Cordell (politician)
Hull, Edith Maude (author--The Sheik)
Hulme, Kathryn (author--Nun's Story)
Hume, Brit (T. V. newsman)

Hume, David (philosopher/essayist--An Inquiry Concerning
Human Understanding,   Dialogues
Concerning Natural Religion, A Treatise of Human Nature)
Hummel, Johann Nepomuk (composer)
Humperdinck, Englebert (composer--Gretel)
Humperdinck, Englebert (singer--Release Me, The Last Waltz)
Humphrey, Hubert Horatio (politician)
Humphries, Kris (basketball)
Humphries, Stan (football)
Hung, Sammo (actor)
Hunt, Ethan (actor--Mission Impossible)
Hunt, Helen (actress)
Hunt, Lamar (football--team owner)
Hunt, Leigh (nee James Henry Leigh Hunt) (author/poet--Abu
Ben Adhem)
Hunt, Linda (actress)
Hunt, Marsha (singer/model/author/actress)
Hunter, Evan (pseudonym--Ed McBain) (author)
Hunter, Holly (actress--Raising Arizona, The Piano)
Hunter, Ian (musician/songwriter)
Hunter, Tab (actor)
Huntley, Chet (newsman)
Hupp, Jana Marie (actress)
Hurd, Douglas (politician)
Hurd, Peter (illustrator)
Hurley, Elizabeth (actress--Hugh Grant's partner)
Hurok, Sol (impresario)
Hurst, Fannie (author--Back Street)
Hurston, Zora Neale (author) (autobiography--Dust Tracks on
a Road, Their Eyes Were   Watching God)
Hurt, Mary Beth (actress--Slaves of New York)
Hurt, William (actor)
Hus/Huss, Jan/John/Johannes
(philosopher/priest/reformer/martyr; Czec.)
Hussein bin Talal (politician--Jordanian king)
Hussein, Ara (politician; Iran.)
Hussy, Olivia (actress)
Huston, Angelica (actress--Mists of Avalon)
Huston, John (director--African Queen)

Huston, Walter (actor/singer)
Hutchins, Will (actor--Sugarfoot)
Hutchinson, Anne (poet/religious dissenter)
Hutchison, Kay (politician)
Hutter, Jacob (Jakob) (Hutterite founder)
Hutton, Gunilla (actress--Petticoat Junction)
Hutton, Jim (actor)
Hutton, Lauren (actress)
Hutton, Timothy (actor)
Huxley, Aldous (author--Antic Hay, Ape and Essence)
Huxtable, Ada Louise (author/critic)
Hwa, Tung Chee (politician; Hong Kong)
Hyde, Douglas (politician--Ireland's first president)
Hyde, Edward (Earl of Clarendon) (historian)
Hyer, Martha (actress--Some Come Running)
Hymes, Bustar (rapper--Pass the Coyrvoisier)
Hynde, Chrissie (singer)
Hyperides (orator) (Plato's pupil)
Hyra, Margaret (nee Meg Ryan) (actress)

--|--

Iacocca, Lee (businessman)
Ian, Janis (singer-songwriter--pop--At 17)
Iba, Hank (basketball)
Ibanez, Blasco (author)
Ibert, Jacques (composer--Angelique)
Ibsen, Henrik (playwright--Ghosts, Peer Gynt, The Wild Duck,
Rosmersholm, The Master Builder,   Hedda Gabler,
Brand, Paa Vidderne, Little Eyolf)
Icahn, Carl (business exec./ former owner of T.W.A.; Am.)
Ice Cube (O'Shea Jackson's pseudonym)
(singer/actor/screenwriter/producer)
Ice-T (Tracy Morrow's pseudonym) (musician--rap--Rhyme
Pays, Original Gangster songs   (O.G.)/actor--Tank Girl, Law
and Order S.U.V., Trespass) (band--Body Count)
Idle, Eric (actor/comedian--Spamalot)

Idol, Billy (singer--rock--Rebel Yell)
Iger, Robert (C.E.O. Walt Disney Company) (Michael Eisner's successor)
Iggy Pop (James Newell Osterberg Jr.'s stage name) (singer/songwriter/actor)
Iglesias, Julio (singer--Amor)
Igoe, Bert A. (Hype) (sport writer/cartoonist)
Ikettes (musical group--I Am Blue)
Ikkidluak, Iola Abraham (artist; Inuit)
Ileo, Joseph (politician; Congo)
Iler, Robert (actor--Sopranos)
Ilg, Frances A. (psychologist) (co-authors--Gesell & Ames)
Iman (model/actress; Somali)
Imhotep (architect--Step Pyramid of Djoser)
Imola, Innocenzo (nee Innocenzo di Petro Francucci) (painter; Bolognese)
Imus, Don (radio host)
In Cargo (musical group--Whip It)
Inarritu, Alejandro (composer/producer/screenwriter--21 Grams)
Inarritu, Alejandro Gonzales (director--21 Grams)
Incaviglia, Pete (baseball)
Ince, Ralph Waldo (actor)
Ince, Thomas (director--Civilization)
Indigo Girls (musical group--Closer to Fine)
Infante, Omar (baseball)
Inge, Milton Thomas (author)
Inge, William (playwright--The Dark at the Top of the Stairs, Little Sheba, Picnic, A Loss of Roses, Bus Stop, Splendor In the Grass, Good Luck Miss Wyckoff)
Ingram, Dan (disc jockey)
Ingram, James (singer--I Don't Have theHeart)
Ingres, Jean-Auguste-Dominique (painter--Odalisque with Slave)
Ink Spots (musical group--Address Unknown)
Inkster, Juli (golfer)
Inman, Henry (artist--Newsboy)
Innes, Hammond (author--The Wreck of the Mary Deare)
Innes, Laura (actress--E.R.)

Inness, George (artist--Rainbow After A Storm, The Delaware Water Gap)
Innis, Roy (Civil Rights leader)
Innisfail, Erin (soccer)
Inonu, Ismet (politician--Turkish leader)
Inouye, Daniel (politician)
Insana, Ron (reporter/analyst--C.N.B.C.)
Inxs (musical group--Suicide Blonde, Need You Tonight, What You Need)
Ione, Skye (actress)
Ionesco, Eugene (playwright--Le Rhinoceros, The Bald Soprano, The Chairs)
Irabu, Hideki (baseball)
Ireland, Jill (actress)
Ireland, John (actor)
Ireton, Henry (General) (King Charles I enemy/Cromwell's son-in-law)
Iron Maiden (musical group--Somewhere in Time)
Irons, Jeremy (actor--Dead Ringers)
Irvan, Ernie (racecar driver)
Irvin, Michael (football)
Irvin, Monte (baseball)
Irvin, Rea (cartoonist)
Irving, Amy (actress)
Irving, John (author--World According to Garp, Owen Meany, A Son of the Circus)
Irving, Washington (diplomat/author--The Sketch Book of Geoffrey Crayon, Astoria,   Brom Bones)
Irwin, Allen (producer/director)
Irwin, Corey (comedian)
Irwin, Hale (golfer)
Irwin, James (astronaut)
Isaac, Oscar (actor--Inside Llewyn Davis)
Isaacs, Jason (actor--Harry Potter)
Isaacs, Susan (author--Magic Hour)
Isaak, Chris (singer--Wicked Game, Heart Shaped World)
Isham, Mark (composer)
Isherwood, Christopher William Bradshaw (author--The Berlin Stories, I Am a Camera,   A Single Man,

Cabaret (musical)/playwright--Treatise on Philosophy) (Don Bachardy's partner)
Ishiguro, Kazuo (author--The Remains of the Day)
Isley Brothers (musical group--R. &. B.--That Lady, It's Your Thing)
Ismay, Hastings (Lord) (politician--NATO Secretary General)
Issa, Darrell (politician)
Issel, Dan (basketball)
Italiano, Anna Maria (a.k.a. Anne Bancroft) (actress--Golda Meir, Miracle Worker)
Ito, Hirobumi (politician; Jap.)
Ito, Lance A. (justice--Simpson trial)
Ito, Midori (skater)
Ito, Robert (actor--Quincy, M.E.)
Iturbi, Jose (pianist)
Ivan I (Moneybags) (Tsar)
Ivan IV (Ivan the Terrible (nee Ivan Marchenko) (Holocaust guard (Dmitry Ivanovich's father)
Ivanisevic, Goran (tennis)
Ivanovic, Ana (tennis)
Ivanovich, Dmitry (Tsar) (Ivan the Terrible's son)
Ivanovna, Anna (Empress of Russia) (Ivan V's daughter)
Ivens, Molly (author--Bill of Wrongs)
Iverson, Allen (basketball)
Ives, Burl Icle Ivanhoe (actor--Big Daddy/songwriter/singer--folk--A Little Bitty Tear,   O For a Thousand Tongues, The Big Country)
Ives, Charles Edward (composer--Three Places in New England/Celestial Country,   Variations on America, Concord Sonata)
Ives, David (playwright--Venus in Fur)
Ives, James Merritt (lithographer--Currier and Ives)
Ivey, Dana (actress)
Ivey, Judith (actress)
Ivey, Phil (poker)
Ivins, Molly (columnist--politics)
Izzard, Eddie (comedian)

--J--

Jackman, Hugh (actor--X-man)
Jackson Five (musical group--A.B.C.)
Jackson Five (musical group--Mama's Pearl, I Am Love)
Jackson, Alan (singer)
Jackson, Andrew (politician)
Jackson, Anne (actress--The Secret Life of an American Wife)
Jackson, Deon (singer--Love Makes the World Go Round)
Jackson, Glenda (actress--Stevie, Mary Queen of Scots)
Jackson, Helen Hunt (author--Ramona)
Jackson, Janet (singer)
Jackson, Jesse (Rev.) (politician/religious leader)
Jackson, Joe (singer/songwriter--Is She Really Going Out with Him, Stepping Out)
Jackson, Kate (director/producer/actress--Charlie's Angels)
Jackson, Latoya (singer)
Jackson, Mahalia (singer) (autobiography--Movin' on Up)
Jackson, Marlon (singer--Jackson Five)
Jackson, Michael (singer--This is It, Thriller, Ben, King of Pop, Bad)
Jackson, Milt (musician--jazz)
Jackson, O'Shea (pseudonym--Ice Cube) (singer/actor/screenwriter/producer)
Jackson, Reginald Martinez (Reggie) (baseball)
Jackson, Samuel L. (actor--Eve's Bayou)
Jackson, Tito (musician)
Jackson, Wanda (singer--country)
Jacob, Mary Phelps (inventor--brassiere)
Jacobi, Derek (actor--I Claudius)
Jacobs, Jane (urbanologist)
Jacobs, Marc (fashion designer)
Jacobsen, Arne (architect)
Jacobsen, Marie Gibbe (author)
Jacoby, Oswald (bridge expert)
Jacopetti, Gualtiero (filmmaker--Mondo Cane)
Jacquet, Luc (director--March of the Penguins)

Jaffe, Rona (author--Mazes and Monsters, Class Reunion)
Jaffe, Sam (actor--Ben Casey)
Jagger, Bianca (model)
Jagger, Mick (singer/musician/actor--Ned Kelly)
Jagr, Jaromir (hockey)
Jahan, Shah (Mogul emperor/Taj Mahal constructor; India)
Jakes, John (author--The Bastard, The Titans)
James, Courtney (Coco) (singer/songwriter/actress)
James, Etta (singer--Good Rockin Daddy)
James, Harry (lyricist--He's My Guy)
James, Henry (author--The Golden Bowl, Portrait of a Lady,
Daisy Miller, The Wings of   the Dove, What
Maisie Knew, The Turn of the Screw)
James, Jesse (outlaw)
James, LeBron (basketball)
James, Otis (orator)
James, Phyllis Dorothy (P.D.) (author--Cover Her Face)
James, Theo (actor--Divergent)
Janacek, Leos (composer; Czech)
Janes, Percy (author)
Janeway, Eliot (economist)
Janis, Byron (pianist)
Janis, Elsie (actress/comedienne)
Jankowski, Horst (pianist--jazz)
Janney, Allison (actress)
Jannings, Emil (actor--The Last Command)
Janowitz, Tama (author--Slaves of N.Y.)
Jansen, Theo (artist; Dutch)
Janssen, David (actor)
Jarnefelt, Eero (painter; Fin.)
Jarre, Maurice (composer--Lawrence of Arabia)
Jarreau, Al (musician)
Jarrett, Keith (musician--pianist--jazz)
Jarrett, Ned (race car driver)
Jarry, Alfred (playwright--absurd--Ubu Roi/King Ubu)
Jaworski, Leon (lawyer--Nixon era)
Jaworski, Ron (football)
Jay Z (musician--rap) (label--roc-a-fella)
Jeanmaire, Renee (dancer)

Jedi Knights (musical group)
Jeeves, Mahatma Kane (W. C. Fields' pseudonym)
(actor/author)
Jefferson, Arthur Stanley (a.k.a. Stan Laurel) (comedian/actor-
-Great Guns)
Jefferson, Margo (critic)
Jefferson, Thomas (The Man of the People) (politician/writer--
Declaration of   Independence)
Jeffreys, Anne (actress)
Jeffries, James J. (boxer)
Jelinek, Otto (politician)
Jemison, Mae (astronaut)
Jeni, Richard (comedian)
Jenkins, Ella (singer)
Jenner, Bruce (decathlete/actor/transitioned to female/author--
I Am Cait)
Jensen, Jim (newsman)
Jeong, Ken (actor--The Hangover)
Jepsen, Carly Rae (singer--Maybe)
Jessell, George (Toastmaster General) (comedian)
Jett, Joan (and the Blackhearts) (singer--rock--I Love Rock &
Roll)
Jewel (singer--Foolish Games)
Jewett, Sarah Orne (author)
Jiles, Paulette (poet)
Jillettte, Penn (magician--Penn & Teller)
Jillian, Ann (actress)
Jinping, Xi (politician; Chin.)
Jobs, Steve (inventor/co-founder--Apple & Pixar) (Tim Cook's
predecessor)
Joel, Alexa (singer-songwsriter/musician-piano) (Billy Joel's
daughter)
Joel, William Martin (Billy) (musician/singer/songwriter--Piano
Man, I Go to Extremes,   It's Still Rock and Roll
to Me, The Downeaster "Alexa", And So It Goes,
              Honesty)
Joelson, Asa (pseudonym--Al Jolson) (singer)
Johansson, Ingemar (boxer)

Johansson, Scarlett (model/singer--Her/actress--A Good
Woman)
John of Gaunt (Duke of England)
John, Elton (Reg) (The Rocket Man) (singer--The One, Can
You Feel the Love Tonight/   pianist--Aida)
John, Robert (singer/songwriter--Sad Eyes)
Johncock, Gordon (race car driver)
Johns, Jasper (artist--pop art)
Johnson, Ben (actor--Last Picture Show)
Johnson, Betsey (fashion designer)
Johnson, Boris (politician; Br.)
Johnson, Claudia Alto (nee Taylor) (Lady Bird) (Lyndon's wife)
Johnson, Dwayne (The Rock) (wrestler/actor)
Johnson, Ernie (sportscaster)
Johnson, Gord (chef)
Johnson, Harold Ogden (Chic) (vaudevillian) (John Sigvard
Olsen's partner)
Johnson, Hugh S. (busnessman--National Recovery
Administration (N.R.A.))
Johnson, Jimmy (race car driver)
Johnson, Ladybird (nee Claudia Alta Taylor) (Lyndon's wife)
Johnson, Lyndon Baines (Landslide Lyndon) (politician--War
on Poverty) (dog--Him, Her)
Johnson, Lynn (cartoonist--For Better Or Worse)
Johnson, Osa (explorer)
Johnson, Philip (architect--A.I.A. group)
Johnson, Rafer (decathlete)
Johnson, Ron (politician; Wisc.)
Johnson, Samuel (Cham)
(lexicographer/author/essayist/editor/literary critic)
Johnson, Trish (golfer)
Johnson, Van (actor)
Johnston, Levi (model/actor/author--Deer in the Headlights)
(Palin's exfiance)
Joliet, Louis (explorer--Lake Erie)
Jolin, Janis (Pearl) (singer)
Joliot-Curie, Irene (chemist/nobelist)
Jolson, Al (Asa Joelson's pseudonym) (singer--Swanee, Toot,
Toot Tootsie, Hallelujah-I'm   a Bum,

Avalon, I Sent My Wife to the Thousand Isles, The One I Love/
actor--The Jazz Singer)
Jonas, Joe (singer--Jonas Brothers)
Jonas, Kevin (singer--Jonas Brothers)
Jonas, Nick (singer--Jonas Brothers)
Jones, Brian (musician--Rolling Stones)
Jones, Carolyn (actress--Adams Family)
Jones, Catherine Zeta (actress/model)
Jones, Chuck (cartoonist--Bugs Bunny)
Jones, Cleon (baseball)
Jones, Ed (Too Tall) (football)
Jones, Etta (singer)
Jones, Gwyneth (singer--soprano--Isolde)
Jones, Inigo (architect)
Jones, Isham (bandleader/composer--It Had To Be You)
Jones, Isola (singer--mezzo-soprano)
Jones, James (author--The Thin Red Line, W.W.II, Some
Came Running)
Jones, Janet (actress)
Jones, Leroi (a.k.a Amiri Baraka) (poet/playwright)
Jones, Leslie (comedian--S.N.L.)
Jones, Norah (singer--jazz--Sunrise, Chasing Pirates)
Jones, Renee (actress--L.A. Law)
Jones, Thad (musician--jazz)
Jones, Tom (singer--She's a Lady)
Jones, Tommy Lee (actor--Men in Black)
Jones, Van (political commentator--C.N.N.)
Jong, Erica (author--Fear of Flying, Fanny)
Jong-Il, Kim (politician--N. Korea)
Jonson, Ben (poet/dramatist--Sweet Swan of Avon)
Jonson, Orare Ben (actor)
Jonze, Spike (director/producer/screenwriter/actor--Her)
Jooss, Kurt (choreographer)
Joplin, Janis (Pearl) (singer--Down on Me, Me and Bobby
McGee)
Joplin, Scott (King of Ragtime) (musician)
Jordan, Neil (writer/director)
Jordan, Sass (singer/songwriter/Can. Idol judge)
Jordan, Yvette (model) (Michael's wife)

Jory, Victor (actor)
Joss, Adruab (Addie) (baseball)
Jovovich, Milla (model/actress--Resident Evil)
Joyce, James (poet/author--The Dead, Finnegan's Wake (Anna Livia Plurabelle), The Dubliners (Eveline)) (Nora's husband)
Joyce, Nora (James Joyce's wife)
Joyce, William (Lord Haw-Haw) (author/illustrator/publisher)
Joyner, Al (track--triple jump)
Joyner, Florence Griffith (Flo Jo) (runner/Olympian)
Juarez, Benito Pablo (politician; Mex.)
Judd, Naomi (singer/musician)
Judge, Arline (actress)
Judge, Mike (actor)
Julia, Raul Rafael (actor)
Jung, Carl (psychoanalyst/author--The Undiscovered Self) (contemporaries Freud & Adler)
Junipero, Serra (missionary--founded San Diego)
Jupitus, Phill (panelist)
Jute (Germanic invader of Kent)
Jutra, Claude (filmmaker)
Juvenal (nee Junius Juvenalis) (satirist)

--K--

Kaat, Billy (baseball)
Kaat, Jim (baseball)
Kabaivanska, Raina (singer--soprano)
Kabalevsky, Dmitri (composer--The Comedians)
Kabibble, Ish (musician--trumpeter--novelty singer--Kay Kyser Band)
Kadar, Janos (politician; Hun.)
Kael, Pauline (film critic--New Yorker/author--I Lost it at the Movies)
Kaelin, Kato (actor--O. J. Simpson trial witness)
Kaepernick, Colin (football)
Kafka, Franz (diarist/author--The Trial, Amerika)

Kagan, Elena (justice)
Kahlo, Frida (artist--self-portraits)
Kahn, Batu (Mongol conqueror)
Kahn, Gus (songwriter--Making Whoopee)
Kahn, Madeline (actress--Blazing Saddles, What's Up Doc)
Kahn, Otto (financier/art patron)
Kahn, Roger (author--The Boys of Summer)
Kain, Karen (dancer--ballet)
Kaine, Tim (politician)
Kai-Shek, Chiang (politician) (Mao's adversary)
Kalb, Bernard (newsman)
Kalb, Marvin (newsman--Meet the Press)
Kaline, Al (baseball)
Kallo, Marvin (newsman)
Kalman, Emmerich (composer--Sari)
Kalmar, Bert (lyricist--Who's Sorry Now) (Harry Ruby's partner)
Kam, Bruce Lee Jun Fan Yuen (a.k.a. Bruce Lee) (actor)
Kamen, Dean (inventor--Segway)
Kamen, Milt (comic/actor)
Kaminska, Ida (actress)
Kamoze, Ini (lyricist/singer--reggae--Here Comes the Hotstepper)
Kandinsky, Wassily (Vasily) (artist--Composition 8)
Kane, Bob (cartoonist--Batman)
Kane, Carol (comedian/actress)
Kane, Paul (painter; Can.)
Kanin, Garson (playwright--Adam's Rib, Where It's At)
Kansas (musical group--Dust in the Wind)
Kant, Immanuel (author--philosophy & ethics--Critique of Pure Reason, Critique of Judgment, Categorically Imperative, The Metaphysics of Morals)
Kaper, Bronislau (composer--Lili)
Kaplan, Gabe (actor--Welcome Back Kotter)
Kaplan, Justin (author--Mr. Clemens & Mark Twain)
Kapp, Colin (author--sci-fi)
Karan, Donna (fashion designer--DKNY)
Karause, Peter (actor)
Kardashian, Khloe (T.V. personality/model)

Kardashian, Kim (T.V. personality)
Kardashian, Kourtney (T.V. personality)
Kardashian, Kris (T.V. personality/manager/producer/author)
Kardashian, Robert Jr. (T.V. personality)
Karina, Anna (actress--Scheherzade)
Karl, George (basketball)
Karlfeldt, Erik (poet)
Karloff, Boris (nee William Henry Pratt) (actor--The Mummy, The Ape)
Karmel, Ilona (author)
Karn, Richard (actor)
Karolyi, Bela (gymnastics--coach)
Karras, Alex (football/ wrestler/actor--Webster, Blazing Saddles)
Karsavina, Tamara (dancer--ballet)
Karsh, Yousef (photographer)
Karzai, Hamid (politician--Afghan.)
Kasdan, Laurence (director--The Big Chill)
Kasem, Casey (disc jockey)
Kashoggi, Adnan (oil man/arms dealer)
Kasi, Lemmons (director--Eve's Bayou)
Kasparov, Gary (chess master)
Kastner, Erich (author--Emil and the Detectives)
Katrina & The Waves (musical group)
Katt, William (actor--Carrie)
Katz, Alex (artist)
Katz, Omri (actor--Dallas's John Ross, Hocus Pocus)
Katzen, Mollie (chef--veg.)
Kaufman, Andy (comedian)
Kaufman, Bel (author--Love Etc.)
Kaufman, Ida (Ada) (Ariel Durant's pseudonym) (author; Am.)
Kaufman, Moises (author--The Laramie Project)
Kavafian, Ani (violinist)
Kavner, Julie (actress)
Kay, Danny (comedian/actor)
Kay, Guy Gavriel (author--Under Heaven)
Kaye, Danny (comedian/actor)
Kaye, Nora (dancer)
Kaye, Sammy (singer--Daddy)

Kazan, Elia (director--East Of Eden, A Streetcar Names Desire)
Kazan, Lainie (actress)
Kazan, Zoe (actress/screenwriter)
Kazantzakis, Nikos (author--Zorba the Greek)
Ke$ha (nee Kesha Rose Sebert) (songwriter/singer--rap--Tiktok)
Keach, Stacy (actor--Mike Hammer)
Kean, Edmund (actor--Shakespearean)
Kean, Thomas (businessman/academic/politician--911 Commission)
Keanan, Staci (actress--Step By Step)
Keane, Bil (cartoonist--Family Circus)
Keane, Margaret (painter--big eyes)
Kearns, Doris (Goodwin) (author--biographer--L.B.J.)
Keating, Kenneth (politician)
Keaton, Buster (actor--Sherlock Jr., Steamboat Bill Jr.)
Keaton, Diane (actress--Annie Hall)
Keaton, Michael (actor--Batman Returns, Mr. Mom)
Keats, John (poet--Ode to Psyche, The Eve of St. Agnes, On First Looking Into Chapman's   Homer, Endymion, Ode On Indolence, Meg Merrilies)
Kedrova, Lila (actress--Zorba the Greek, Torn Curtain)
Keefe, Tim (baseball)
Keel, Howard (singer)
Keeler, Ruby (nee Ethel Keeler) (dancer/singer/actress--No No Nanette)
Keeler, Willie (baseball)
Keene, Laura (actress)
Keener, Catherine (actress--Full Frontal)
Keeshan, Robert James (Bob) (actor--Clarabell the Clown)
Kefauver, Estes (politician--senator--Adlai's running mate)
Keibler, Stacy (model/actress)
Keillor, Gary Edward (Garrison) (radio personality/storyteller--anecdotes/   author--Lake Wobegon Days)
Keino, Kip (runner/Olympian; Kenya)
Keir, Dullea (actor--2001 The Space Odyssey)
Keir, Udo (actor)

Keita, Ibrahim (politician; Mali)
Keitel, Harvey (actor--The Piano, Reservoir Dogs, Taxi Driver)
Keith Vicki (swimmer; Can)
Kell, George (baseball)
Keller, Helen (activist/lecturer/author) (Anne Sullivan's blind pupil)
Kellerman, Sally (actress)
Kelley, David E. (actor--Snoops)
Kelley, Stella (actress)
Kellogg, Will Keith (surgeon/cereal brand founder)
Kelly, Emmett (clown)
Kelly, Gene (singer/dancer/actor--Les Girls, Singing in the Rain)
Kelly, George (playwright--Craig's Wife)
Kelly, Grace (actress--Rear Window--Monaco)
Kelly, M. T. (author--A Dream Like Mine)
Kelly, Moira (actress--Chaplin, The West Wing)
Kelly, Ned (outlaw)
Kelly, Patsy (comedian)
Kelly, Robert Sylvester (singer--I'm Your Angel, Love Letters) (Celine Dion's duet partner)
Kelly, Walt (cartoonist--Pogo)
Kemal, Mustafa (politician; Turkey)
Kemble, Frances Anne (Fanny) (author/actress/abolitionist)
Kemp, David (politician)
Kemp, Jack (politician)
Kemp, Shawn (basketball)
Kemperer, Werner (singer/musician/actor--Hogan's Heroes)
Kempson, Rachel (actress) (Sir Michael Redgrave's wife)
Kempton, Murray (reporter)
Kenan and Kel (comedy duo)
Kendrick, Anna (actress--Up In the Air)
Kennan, George (author--Russia Leaves the War)
Kennedy, Edgar (Slow Burn) (actor/comedian)
Kennedy, Edward Moore (politician)
Kennedy, John Fitzgerald (politician/author--Why England Slept)
Kennedy, Mimi (actress)

Kennedy, Rory Elizabeth Katherine (filmmaker--documentary) (Robert's daughter)
Kennedy, Rose Fitzgerald (philanthropist/socialite) (John Francis (Honey) Fitz's daughter)
Kennedy, William (author--Ironweed)
Kensit, Patsy (actress)
Kent, Allegra (dancer--ballet)
Kenton, Erle C. (director)
Kenton, Stan (actor)
Kenton, Stan (musician--jazz)
Kenyatta, Jomo (politician; Kenya)
Kenyatta, Uhuru (politician; Kenya)
Keonig, Walter (actor--Star Trek)
Kepler, Johannes (astronomer)
Kerensky, Alexander (politician)
Kern, Jerome (composer/lyricist--A Fine Romance, Smoke Gets in Your Eyes, Try to Forget,   Roberta, Nobody Else But Me, Very Good Eddie, Sunny, The Last Time I Saw Paris,   No One But Me)
Kerns, Joanne (actress--Growing Pains)
Kerouac, Jack (author--On the Road, Big Sur)
Kerr, Anita (singer)
Kerr, Christie (golf)
Kerr, Deborah (actress--An Affair to Remember, Tea and Sympathy)
Kerr, Graham (Galloping Gourmet) (chef)
Kerr, Jack (actor)
Kerr, Jean (author--Please Don't Eat the Daisies/playwright--Lunch Hour)
Kerr, Steve (basketball)
Kerr, Walter (author--The Silent Clowns)
Kerrigan, Nancy (skater)
Kerry, John (politician) (John Edward's running mate)
Kerry, Teresa Heinz (businesswoman)
Kersee, Jackie Joyner (runner)
Kert, Larry (actor--West Side Story)
Kertesz, Imre (author)
Kesey, Ken (author--One Flew Over the Cuckoo's Nest)
Kesha (singer--Tik-Tok)

Keshishian, Alek (director)
Kesselring, Albert (German Marshal)
Kesselring, Joseph (playwright--Arsenic and Old Lace)
Key, Francis Scott (songwriter--Star Spangled Banner/poet--Defense of Fort M'Henry)
Key, Ted (cartoonist--Hazel)
Keye, Luke (actor)
Keyes, Daniel (author--Flowers for Alernon)
Keyes, Francis Parkinson (author)
Keynes, John Maynard (Lord) (advocate--Mixed Economy)
Keys, Alicia (pianist/songwriter-singer, record producer--Songs in A Minor, As I Am)
Khachaturian, Aram (composer)
Khamenei, Sayyed Ali (politician--Iran)
Khan, Aga (Mongol ruler)
Khan, Ali (Aly) (Prince) (Rita Hayworth's lover)
Khan, Ayub (military leader; Afgh.)
Khan, Batu (The Good Khan) (Mogul ruler)
Khan, Chaka (singer) (band--Rufus)
Khan, Genghis (Mongol ruler)
Khan, Jemima Marcelle (heiress/author/campaigner/magazine editor--Vanity Fair)
Khan, Kublia (Mongol ruler) (Genghis grandson)
Khan, Salman (Sal) (entrepreneur/educator--Online Academy)
Khan, Yasmin Aga (princess) (philanthropist--Alzheimer's) (Rita Hayworth/Prince   Aly Khan's daughter)
Khashoggi, Jamal (author/columnist/Saudi Arabian dissident)
Khayyam, Omar (poet--A Book of Verses Underneath the Bough)   (translated by Edward Fitzgerald)
Khnum-Khufu (pharaoh--built Giza Pyramid)
Khosrow, Amir (poet--Nine Heavens)
Khruschev, Nikita (politician) (Alexei Kosygin's/Leonid Breznev's predecessor)
Kid Edward (Ory) (bandleader/musician--trombonist--jazz)
Kid Rock (Robert James "Bob" Ritchie's pseudonym) (singer/songwriter--All Summer Long)
Kidd, Jason (basketball)

Kidd, Michael (choreographer)
Kidder, John Tracy (author--Among School Children, The Soul of a New Machine)
Kidder, Margot (actress--Lois Lane)
Kidman, Nicole (actress--Malice, Practical Magic)
Kiel, Richard (actor--Bond movies--Jaws)
Kielburger, Craig (columnist/activist/author--Free the Children)
Kieran, John (radio personality--Information Please)
Kierkegaard, Soren (Father of Existentialism) (author/philosopher--The Sickness Unto Death)
Kilborn, Craig (comedian)
Kilbride, Percy (actor--Pa Kettle)
Kiley, Brian (comedian)
Killy, Jean-Claude (skier)
Kilmer, Joyce (poet--Trees)
Kilmer, Val (actor--The Doors, Wyatt Earp)
Kim, Daniel Dae (actor--Hawaii Five-O)
Kim, Lil (singer--rap)
Kimbraugh, Emily (author/journalist)
Ki-moon, Ban (politician--U. N. Secretary General)
Kincaid, Jamaica (author)
Kiner, Ralph (baseball)
King Cole Trio (musical group)
King, Alan (comedian/author--Matzo Balls for Breakfast/ Great Jewish Joke Book)
King, Alyce (singer--King Sisters)
King, B. B. (Riley B.) (musician--guitarist--blues--The Thrill is Gone)
King, Ben E. (Bene) (musician--pop)
King, Betsy (golfer)
King, Carole (singer/songwriter)
King, Coretta (Martin Luther King's widow)
King, Gayle (T.V. personality--C.B.S. This Morning/editor--Oprah Magazine)
King, Leslie Lynch (Gerald Ford's father)
King, Martin Luther (activist) (Coretta's husband)
King, Peter (author/analyst/reporter)
King, Rufus (politician; Am.)

King, Stephen (author--Stride Toward Freedom, Wolves of the Calla, Misery, Firestarter,   Carrie, Salem's Lot, Christine)
Kingman, Dong (artist)
Kingsley, Amis (author)
Kingsley, Charles (priest/professor/historian/poet/author--Westward Ho)
Kingsley, Sidney (author--Men in White)
Kingston Trio (musical group--M. T. A., Tom Dooley, Scotch and Soda)
Kingston, Sea (singer/songwriter--Eenie Meenie) (Bieber collaborator)
Kinks (musical group--Lola)
Kinnear, Greg (actor--As Good As It Gets)
Kinnock, Neil (politician; Br.)
Kinsella W. P. (author-Shoeless Joe)
Kinsey, Alfred (biologist--sex)
Kinski, Klaus (actor--Acquirre; Wrath of God)
Kinski, Natassia (actress--Tess)
Kinsolver, Barbara (poet/essayist/author--The Poisonwood Bible)
Kipling, Rudyard (author-- The Maltese Cat, Soldiers Three/poet--L'Envoi, Mandalay,   Follow Me Ome, Shere Khan, Boots, Mother O Mine)
Kipnis, Igor (harpsichordist/pianist/conductor)
Kiraly, Karch (volleyball)
Kirby, Bruno (actor--City Slickers)
Kirk, Lisa (comedian/actress/singer)
Kirkland, Gelsey (dancer--ballet)
Kirkman, Rick (cartoonist--Baby Blues)
Kirkpatrickk, Jeane (politician--U. N. Ambassador)
Kirschner, Mia (actress)
Kiss (musical group--Beth)
Kissinger, Henry (politician/author--A World Restored) (Tho Le Duc's co-nobelist)
Kitchener, Horatio Herbert (Lord Kitchener of Khartoum) (Boeu War commander)
Ki-Tse (politician--Korea founder)
Kitt, Eartha (singer--Santa Baby)

Kittle, Ron (baseball)
Klas, Eri (conductor)
Klee, Paul (painter/designer--Bauhaus school--Fish Magic, Twittering Machine)
Klein, Anne (fashion designer)
Klein, Calvin (fashion designer) (bio--A Stylish Obsession)
Klein, Chris (actor)
Klein, Ezra (journalist/author/political commentator--VOX co-founder)
Klein, Lawrence (economist)
Klein, Marci (producer)
Kleist, Heinrich von (author/playwright--The Broken Jug)
Klemperer, Otto (maestro)
Klemperer, Werner (actor/narrator/operatic performer)
Klensch, Elsa (author--fashion /producer & host--Style)
Kliban, Bernard (cartoonist--cats)
Klimt, Gustav (painter--Portrait of Adele Bloch-Bauer I)
Kline, Franz Joseph (painter; Am.)
Kline, Kevin (actor--Dave, January Man, In & Out, A Fish Called Wanda, Violets Are Blue)
Klug, Gunther Adolf Ferdinand (German field marshal--W.W.II)
Klum, Heidi (model/T.V. personality--America's Got Talent)
Knack (musical group--Sharona)
Knievel, Evel (stuntman)
Knight, Eric (author--Lassie)
Knight, Gladys (singer--If I Were a Woman)
Knight, Phil (businessman--Nike)
Knight, Ted (actor)
Knightley, Keira (actress--Cecilia & Robbee, Bend it Like Beckham)
Knights (musical group)
Knopf, Alfred A. (publisher)
Knott, Frederick (playwright--Dial M for Murder)
Knotts, Don (actor/comedian--Barney Fife)
Knowles, John (author--A Separate Place)
Knowles, Solange (singer)
Knut (King; Den.)
Kobo, Abe (author)
Koch, Ed (poltician--N.Y. mayor/author--Mayor)

Kodaly, Zoltan (composer--Hary Janos)
Kodes, Jan (tennis)
Koehler, Ted (lyricist)
Koerber, Leila (Marie Dressler's pseudonym) (actress)
Koestler, Arthur (author--Darkness at Noon; Br.)
Kogawa, Joy (author)
Kohl, Helmut (first Chancelor of united Germany) (Schmidt's successor)
Kohler, Wolfgang (psychologist--Gestalt)
Koko (gorilla--talking)
Kokoschka, Oskar (painter/author/playwright)
Kollwitz, Kathe (artist)
Kondabolu, Hari (comedian)
Koner, Pauline (dancer)
Konev, Ivan (Marshall--W.W. II; Rus.)
Kook, Abraham Isaac (rabbi--first chief rabbi of Palestine)
Kool Moe Dee (musician--rap)
Koontz, Dean (author)
Koop, C. Everett (Surgeon General)
Kopp, Sheldon (psychologist--pop)
Korbut, Olga (gymnast)
Korda, Alexander (producer/director)
Korda, Petr (tennis)
Korda, Zoltan (director--Elephant Boy, Sahara)
Korin, Ogata (painter--Irises)
Korn (musical group--Freak on a Leash)
Korngold, Erich (composer)
Korvald, Lars (politician; Nor.)
Korver, Kyle (basketball)
Koss, Johann Olav (skater)
Kostick, Ken (chef)
Kosygin, Aleksei/Alexei (politician; Ru.)
Kotb, Hoda (T.V. personality--Today Show)
Kottke, Leo (musician--guitar--folk)
Koufax, Sanfoud (Sandy/#32) (baseball)
Kournikova, Anna (tennis)
Koussevitzky, Serge (conductor)
Kovacs, Ernie (writer/producer/actor/comedian) (Edie Adam's husband)

Kovic, Ron (actor--Born on the Fourth of July, Hurricane
Street, A Dangerous Country)
Kraft, Norbert (musician--guitarist)
Krakauer, Jon (author--Into the Wild)
Krall, Diana (singer--jazz)
Kramer, Erik (football)
Kramer, Ilona (author)
Kramer, Jerry (author--Instant Replay)
Kramer, Sven (skater--long track)
Krantz, Judith (author--Scruples)
Krasner, Lee (painter--abstract)
Kraus, Alfredo (singer--tenor)
Kraus, Karl
(journalist/satirist/essayist/aphorist/playwright/poet)
Krause, Peter (actor)
Krauss, Alison (singer)
Kravchenko, Victor (defector/author--I Chose Freedom
Kravitz, Lenny (singer/songwriter)
Kravitz, Zoe (model/singer/actress--Divergent Series, Mad
Max: Fury Road)
Kreisky, Bruno (author/politician)
Kresge, Sebastian Spering (businessman--K. Mart)
Kreuger, Ivar (inventor--matches)
Kreuk, Kristin (actress)
Krieg, Dave (football)
Krieger, Ali (soccer)
Kripke, Saul (author)
Kristen, Ilene (actress--Ryan's Hope)
Kristofferson, Kris (singer)
Kroc, Joan (philanthropist)
Kroc, Ray (McDonald's founder/Padre owner
(once)/philanthropist)
Krone, Julie (jockey)
Kross, Kris (musical group--rap)
Krueger, Ivar (The Match King) (businessman)
Kruger, Lon (basketball)
Kruger, Otto (actor)
Kruger, Paul (Oom--Uncle) (Africaaner Nation builder/S.Africa)
Krugman, Paul (economist/columnist--op. eds.)

Krupa, Gene (musician--drum)
Krzyzewski, Mike (Coach K) (baseball)
Kubek, Tony (baseball)
Kubelik, Rafael (conductor)
Kubrick, Stanley (producer/director--Full Metal Jacket, 1001, Lolita)
Kudrow, Lisa (actress)
Kuerti, Anton (musician--pianist)
Kuhn, Bowie (baseball)
Kukoc, Toni (basketball)
Kulik, Ilia (skater)
Kulp, Nancy (actress--Beverly Hillbillies)
Kun, Bela (revolutionary--communism; Hung.)
Kunderi, Milan (author--The Unbearable Lightness of Being)
Kung, Fu-Tse (philosopher)
Kunis, Mila (actress--That 70's Show, Black Swan, Bad Moms)
Kunitz, Stanley (poet)
Kupcinet, Irv (talk show host)
Kuralt, Charles (newsman/author--On the Road) (Osgood predecessor)
Kurchatov, Igor (physicist)
Kurie, Franz Newell (physicist)
Kurosawa, Akira (director--Seven Samurai, Ran)
Kurtz, Swoosie (actress--Sisters, Man With a Plan)
Kurylenko, Olga (actress--Oblivion)
Kushner, Tony (playwright--Angels in America)
Kutcher, Ashton (actor--That 70's Show, Two and a Half Men, The Ranch)
Kwa, Tung Chee (politician--Hong Kong)
Kweli, Talib (singer--hip-hop/activist)
Kwong-Song, Chan (pseudonym--Jackie Chan) (actor/stuntman)
Kyd, Thomas (playwright--The Spanish Tragedy)
Kyl, Jon (politician)
Kyser, Kay (bandleader)

--L--

L L Cool J (nee James Todd Smith) (singer--rap--Going Back to Cali, I Need Love/actor--NCIS Los Angeles)
L. F. O. (musical group--Summer Girls)
L'Amour, Louis Dearborn (author--The Haunted Mesa)
L'Engle, Madeline (author--A Wrinkle in Time)
La Belle, Patti (singer--Lady Marmalade)
La Beouf, Sabrina (actress--The Cosby Show)
La Beouf, Shia (actor--Transformers, Disturbia)
La Lanne, Jack (fitness expert, author--Live Young Forever)
La Paglia, Anthony (actor--Without a Trace)
La Rocca, Frank (composer--Dybbuk)
La Rue Eva (actress--C.S.I. Miami)
La Rue, Jack (actor)
La Salle, Eriq (actor--E. R.)
Labine, Clem (baseball)
Lacoste, Rene (Crocodile) (tennis; Fr.)
Ladd, Alan (actor--This Gun for Hire, The Blue Dahlia, The Glass Key, Shane, O.S.S., China)
Ladd, Cheryl (actress)
Ladd, Diane (actress--A Kiss Before Dying)
Lady Gaga (singer--Born This Way)
Laennec, Rene (inventor--stethoscope)
Lafitte (Laffitte), Jean (pirate--Andrew Jackson era)
Lagasse, Emeril (chef/author--Farm to Fork, Louisiana Real Rustic, Kicked-Up Sandwiches)
Lagerfeld, Karl (fashion designer)
Lagerlof, Selma (author; Swed.)
Lagrange, Joseph Louis (mathematician/astronomer) (Euler's contempory)
Lahm, Frank P. (aviator, balloon racer)
Lahr, Bert (actor--The Night They Raided Minsky's, The Wizard of Oz, Waiting for Godot /singer--If I Only Had the Nerve)
Lahr, John (author/critic)

Lahti, Christine (actress--Running on Empty, Swing Shift, The Blacklist, The Good Fight)
Lai, Frances (composer--Love Story, A Man and a Woman)
Laine, Cleo (singer--jazz)
Laine, Frankie (singer--Mule Train, Moonlight Gambler, I Believe)
Laing, Robert David (psychiatrist/author--Knots, The Divided Self; Br.)
Laird, Melvin (Defence Sect.)
Lake, Arthur (actor)
Lake, Ricki (actress/talkshow host)
Lake, Sanoe (actress)
Lake, Veronica (Peek-a-Boo Girl) (actress)
Laker, Freddie (Sir) (businessman--Sky Train Airlines)
Lakshmi, Padma (chef/T.V. personality--Top Chef)
Lal (poet; India)
Lalique, Rene (designer--jewelry--art nouveau)
Lalo, Edourd (composer--Symphonic Espagnole, Le Roi d'Ys'; Fr.)
Lama, Dalai (religious leader; Tibet)
Lama, Panchen (spiritual leader)
Lamar, Kendrick (singer--rap--King Kunta)
Lamarr, Hedy (actress--Samson & Delilah.Tortilla Flat)
Lamas, Carlos Saavedra (academic/politician; Arg.)
Lamas, Fernando (actor--Sangaree)
Lamas, Lorenzo (actor--Falcon Crest, Final Impact) (Arlene Dahl's son)
Lamaze, Fernand (author--childbirth)
Lamb, Caroline (Lady (author) (Lord Byron's lover)
Lamb, Charles (pseudonym--Elia) (author--Tales from Shakespeare, The Praise of the Chimney Sweepers, Essays of Elie, Dream Child)
Lamb, Mary Ann (author--Tales from Shakespeare)
Lambeau, Earl Louis (Curly) (football)
Lambert, Adam (singer)
Lamer, Antonio (justice--Supreme Court)
Lamonica, Daryle (football)
Lamotta, Jake (The Raging Bull) (boxer)
Lancaster, Burt (actor--Elmer Gantry)

Lancelot Du Lac (also Launcelot) (knight in King Arthur's court) (lady--Elaine)
Lanchester, Elsa (actress--Bride of Frankenstein) (Charles Lauthton's wife)
Land, Edwin (scientist/inventor--Polaroid camera)
Landers, Ann (Esther Lederer's pseudonym (Eppie) (advice columnist)
Landi, Elissa (actress)
Landis, Carole (actress)
Landis, Floyd (cyclist)
Landis, Kenesaw Mountain (jurist/first baseball commissioner)
Landon, Alf (politician--Kansas)
Landor, Walter Savage (author; Br.)
Landowska, Wanda (musician--harpsichord)
Landry, Ali (actress)
Landseer, Edwin (Sir) (painter--Stag at Bay)
Landsend (merchant--L.L. Bean rival)
Lane, Abbe (singer)
Lane, Allan (Rocky) (voice--Mr. Ed)
Lane, Burtan (composer--On A Clear Day)
Lane, Diane (actress--Unfaithful)
Lane, Harriet (Buchanan's First Lady stand in)
Lane, Nathan (singer/actor/comedian)
Lane, Patrick (poet)
Lane, Priscilla (actress--Four Daughters)
Lane, Rocky (actor--Mr. Ed's voice)
Lang, Artie (actor)
Lang, Fritz (director--Ministry of Fear, Spies, Metropolis, The Big Heat, "M")
Lang, Helmut (fashion designer)
Lang, K. D. (singer--Constant Craving) (Roy Orbison's duet partner--Crying)
Langdon, Harry (actor/writer/director/producer)
Langdon, Sue Ann(e) (actress)
Lange, Dorothea (photojournalist)
Lange, Hope (actress)
Lange, Jessica (actress)
Langer, Susanne (philosopher)
Langtry, Lillie (Jersey Lilly) (actress)

Lanier, Sidney (musician/poet)
Lanin, Lester (bandleader)
Lansbury, Angela (actress--Mame)
Lansky, Meyer (gangster)
Lanza, Mario (singer/actor--Caruso, Be My Love)
Lao-Tzu/Laozi (philosopher--Taoism/author--Tao Te Ching
(The Book of the Way))
Laplace, Pierre-Simon (astronomer)
Lara, Helen (actress)
Lardner, Ring (author--You Know Me All, Alibi Ike)
Laredo, Jaime (musician--violinist)
Larosa, Julius (singer--Domani)
Larouche, Pierre (Lucky) (hockey)
Larsen, Don (baseball)
Larson, Erik (journalist)
Larson, Gary (cartoonist--The Far Side)
Larson, Nicolette (singer--A Lotta Love)
Larsson, Stieg (author--The Girl With the Dragon Tattoo)
Larter, Ali (actress)
Larue, Alfred (Lash) (actor--westerns--King of the Bullwhip)
Larussa, Tony (baseball)
Lash, Joseph P. (author--Eleanor and Franklin)
Lasker, Emanuel (chess master)
Laski, Harold (political theorist/economist/lecturer/author)
Lasky, Kathryn (author)
Laslo, Ilsa Lund (actress)
Lasorda, Tommy (baseball)
Lasser, Louise (actress--Mary Hartman)
Laszlo, Erno (beautician)
Lateef, Yusef (musician--jazz)
Lathen, Emma (author--mystery)
Latini, Brunetto (Dante's guardian & teacher)
Lattisaw, Stacey (singer--Let Me Be Your Angel)
Lau, Charlie (baseball)
Lauch, Chester (pseudonym--Lum) (actor) (Abner's partner)
Lauda, Niki (racecar driver)
Lauder, Estee (manufacturer--cosmetics)
Lauer, Andy (actor)
Lauer, Matt (broadcast journalist--N.B.C. Today Show)

Laughton, Charles (actor--Nero) (Elsa Langcaster's husband)
Lauper, Cyndi (singer--True Colors, She Bop, Time After Time, She's So Unusual)
Laurance, Ewa Mataya (billiards)
Laurel, Stan (nee Arthur Stanley Jefferson) (comedian/actor--Great Guns)
Lauren, Ralph (nee Lifshitz) (fashion designer)
Laurence, Margaret (author--The Olden Days Coat)
Laurie, Hugh (author/comedian/writer/musician/director/actor--House)
Laurie, Piper (actress)
Laurier, Wilfred (Sir) (politician; Can.)
Laver, Rod (tennis)
Lavin, Linda (actress--Alice)
Lavoisier, Antoine-Lurent de (Father of Modern Chemistry) (chemist)
Law, Bernard (Cardinal) (Boston Archbishop/author)
Law, Jude (actor--Alfie)
Lawes, Adrianus Lewis Edward) (penologist/warden--Sing Sing)
Lawford, Peter (actor--Ocean's Eleven)
Lawless, Lucy (actress--Xena)
Lawrence, David Herbert (D. H.) (author--Women in Love, Aaron's Rod, Sons and   Lovers)
Lawrence, Ernest Orlando (physicist)
Lawrence, Gertrude (Stage Queen) (actress--Star/singer--Someone to Watch Over Me,   Oh, So Nice)
Lawrence, Jack (songwriter--Tenderly)
Lawrence, Joey (actor--Melissa and Joey)
Lawrence, Judith A. (puppeteer--Casey and Finnigan on Mr. Dressup)
Lawrence, Martin (actor--Big Momma's House)
Lawrence, Steve (nee Sidney Leibowitz) (singer/actor)
Lawrence, Vicki (actress--Mama's Family)
Lawton, Chiles (Gov. of Florida)
Layne, Bobby (football)
Lazarus, Emma (poet--The New Colossus (Statue of Liberty; Am.)
Lazarus, Mell (cartoonist--Momma, Miss Peach)

Lazenby, George (actor--007)
Lea, Tom (artist/muralist/author--The King Ranch, The Brave Bulls)
Leach, Robin (T. V. personality)
Leacha, Christopher (author--A Killing Frost)
Leachman, Cloris (actress--Mary Tyler Moore Show, Phyllis)
Leacock, Stephen (author--humor)
Leal, Sharon (actress--Boston Public)
Lean, David (director--Ryan's Daughter, A Passage to India)
Lear, Edward (author--limericks)
Lear, Evelyn (singer--soprano)
Lear, Norman (T.V. writer/producer)
Learned, Michael (actress--The Waltons--Mama)
Leary, Denis (actor--Rescue Me, The Ref)
Leary, Timothy (author--Politics of Ecstasy, Psychedelic Reader)
LeBeau, Charles Richard (Dick) (football)
Lebed, Alexander (politician)
LeBlanc, Matt (actor--Friends)
Leblanc, Maurice (author--Arsene Lupine)
Lebon, Simon (musician--Duran Duran)
Lebowitz, Fran (author)
LeBrun, Denis (cartoonist--Blondie)
LeCain, Errol (author--children)
LeCarre, John (David John Moore Cornwell's pseudonym) (author--Smiley's People,   The Tailor of Panama, A Perfect Spy, The Night Manager, A Murder of Quality)
Lech, Archibald (Cary Grant's pseudonym) (actor)
LeClaire, Jean-Marie (composer--baroque)
Leclerc, Charles Victoire Emmanuel (Gen.--Napoleonic Wars) (Napoleon's in-law)
Lecuona, Ernesto (composer--Jungle Drums)
Lede (monk/historian; Br.)
Lederer, Esther (pseudonym-Ann Landers) (Eppie) (advice columnist)
Ledger, Heath (actor)
Ledru-Rollin, Alexandre Auguste (politician; Fr.)
LeDuc, Tho (Phan Dinh Khai's pseudonym) (politician/revolutionary/nobelist)

Lee, Amos (singer--Mission Bell)
Lee, Ang (director--Crouching Tiger, Hidden Dragon; Sense & Sensibility,   Eat Drink Man Woman, Life of Pi)
Lee, Ann (Shaker's founder)
Lee, Brandon (actor)
Lee, Brenda (singer--I'm Sorry)
Lee, Bruce (born Bruce Lee Jun Fan Yuen Kam) (actor)
Lee, Chang-Rae (author)
Lee, Christopher (actor; Br.)
Lee, Dennis (poet--Alligator Pie)
Lee, Harper (author--Go Set a Watchman, To Kill A Mockingbird)
Lee, Henry (Light-Horse Harry) (soldier)
Lee, Jennifer Jason (actress)
Lee, Johnny (singer--Looking for Love)
Lee, Kathie (actress/singer/T.V. personality) (Frank Gifford's wife)
Lee, Lila (actress--Blood and Sand)
Lee, Manfred B. (pseudonym--Ellery Queen) (author--mystery)
Lee, Nelle (Harper) (author--To Kill a Mockingbird)
Lee, Peggy (singer--Fever, He's a Tramp)
Lee, Pinky (Pincus Leff's pseudonym) (comedian)
Lee, Robert E. (military officer) (Mary Custis's husband)
Lee, Ruta (actress--Funny Face)
Lee, Sandra (T.V. personality--Food Network)
Lee, Spike (director--She's Gotta Have It, When the Levees Broke, Malcolm X)
Lee, Stan (author/editor--Marvel Comics--Superman, Iron Man)
Leeuwenhoek, Anton van (microbiologist/inventor--microscope)
Leeves, Jane (actress--Frasier)
Leff, Pincus (pseudonym--Pinky Lee) (comedian)
Left Banke (musical group--Walk Away Renee)
LeGallienne, Eva (actress/producer/director)
Leger, Fernand (artist--La Grande Parade)
Legis, Alexis (pseudonym--St. John Perse) (diplomat/poet/nobelist; Fr.)

LeGrand, Michel (composer--Thomas Crown Affair)
LeGuin, Ursula (author--Earthsea)
Leguizamo, John (actor/comedian--Super Mario Bros.)
Lehane, Dennis (author--Gone Baby Gone)
Lehar, Franz/Ferenc (composer--Paganini, Zigeanerliebe, Gypsy Love, Gold and Silver Waltz,   You Are My Heart's Delight, Eva, Vilia, The Merry Widow)
Lehman, Adele (medicine/teacher--Harvard)
Lehman, Ernest Paul (screenwriter--West Side Story)
Lehmann, Lilli (singer--soprano)
Lehmann, Lotte (singer--soprano)
Lehne, John (actor)
Lehr, Lew (comedian)
Lehrer, James Charles (Jim) (journalist/newsman) (MacNeil's partner)
Leibovitz, Annie (painter--portrait)
Leibowitz, Rene (conductor)
Leigh, Janet (actress--Psycho) (Jamie Lee Curtis's mother)
Leigh, Mike (author/director--Life is Sweet)
Leigh, Vivien (actress--Gone With the Wind, Ship of Fools)
Leinsdorf, Erich (conductor/pianist)
Leiter, Al (baseball)
Leland, Henry (auto pioneer--Cadillac)
Lem, Stanislaw (author--sci-fi--The Invinsible, One Human Minute)
Lema, Tony (golfer)
Lemay, Curtis (Gen.) (politician--Wallace's running mate)
Lemieux, Mario (hockey)
Lemmon, Jack (actor--Luv, Some Like It Hot, Avanti, The Apartment)
Lemon, Elizabeth Miervaldis (Liz) (actress, comedian--30 Rock)
Lemper, Ute (singer)
Lenard, Alexander (author--Winnie Ille Pu)
Lendl, Ivan (tennis)
Lenin (Vladimir Ulyanov's pseudonym) (politician; Ru.)
Lennon Kathy (singer--Lennon Sisters)
Lennon, Diane (singer--Lennon Sisters)
Lennon, Janet (singer--Lennon Sisters)

Lennon, John Winston Ono (musician--The Beatles--Bad to Me, How Do You Sleep/ author--In His Own Write)
Lennon, Peggy (singer--Lennon Sisters)
Lennon, Sean Ono (musician--Friendly Fire)
Lennox, Annie (singer--No More I Love You's)
Leno, Jay (nee James Douglas Muir) (Iron Jay) (talkshow host/ author--Leading with My Chin)
Lenoir, Etienne (inventor--internal combustion engine)
Lens, Kay (actress--Breezy)
Lenska, Rula (actress)
Lenya, Lotte (singer/actress) (Kurt Weill's wife)
Lenz, Kay (actress--Physical Evidence, Rich Man, Poor Man)
Lenz, Sidney (author/bridge expert)
Leo VI (The Philosopher) (Byzantine Emperor)
Leonard, Elmore (author--Get Shorty)
Leonard, Herman (playwright--A Life)
Leonard, Hugh (playwright--Da)
Leonard, Sheldon (actor)
Leone, Sergio (director)
Leoni, Tea (actress--Family Man, Spanglish, Ghost Town)
Leonidas (warrior king--Sparta)
Leonowens, Anna (author/educator/feminist)
Leopardi, Giacoma (poet)
Leopold, Nathan Freudenthal (criminal) (Loeb's cohort)
Leowe, Frederick (composer--Camelot)
Lepage, Robert (playwright/actor/director)
Lerner, Alan Jay (lyricist--Brigadoon, My Fair Lady, On a Clear Day)
LeRoy, Mervyn (director--Anthony Adverse)
Lesage, Alain Rene (author--Gil Blas)
LeShan, Eda (psychologist/author--When Your Child Drives You Crazy)
Leslie, Edgar (composer--Moon Over Miama) (Joe Burke's co-writer)
Leslie, Lisa (basketball)
Lesser, Len (actor--Seinfeld (Leo))
Lesser, Sol (producer--Tartan)

Lessing, Doris (author)
Less-than-Ruthian (musical group--Bloops)
Lester, Mark (actor--Oliver Twist)
Lester, Richard (director--Help! It's A Hard Day's Night)
Leto, Jared (actor--Mr. Nobody, Panic Room, Dallas Buyers Club, Suicide Squad/ musician--band-30 Seconds to Mars)
Lettermen (musical group--When I Fall In Love)
Levant, Oscar (musician--pianist)
Levene, Sam (singer)
Levenson, Sam (author)
Leverson, Ada (author)
Levertov, Denise (poet)
Levesque, Rene (politician; Can.)
Levi, Carlo (journalist/artist/author/physician--Christ Stopped at Eboli)
Levi, Ivo (Yves Montand stage name) (actor)
Levi, Primo (chemist/author)
Levin, Ira (author--Sliver, Rosemary's Baby, Death Trap, Stepford Wives)
Levin, Meyer (author--Eva)
Levine, Adam (singer/songwriter/musician/producer/actor) (band--Maroon 5)
Levinson, Barry (author/director--Diner)
Levit, Igor (musician--piano)
Levitt, Steven (author--Freakonomics)
Levy, Ethel (actress) (George M. Cohan's first wife)
Levy, Marv (football)
Lew, Jack (politician--Treasury Sect.)
Lewis, Al (actor--The Munsters)
Lewis, Carl (runner)
Lewis, Clairemonte Christopher (author/autobiographer--Surprised by Joy)
Lewis, Clea (actress)
Lewis, Clive Staples (C.S.) (Jack) (author--The Allegory of Love, The Screwtape Letters, Mere Christianity)
Lewis, Huey (singer--Hip To Be Square)
Lewis, Jerry Lee (singer--Great Balls of Fire, Breathless)

Lewis, John (activist--Civil Rights)
Lewis, Leona (singer--Bleeding Love, Avatar)
Lewis, Michael (author--Moneyball)
Lewis, Reggie (basketball)
Lewis, Shari (puppeteer)
Lewis, Sinclair (Red) (playwright/author--Elmer Gantry, Ann
Vickers, Cass Timberlane,   Arrowsmith)
Lewis, Stacy (golf)
Lewis, Ted (musician/bandleader--Me and My Shadow)
Lewis, Wyndham (author--Tarr)
Lewit, Sol (artist)
Ley, Bob (sportscaster)
Ley, Robert (Nazi leader)
Ley, Willy (rocketeer/The Conquest of Space)
Li, Jet (actor--The One, Kiss of the Dragon, Romeo Must Die)
Liasson, Mara (political correspondent)
Lichtenstein, Roy (artist--dots)
Liddell, Eric (runner/Olympian)
Liddy, George Gordon (politician/radio host)
Lie, Trygve (politician--first U. S. Sect. General/author)
Lieber, Fritz (author--sci-fi)
Lieber, Jerome (Jerry) (songwriter) (Mike Stroller's partner)
Lieber, Larry (co-creator of the Iron Man)
Lieberman, Nancy (basketball)
Liebig, Justus von (scientist--discovered chloroform)
Lieblich, Amia (psychologist/author)
Liebling, Abbott Joseph (journalist)
Liebman, Ron (actor/writer)
Lieder, Dietrich Fischer Dieskau (singer--baritone)
Lifar, Serge (dancer--ballet)
Lifshin, Lyn (author)
Lifshitz, Ralph (a.k.a. Ralph Lauren) (fashion designer)
Light, Judith (actress--Who's the Boss)
Lightfoot, Gordon (singer/songwriter)
Lil Jon (singer--rap--Get Low)
Lil Kim (singer--rap)
Lil Nas X (singer--rap)
Lili'uokalani (Hawaiian Queen)
Lilienthal, Otto (aviator)

Lillie, Bea (actress)
Lilly, Eli (pharmaceutical manufacturer)
Lilly, Evangeline (actress--Lost)
Lima, Adriana (model/actress)
Limon, Jose (choreographer/dancer)
Lin, Jeremy (basketball)
Lin, Maya Ling (artist/designer/architect--Vietnam Memorial)
Lincicome, Brittany (golfer)
Lincoln, Abbey (singer--jazz)
Lincoln, Abraham (Abe) (The Great Emancipator
(lawyer/politician)
Lincoln, Elmo (actor--Tarzan)
Lincoln, Joseph Crosby (author--Cap'n Eri)
Lincoln, Thomas (Tad) (Abe & Mary Todd's son)
Lind, Jenny (Swedish Nightingale) (singer--opera--Lucia)
Lindbergh, Anne Morrow (author--The Wave of the Future,
North to the Orient) (Charle's wife)
Lindbergh, Charles (Lone Eagle, Slim Lucky Lindy)
(aviator/author)   (Anne
Morrow's husband)
Linden, Hal (actor--Barney Miller)
Lindgren, Astrid (author--Pippi Longstockings)
Lindley, Audra (actress)
Lindsay, Anne (Lady) (poet--Auld Robin Gray)
Lindsay, Howard (actor/director/playwright--Call Me Madame)
Lindstrom, Pia (journalist) (Ingrid Bergman's daughter)
Ling, Bai (actress--Anna and the King, The Crow)
Ling, Lisa (television journalist--The View)
Linklater, Eric (author)
Linkletter, Art (actor)
Lin-Manuel, Miranda (actor/playwright/lyricist/composer--
Heights and Hamilton)
Linn, Bambi (dancer/ choreographer/actress)
Linn, George (philatelist)
Linnaeus, Carl (botanist; Swed.)
Linney, Laura (actress--The Truman Show, The Savages,
Love Actually)
Liotta, Ray (actor)
Lipinski, Tara (figure skater)

Lipman, Elinor (author--The Ladies Man)
Lipo (poet; Chin.)
Lippershey, Hans (inventor--telescope)
Lippi, Fra Filippo (painter--Adoration of the Magi)
Lipton, Thomas (Sir) (tea merchant)
Liquori, Marty (runner-miler)
Lisa Lisa (nee Lisa Velez) (musician--Cult Jam band--Lost in Emotion)
Lisi, Virna (actress--The Statue)
Lisle, Rouget de (composer--La Marseillaise)
Lister, Joseph (inventor--water bag/army surgeon; Br.)
Liston, Sonny The Bear) (boxer)
Liszt, Franz (composer--Les Preludes, Transcendental Etudes, Piano Sonata in B Minor, Mephisto Waltz, Hungarian Rhapsody)
Lithgow, John (musician/singer/poet/author/actor)
Little Richard (singer--Rip It Up, Tutti Frutti)
Little, Larry (football)
Little, Omar (The Wire) (gangster)
Littler, Gene (golf)
Liu, Lena (painter--watercolours)
Liu, Lucy (actress--Ally McBeal)
Lively, Blake (actress--Adaline)
Livy (nee Titus Livius) (historian)
Lizette, Reese (poet)
Llosa, Mario Vargas (author)
Lloyd, Christopher (actor)
Lloyd, Frank (director--Love of Alion)
Lloyd, Harold (actor--Safety Last)
Lobo, Rebecca (basketball)
Locke, Alain (Dean of the Harlem Renaissance) (philosopher/writer/educator)
Locke, John (Father of Liberalism) (philosopher--empirical--Social Contract, Two Treatises of Government, An Essay Concerning Understanding; Br.)
Locke, Sandra (actress)
Lockheart, Keith (conductor)
Loeb, Lisa (actress/singer-songwriter--Stay (I Missed You), I Do)

Loeb, Richard Albert (criminal) (Leopold's cohort)
Loeb, William (publisher--financial)
Loesser, Frank (songwriter--Once In Love with Amy, Baby It's Cold Outside, Luck   Be a Lady, Guys and Dolls, How to Succeed in Business…)
Loeveberg, Amelita (singer--soprano)
Loew, Marcus (movie mogul--M. G. M. founder)
Loewe, Frederick (composer--My Fair Lady, Camelot)
Loewenstein, Leszlo (Peter Lorre's stage name) (actor--"M", Casablanca--Ugarte)
Lofgren, Nils (quitarist)
Lofts, Norah (author)
Logan, Ella (actress--Finian's Rainbow)
Logan, Josh (singer/songwriter/musician--guitar)
Logan, Joshua (stage-film direcor--Picnic/writer--South Pacific, Mister Roberts)
Logan, Lara (newswoman)
Logue, Donal (actor--Blade)
Lohan, Lindsay (actress--Freaky Friday, Mean Girls)
Lom, Herbert (actor--The Ladykillers, Ten Little Indians, The Phantom of the Opera)
Lomax, Alan (musician/historian/activist/filmmaker/ethnomuciologist--Jelly Roll Morton)
Lomax, John (historian--folk music)
Lombard, Carole (actress)
Lombardo, Gaetano Albert (Guy) (musician--violin/bandleader--So Rare)
London, Jack (author--Martin Eden, The Sea Wolf) (boat--Snark)
London, Julie (singer/actress)
Long, Eli (Gen.--Union of the Civil War)
Long, Howie (football)
Long, Huey (The Kingfish) (politician--Louisiana) (Russell's father)
Long, Nia (actress--Made in America, Soul Food, Big Momma's House, Love Jones, Boyz   N the Hood)
Long, Russell Billiu (politician) (Huey's son)

Longfellow, Henry Wadsworth (poet--A Bell for Adano, The Alarm Bell of Atri, Paul   Revere's Ride)
Longley, Luc (basketball))
Longoria, Eva (actress--Desperate Housewives)
Longoria, Evan (baseball)
Loopner, Lisa (actress)
Loos, Anita (playwright/screenwriter/author--Gentlemen Prefer Blondes, Lorelei Lee, Gigi)   (autobiog.--A Girl Like I)
Lopat, Eddie (Steady Eddie) (baseball)
Lopes, Lisa (Left Eye) (singer--hip-hop)
Lopez, Jennifer (actress--Gigli, The Cell, Maid in Manhattan, J to Tha L-O)
Lopez, Nancy (golfer)
Lopez, Trini (singer)
Lopez, Vincent (singer--Nola)
Lor, Denise (singer/actress--Garry Moore Show)
Lorca, Federico Garcia (poet--Dona Rosita La Soltera, Romancero Gitano; Sp.)
Lord, Walter (author--A Night to Remember)
Lorde (nee Ella Marija Lani Yelich-O'Connor) (producer/singer-songwriter)
Lorde, Audre (poet)
Lords, Traci (actress)
Loren, Sophia (actress--The Millionairess, El Cid, Marriage Italian Style, Two Women)   (Carlo Ponti's wife) (Anna Maria Villani Scicolone's sister)
Lorrain, Claude (a.k.a. Claude Gellee) (etcher/painter/printmaker/art theorist)
Lorre, Peter (nee Leszlo Loewenstein) (actor--"M", Mr. Moto, Casablanca--Ugarte, Nero)
Los Lobos (musical group--La Bamba)
Lothair (emporer of Rome, 1840-1855)
Loti, Pierre (Louis Marie-Julien Viaud's pseudonym) (naval officer/author--Fin de Siecle)   (Anet's contemporary)
Lott, Felicity (singer--soprano)
Lott, Ronnie (football)

Lott, Trent (politician/author--Herding Cats: A Life in Politics)
(Dole's successor)
Lotte, Lenya (singer)
Loudon, Dorothy (actress)
Loughin, Lori (actress)
Louis, Joe (boxer) (defeated--Tommy Farr)
Louise, Anita (actress)
Louise, Tina (actress)
Lovato, Demi (singer--Give Your Heart a Break)
Love, Courtney (musician/band--Hole) (Kurt Cobain's
wife/Frances Bean Cobain's mother)
Love, Davis (golfer)
Love, Jennifer (actress)
Love, Loni (comedian/actress/author/T.V. host--The Real)
Lovecraft, Howard Phillips (author--horror, fantasy, sci-fi)
Lovelace, Ada (computer pioneer)
Lovelace, Richard (poet--To Althea from Prison)
Lovelock, James (author--Gaia (theory)
Lovett, Lyle Pearce (singer/songwriter/actor)
Low, David (cartoonist--Colonel Blimp)
Low, Juliette (activist--Girl Scouts of America)
Lowe, Chad (actor)
Lowe, Edmond (actor--Around the World in 80 Days)
Lowe, Edwin (producer--theater)
Lowe, Nick (singer-songwriter--Cruel to be Kind)
Lowe, Rebecca (soccer)
Lowe, Rob (actor--St. Elmo's Fire, Youngblood, Parks &
Recreation, Frank and Jesse/   director--
Oxford Blues)
Lowell, Amy (poet--imagist--Lilacs)
Lowell, James Russell (diplomat/critic/poet--Bigelow Papers)
Lowell, Percival (astronaut)
Lowry, Clarence Malcolm (author--Under the Volcano; Br.)
Lowry, Kyle (basketball)
Lowry, Lois (author--children's)
Lowther, Pat (poet) (killed by spouse)
Lowy, Otto (T. V. personality--The Transcontinental)
Loy, Myrna (actress--The Best Years of our Lives, The Thin
Man, Love Crazy)

Loy, Tommie (musician--trumpet)
Lubitsch, Ernst (director)
Lubovitch, Lar (dancer/choreographer)
Lucan (poet; Roman)
Lucas, Craig (playwright--Prelude to a Kiss)
Lucas, George (author/director/producer)
Lucas, Paul (author)
Lucci, Susan (actress--All My Children--Erica)
Luce, Clare Boothe (author--Stuffed Shirts/playwright--Women/editor--Vanity Fair)
Luce, Henry (publisher--Time-Life)
Luce, Robert E. (publisher)
Lucian (Lucianos; Lucianus of Samosata) (author--satirist--Dialogues of the Gods)
Lucine, Amara (singer--opera)
Luckman, Sidney (Sid) (football)
Lucullus, Lucius Licinius (politician)
Ludd, Ned (revolutionary--Luddite)
Ludwig, Emil (biographer/author--The Nile: The Life Story of a River)
Luft, Lorna (singer) (Judy Garland's daughter/Liza Minelli's sister)
Lugar, Richard (politician--Indiana senator)
Lugosi, Bela (actor--Mark of the Vampire, The Black Cat, Dracula)
Lulu (singer--To Sir With Love)
Lum (Chester Lauck's pseudonym) (actor--Abner's partner)
Lumbard, Carole (actress--In Name Only)
Lumet, Sidney (director--Twelve Angry Men, Network, Pawnbroker, Dog Day Afternoon,   The Wiz))
Lumiere, Auguste (inventor--motion pictures)
Lumiere, Louis (inventor--motion pictures)
Lumumba, Patrice (politician; Congo)
Lun, Ts'ai (inventor--paper)
Lund, Ilsa (Ilsa Lund Laslo) (actress)
Lund, John (actor)
Lundgren, Dolph (actor--Rocky IV, He-Man)
Lunn, Janet (author--The Root Cellar)

Lunt, Alfred (actor--Marco's Millions, The Guardsman/director--O Mistress Mine)   (Lynn Fontanne's husband)
Lunt, Lynn (actress)
Lupino, Ida (actress--High Sierra)
LuPone, Patti (singer--Broadway--Evita)
Luria, Salvador (microbiologist/nobelist--medicine)
Lurie, Alison (author--Foreign Affairs, The Black Prince, The War Between the Tates)
Lustbader, Eric (author)
Luther, Martin (religious reformer/author--Thesis) (Calvin's contemporary)
Luxemburg, Rosa (economist/philosopher--Marxism)
Luyendyk, Arie (racecar driver)
Luzinski, Greg (baseball)
Lycurgus (lawyer; Spartan)
Lyell, Charles (geologist)
Lyle, Sandy (baseball)
Lyle, Sparky (baseball/author--Bronx Zoo)
Lynch, David (director--Blue Velvet, Twin Peaks, Dune, Eraserhead)
Lynch, Kelly (actress)
Lynch, Loretta (politician) (Holder's successor)
Lyne, Adrian (director--Unfaithful)
Lynn, Fred (baseball)
Lynn, Loretta (singer--country)
Lynne, Jeff (musician--E. L. O.--Traveling Wilburys)
Lynne, Shelby (actress/singer/songwriter--country)
Lynskey, Melanie (actress)
Lynyrd Skynyrd (musical group)
Lyon, Ben (actor--Hell's Angels)
Lyon, Mary (chemist/educator--Mount Holyoke Female Siminary founder)
Lyon, Sue (actress--Lolita)
Lysimachus (General under Alexander the Great)

--M--

M.I.A. (musician--rap--Paper Planes)
Ma, Yo-yo (musician--cellist)
Maar, Dora (photographer/poet/artist) (Picasso's Weeping
Woman muse) (Picasso's   lover)
Maas, Peter (author--Serpico, Valachi Papers)
Maass, Clara (nurse--Yellow Fever)
Maathai, Wangari (activist; Kenya)
Maazel, Lorin (conductor)
Mabius, Eric (actor)
Mabus, Ray (politician)
Mac, Bernie (comedian/actor--Oceans Eleven)
Macaulay, Thomas Babington (author--Lays of Ancient Rome)
Macchio, Ralph (actor)
MacDonald, Jeanette (singer) (Maurice Chevalier's/Nelson
Eddy's duet partner)
MacDonald, John (author--Travis McGee)
MacDonald, Nora (actress)
MacDonald, Norm (actor)
MacDonald, Ross (Kenneth Millar's pseudonym) (author--
crime fiction)
MacDowell, Andie (actress)
MacDowell, Edward (composer--To a Wild Rose)
MacDowell, Rosalie Anderson (Andie) (actress--Groundhog
Day, Four Weddings and   a Funeral)
Macero, Teo (composer/musician--sax--jazz)
MacFarlane, Seth (producer/author/comedian/singer/creator--
Family Guy)
MacGraw, Ali (actress--The Getaway, Goodbye Columbus)
Mach, Ernst (physicist/philosopher)
Mack, Charles (radio personality--The Two Black Crows)
(Moran's partner)
Mack, Connie (baseball)
Mack, Ted (T. V. personality)
Mackenzie, Gisele (singer)
Macklemore (musician--rap)
MacLachlan, Kyle (actor)
MacLaine, Shirley (actress--Guarding Tess)
MacLane, Barton (actor--I Dream of Jeannie)

MacLean, Alistair (author--Bear Island, The Guns of Navarone)
MacLennan, Hugh (author--Two Solitudes)
MacLeod, Alistair (author--The Lost Salt Gift of Blood)
MacLeod, Gavin (actor--Love Boat)
MacMahon, Aline (actress)
Macmillan, Harold (politician; Br.)
MacMurray, Fred (actor)
Macnee, Patrick (actor--Steed in the Avengers)
MacNeil, Rita (singer)
MacNeil, Robert Breckenridge Waren (Robin) (author/journalist/news anchor) (Jim
          Lehrer's partner)
MacNelly, Jeff (cartoonist--Shoe)
MacNicol, Peter (actor--Ally McBeal)
Macon, Emmanuel Jean-Michel Frederic (politician; Fr.)
MacPherson, Elle (model/actress--Sirens)
MacRae, Gordon (actor/singer--Oklahoma)
MacRae, Meredith (actress--Petticoat Junction)
Macy, Bill (actor--Maude)
Macy, Rowland Hussey (retailer)
Madero, Francisco (politician; Mex.)
Madigan, Amy (actress--Field of Dreams)
Madison, Donney (James's wife)
Madison, James (politician)
Madness (musical group--Our House)
Madonna (actress/singer--La Isla Bonita, Erotica) (record label--Sire)
Madsen, Michael (actor--Reservoir Dogs)
Madur, Kurt (conductor)
Maentyranta, Eero (skier; Fin.)
Magee, Patrick (actor--Marat/Sade)
Maglie, Sal (baseball)
Magnani, Anna (actress)
Magnussen, Karen (skater)
Magritte, Rene (artist--The Treachery of Images)
Maguire, Tobey/Tobias (actor--Spiderman, The Great Gatsby)
Mahal, Taj (musician--blues)

Mahan, Alfred Thayer (historian/author --Admiral Farragut/The
Influence of Seapower   Upon History)
Mahan, Lori (rodeo)
Maharis, George (actor--Route 66)
Maher, Bill (actor--D.C. Cab/T. V. host--Politically Incorrect,
Real Time with Bill Maher)
Mahler, Gustav (composer--Das Lied Von Der Erde,
Symphony of a Thousand,   Song of the
Earth)
Mahony, Francis Sylvester (a.k.a. Father Prout)
(humourist/journalist)
Mahre, Phil (skier)
Mahre, Steve (skier)
Maier, Hermann (skier)
Maier, Tomas (fashion designer--swimwear)
Mailer, Norman (author--Deer Park, The Executioner's Song,
The Naked and the Dead,   The Fight, The
Armies of the Night)
Maillard, Keith (author--Gloria)
Maillet, Antonine (author--Evangeline Home, Grand Pri)
Maimonides, Moses (philosopher)
Main, Marjorie (actress--Ma Kettle)
Maines, Natalie (singer--Dixie Chicks)
Majoli, Iva (tennis)
Major, Kevin (author--Hold Fast)
Majorino, Tina (actress--Corrina, Corrina)
Majors, Lee (actor)
Makarov, Oleg (cosmonaut)
Makarova, Elena (tennis)
Makarova, Natalia (dancer--ballet)
Makeba, Miriam (singer; S. African)
Malamud, Bernard (author--The Natural, The Fixer)
Malden, Karl (actor--Streets of San Francisco)
Malek, Rami (actor--Mr. Robot, Bohemian Rhapsody)
Malenkov, Georgy (politician--Communist Party leader)
Malfi, Theodore (director--St. Vincent)
Malkovich, John (actor--Eleni)
Mallarme, Stephane (poet--L'Apres-Midi de Un Faune)
Malle, Louis (director--My Dinner with Andre, Damage)

Malone, Dorothy (Maloney, Dorothy) (actress)
Malone, Karl (actor)
Malone, Karl (basketball)
Malone/Maloney, Dorothy (actress)
Malory, Thomas (author--Morte d'Arthur)
Malraux, Andre (author)
Mamet, David (director/playwright--State and Main,
Cryptogram, Oleanna, Speed-The-Plow)
Mancinelli, Luigi (composer--opera--Ero E Leandro)
Mancini, Henry (composer--Moon River, Dear Heart)
Mandel, Harvey (musician--guitar--blues)
Mandel, Howie (comedian)
Mandela, Nelson (politician/author--Long Walk to Freedom; S.
Africa)
Mandelstam, Osip (poet)
Manden, Robert (actor--Soap)
Mandlikova, Hana (tennis)
Mandrell, Irlene (singer)
Manet, Edouard (painter--Olympia, The Fife Player, Café
Concert, Nana, Le Dejeuner Sur L'Herbe   Luncheon on
the Grass, A Bar At the Follies Bergere, In A Boat)
Mangione, Chuck (musician--flugelhorn)
Manguel, Alberto (author/anthologist)
Manheim, Camryn (actress)
Maniac (musical group--In My Tribe)
Manilow, Barry (singer--Could It Be Magic, I Made It Through
the Rain)
Mankiewicz, Herman (screenwriter)
Mann, Aimee (singer--Save Me, Voices Carry)
Mann, Barry (songwriter--On Broadway) (co-writer/wife
Cynthia Weil)
Mann, Delbert (director--The Outsider, Marty)
Mann, Dylan (singer--Voices Carry)
Mann, Hank (actor--Keystone Cops with Chaplin)
Mann, Herbie (musician--jazz)
Mann, Horace (educator/politician)
Mann, Manfred (singer--pop--Sha la la)
Mann, Michael (director--The Insider)
Mann, Sheldon (Shelley) (drummer--jazz)

Mann, Theodore (producer)
Mann, Thomas (author--Confessions of Felix Krull, Dr. Faustus, Tonio Kroger,   Der Tod in Venedig/Death in Venice, Joseph and His Brothers A Man and His   Dog) (Hans Castrop's/Buddenbrook's creator)
Manne, Shelly (musician--drummer)
Manning, Eli (football)
Manolete (nee Manuel Laureano Rodriguez Sanchez) (matador)
Manray, Caxton (artist--dada)
Mansfield, Jane (actress)
Mansfield, Peter (author--The Arabs)
Mantle, Mickey (The Commerce Comet) (baseball)
Mantovani, Annunzio Paolo (composer/conductor)
Manush, Heinie (baseball)
Manzoni, Alessandro (author--I Promessi Sposi/The Betrothed)
Mao-Tze (philosopher/military revolutionary--P.L.A.) (Hua's predecessor)
Mapes (poet; Welsh)
Maples, Marla (actress) (Donald Trump's ex)
Mapother, William (actor)
Mara, Adele (actress)
Mara, Kate (actress--Transcendence, the Martian)
Mara, Tim (football--founder of N. Y. Giants)
Marat, Jean-Paul (politician--Corday victim; Fr.) (Danton's colleague)
Maravich, Pete (Pistol Pete) (basketball)
Marc, Franz (artist--Blue Horses)
Marceau, Marcel (mime--Bip)
Marceau, Sophie (actress--Braveheart)
March, Fredric (actor--Inherit the Wind, Mark Twain)
March, Hal (T. V. game show host)
Marchenko, Ivan (Ivan the Terrible) (Holocaust guard)
Marchetti, Gino (football)
Marciano, Rocco (Rocky) (boxer)
Marcil, Vanessa (actress)
Marcille, Eva (model)

Marconi, Guglielmo (inventor)
Marcos, Ferdinand (politician--Philippines)
Marcos, Imelda (Ferdinand's spouse)
Marguand, George (author--George Apley)
Marichal, Juan (baseball)
Marie, Teena (singer--Lady T, Lover Girl)
Marin, Cheech Richard (actor/comedian--Cheech and Chong)
Marin, John (painter--Lower Manhattan)
Marino, Dan (football)
Marion, Francis (Swamp Fox) (military officer)
Maris, Ada (actress)
Maris, Roger (baseball)
Markevitch, Igor (composer/conductor)
Markey, Enid (actress--Tarzan)
Markham, Beryl (aviator)
Markham, Monte (actor)
Markova, Alicia (dancer--ballet)
Marley, Bob (Rastafarian/musician--The Wailers, One Love,
Stir It Up, Is This Love)   (Damian's father)
Marley, Christopher (author--Kitty Foyle)
Marley, Damian (musician) (Bob's son)
Marley, David Nesta (Ziggy) (musician/bandleader; Jam.)
Marlowe, Christopher (author--The Jew of Malta)
Marlowe, Derek (author)
Marmont, Percy (actor--Lord Jim)
Maron, Mark (comedian/actor/wrter/podcaster)
Marquand, John Phillips (author--Moto, The Late George
Apley)
Marquand, Ross (actor--Walking Dead)
Marquette, Jacques (Pere) (missionary/explorer) (Louis
Jolliet's partner)
Marquez, Gabriel Garcia (author--A Hundred Years of
Solitude)
Marquis, Don (author--Archy)
Marr, Dave (golfer)
Marrow, Tracy (Ice. T.) (musician--hip hop)
Marsalis, Branford (musician--saxophone)
Marsalis, Ellis (musician--piano--jazz)
Marsden, James (actor--X-Men)

Marsh Edith Ngaio (author--detective/theater director; N.Z.)
Marsh, Mae (author--The Birth of a Nation)
Marshall, George C. (author--European Recovery plan)
Marshall, Lois (singer--soprano)
Martel, Charles (The Hammer) (statesman/military leader--Franks)
Martel, Yann (author--Life of Pi)
Marti, Jose (poet/journalist/patriot; Cuban)
Martin, Amis (author--Yellow Dog, The Information)
Martin, Andrea (actress--S.C.T.V.)
Martin, Dean (singer--That's Amore, Volare/actor--Ocean's Eleven) (band--Dino, Desi & Billy)
Martin, Dick (comedian--Laugh In) (Dan Rowan's partner)
Martin, Frank (cartoonist--Born Loser)
Martin, Kiel (actor--Hill Street Blues)
Martin, Leila (actress)
Martin, Lori (actress--National Velvet)
Martin, Mardik (screenwriter--Mean Streets)
Martin, Mark (racecar driver)
Martin, Mary (actress--Peter Pan, I Do, I Do)
Martin, Pamela Sue (actress--Dynasty)
Martin, Perl (physicist--discovered tauon)
Martin, Ricky (singer--She Bangs)
Martin, Steve (actor--King Tut, L. A. Story, All Of Me, My Blue Heaven, Roxanne)
Martin, Tony (singer--I Get Ideas)
Martinez, Mel (politician)
Martinez, Pedro (baseball)
Martinez, Ramon (baseball)
Martinez, Tino (baseball)
Martini, Nino (actor/singer--tenor)
Martini, Simone (painter)
Martins, Peter (dancer--ballet)
Marton, Eva (singer--soprano)
Marvelettes (musical group--Please Mr. Postman)
Marvin, Lee (actor--Big Red One)
Marx, Anne (poet)
Marx, Chico Leonard (actor/comedian)

Marx, Groucho (nee Julius) (actor/comedian--A Girl in Every Port)
Marx, Harpo (actor/comedian)
Marx, Karl (author/revolutionist) (Fredrick Engels collaborator)
Marx, Zeppo (Herbert) (actor/comedian)
Masaryk, Tomas Garrigue (politician; Czech.)
Mascagni, Pietro (composer--opera--Nero)
Masefield, John (author--All Ye That Pass By, The Tragedy of Nan, Dead Ned, ODTAA)
Maserati, Ernesto (automaker)
Mason, Bobbie Ann (author)
Mason, Jackie (actor)
Mason, James (actor/author) (Pamela's husband)
Mason, Marsha (actress--Goodbye Girl)
Mason, Pamela (actress/author/screenwriter) (James's wife)
Massen, Osa (actress--Tokyo Rose)
Massenet, Jules Emile Frederic (composer--opera--Manon, Thais, Ariane, Eve, Le Roi   de Lahore, Le Reve)
Massey, Abe (actor)
Massey, Ilona (actress--Rosalie, Ziegfeld Follies)
Massey, Raymond (actor--Dr. Kildare, East of Eden)
Massimo, Carlotto (author--The Goodbye Kiss)
Masson, Elle (author--romance)
Masson, Paul (vintner)
Masters, Edgar Lee (poet/dramatist/author--Spoon River Anthology)
Masterson, Bat (lawman--U. S. Marshall)
Mastroianni, Marcello (actor--La Dolce Vita)
Mastsumoto, Chizuo (pseudonym--Shoko Asahara) (cult figure--gas attacks)
Masur, Kurt (conductor)
Masur, Richard (actor)
Matalin, Mary (actress--Equal Time)
Matarazzo, Heather (author--Welcome to the Dollhouse)
Matchbox 20 (musical group)
Mather, Increase (moralist/preacher)
Mather, Richard (clergyman)
Mathers, Jerry (actor--Beaver Cleaver)

Mathers, Marshal Bruce (Eminem, M & M, Slim Shady)
(singer)
Matheson, Richard (author)
Mathewson, Christy (basketball)
Mathieu, Andre (composer)
Mathis, Johnny (singer--Itsy Bitsy World, Ole, Chances Are)
Matisse, Henri (painter--fauvist--The Dance, The Piano
Lesson, Sailboat Reflection,   Le
Bateau, Le Bonheur de Vivre (The Joy of Life))
Matlin, Marlee (actress--deaf)
Matsuhisa, Nobu (chef)
Matsui, Kazuo (Kaz) (baseball)
Mattea, Kathy (singer--country--18 Wheels and a Dozen
Roses)
Matthau, Walter (actor)
Matthews, Chris (actor--Hardball)
Matthews, Dave (singer)
Matthews, Pauline (a.k.a. Kiki Dee) (singer)
Mauer, Joe (baseball)
Maugham, William Somerset (author--Our Betters, Ashenden,
                Of Human Bondage--Norah Nesbit)
                Cakes and Ale/The Skeleton in the Closet
Maura, Carmen (actress; Sp.)
Maurel, Victor (singer--baritone)
Mauresmo, Amelie (tennis)
Mauriac, Francois (author--Flesh & Blood)
Mauro, Philip (author--religious)
Maurois, Andre (author--Terre Promise/biographer--Shelley--
Ariel)
Maurras, Charles (poet, author, critic--politics)
Mauve, Anton (artist--landscapes; Dutch)
Max, Peter (painter--pop art)
Maxwell, Elsa (author/hostess)
May, Brian (musician--guitar) (band--Queen)
May, Elaine (author/actress/director)
May, Rollo (psychologist/author--Love and Will)
Mayall, John (musician--Fleetwood Mac)
Mayall, Rik (actor--Drop Dead Fred)
Maye, Lee (baseball)

Mayer, Dina (actress--Starship Troupers)
Mayfield, Curtis (singer--impressions)
Mayle, Peter (author--A Year in Provence)
Mayo, Virginia (actress)
Mayr, Ernst (zoologist)
Mays, Billy (pitchman--infomercials--OxiClean)
Mays, Willie (Say Hey Kid/#24) (baseball)
Mazar, Debi (actress)
Mbeki, Thabo (politician; S. Afr.)
Mboya, Tom (politician; Kenya)
MC Ren (singer--rap)
McAdam, John Loudon (engineer/road-builder)
McAdams, Rachel (actress--Mean Girls, Sherlock Holmes)
McAn, Thom (retailer--shoes)
McArdle, Andrea (singer/actress--Annie)
McAvoy, James (actor--X-men, Cecilia & Robbee)
McBain, Ed (Evan Hunter's pseudonym) (author--87th
Precinct)
McBride, Chi (actor--Boston Public)
McBurney, Alvin (pseudonym--Rey, Alvino) (bandleader--jazz)
McCaffrey, Anne (author--Pern)
McCann, Brian (baseball)
McCann, Les (musician/composer)
McCann, Lila (singer)
McCarthy, Clem (radio sportscaster/public address
announcer)
McCarthy, Cormac (author--All The Pretty Horses, The Road)
McCartney, Linda (photographer/musician/activist) (Paul's
wife/Stella's mother)
McCartney, Paul (musician/singer--Bad to Me, Eat at Home,
Ram, Uncle Albert,   This One) (band--
Beatles, Jets)
McCartney, Stella (fashion designer) (Paul & Linda's
daughter)
McCartyney, Paul (singer) (band--Wings/Jet/Beatles)
McCarver, Tim (baseball)
McCaskill, Claire (politician)
McCauly, Mary Hays (a.k.a. Molly Pitcher) (activist--American
Revolution)

McCay, Winsor (author--Little Nemo)
McClanahan, Rue (actress--Golden Girls)
McClintock, Mike (author--A Fly Went By)
McClure, Doug Osbourne (actor--The Virginian)
McClurg, Edie (actress)
McConaughey, Matthew (actor--Ed T.V.)
McConnell, Mitch (politician)
McCoo, Marilyn (singer--Wedding Bell Blues/T.V. host--Solid Gold)
McCord, Kent (actor)
McCorvey, Norma (a.k.a. Jane Roe) (plaintiff--Roe vs. Wade)
McCourt (McCort), Frank (author--Angela's Ashes, Tis)
McCowen, Alec (actor)
McCoy, Neal (singer--country)
McCrae, John (physician/poet--Flanders Fields)
McCrea, Joel (actor/singer/dancer)
McCrindle, Ronald (Mrs.) (pseudonym--Susan Ertz) (author--Madame Claire)
McCullers, Carson (author--Clock without hands)
McCulley, Johnston (author--Zorro (Don Diego de la Vega))
McCullough, Colleen (author--The Thorn Birds)
McCullough, David (author--Adams)
McDaniel, Hattie (actress--Gone With the Wind)
McDaniel, Mel (singer--country)
McDonald, Audra (actress)
McDonald, Enos William (Skeets) (singer/songwriter)
McDonald, John D. (author--The Long Lavender Look, Det. Travis McGee)
McDonough, Alexa (politician; Can.)
McDonough, Neal (actor--Medical Investigation)
McDowall, Roddy (actor)
McDowell, Malcolm (actor--Aces High)
McEachern Lon (sportscaster)
McEldowney, Brooke (cartoonist--9 Chickweed Lane)
McElhenney, Jane (pseudonym--Ada Clare (actress--Bleak House)
McEntyre, Reba (actress, singer--country)
McEvoy, Trish (makeup artist)
McEwan, Ian (author--Atonement)

McFadden, Cyra (author)
McGann, Eileen (singer--Celtic)
McGavin, Darren (actor)
McGee, Frank (newscaster)
McGee, Patrick (actor--Marat/Sade)
McGillis, Kelly (actress--Reuben-Reuben, Witness)
McGinnis, Joe (journalist/author--Fatal Vision)
McGinnis, Susan (newsreporter)
McGrath, Frank (actor--Wagon Train)
McGraw, John (Little Napoleon/Mugsy) (baseball)
McGraw, Tim (singer--Just to See You Smile)
McGraw, Tug (baseball)
McGregor, Ewan (actor--Obi Wan Kenobi)
McGruder, Aaron (cartoonist--The Boondocks)
McGuane, Thomas (author--The Bushwacked Piano)
McGuffey, William Holmes (publisher--readers)
McGuinn, Roger (singer--It's Gone)
McGwire, Mark (baseball)
McIlory, Rory (golfer)
McInerney, Jay (actor--Bright Lights, Big City)
McKay, Claude (author--Home to Harlem)
McKay, Jim (sportscaster)
McKellen, Ian (actor)
McKenna, Lori (singer)
McKenna, Siobhan (actress--Dr. Zhavigo; Irish)
McKenna, Virginia (actress--A Town Like Alice)
McKennitt, Loreena (singer)
McKenzie, Robert Tail (sculptor)
McKern, Leo (actor)
McKerrow, Amanda (dancer--ballet)
McKinley, Ida (William's wife)
McKinley, William (politician) (Ida's husband)
McKinnon, Kate (nee Berthold) (actress/comedian--S.N.L.)
McKnight, Brian (singer--R & B)
McKuen, Rod (poet/songwriter/singer)
McLachlan, Sarah (singer--Adia)
McLaglen, Victor (actor--The Informer)
McLean, Don (songwriter--American Pie)
McLean, Stuart (actor--Vinyl Café)

McMahon, Ed (T. V. personality)
McMurtry, Larry (author--Streets of Laredo, Lonesome Dove)
McNair, Ronald E. (astronaut)
McNairy, John Marcus (Scoot) (actor--True Detective)
McNally, Rand (mapmaker)
McNeill, Don (radio personality--The Breakfast Club)
McPherson, Aimee Semple (evangelist)
McPherson, John (cartoonist--Close to Home)
McQueen, Steve (actor--The Blob, The Getaway, The Great Escape)   (Neile Adam's husband)
McRae, Carmen (singer--jazz)
McRae, Hal (baseball)
McRaney, Gerald (actor)
McTeer, Janet (actress/model)
McVie, Christine (musician--Fleetwood Mac)
McVie, John (musician--Fleetwood Mac)
Mead, Edward (pubisher) (Frank Howard Dodd's partner)
Mead, George (biologist/author)
Mead, Margaret (anthropologist/author)
Meade, George (General--Union Army)
Meadows, Audrey (actress--Honeymooners) (Jayne's sister)
Meadows, Jayne (actress) (Steve Allen's wife) (Audrey's sister)
Meany, William George (labor leader--AFL-CIO) (Gomper's successor)
Meara, Anne (actress/author--The Other Woman) (Ben Stiller's wife)
Mears, Rick (race car driver)
Meat Loaf (Marvin Lee Aday's pseudonym) (musician--Bat Out of Hell/actor--Rocky Horror   Picture Show (Eddie)
Mecom, Jane (Benjamin Franklin's sister)
Medeiros, Elli (diva; Persian)
Mediate, Rocco (golfer)
Medley, Bill (singer/songwriter)
Mee, Arthur (author/editor)
Mee, Charles L. (author--Meeting at Potsdam)
Meek, Donald (actor)
Meeker, Ralph (actor)

Meer Van Delft, Johannes/Jan/Johan (painter)
Meese, Edwin (politician--Attorney General/author--With Reagan: The Inside Story)   (Thornburgh's predecessor)
Meester, Leighton (singer, actress--Gossip Girl)
Mehemet, Ali (politician; Egyptian)
Mehta, Zubin (conductor)
Meier, Richard Alan (architect--Getty Center)
Meir, Golda (politician/author--My Life; Isr.) (Levi Eshkol's successor)
Melba, Nellie (Dame) (diva/author--Melodies and Memories)
Melber, Ari (journalist/newsman--The Beat)
Melchizedek (King of Salem)
Mellon, Andrew (politician/financier)
Melville, Herman (author--Omoo, Typee, Benito Cereno, Billy Budd, Mardi)
Men At Work (musical group)
Mencken, Henry Louis (author)
Mendel, Gregor (botanist)
Mendeleev, Dmitri (chemist/inventor--formulated periodic table)
Mendelssohn, Felix (Jakob Ludwig) (composer--Octette, Violin Concertoin E Minor)
Mendes, Eva (model/actress--2 Fast, 2 Furious, Hitch)
Mendes, Sam (director--American Beauty)
Mendes, Sergio (pianist/bandleader--The Look of Love, Mas Que Nada)
Menen, Aubrey (author--The Prevalence of Witches)
Menes (Egyptian 1st dynasty founder)
Menjou, Adolphe (actor)
Menken, Adah Isaacs (painter/poet/actress)
Menken, Alan (composer--Disney)
Menon, Krisna (statesman/diplomat)
Menotti, Gian Carlo (composer--The Consul, Amahl & the Night Visitors, The Telephone,   Amelia Goes to the Ball)
Menuhin, Yehudi (musician--violin) (Auer's student)
Menzel, Idina (actress--Elsa, Wicked)
Mercer, Jack (voice actor--Popeye)

Mercer, Johnny (singer/songwriter--I Lost My Sugar in Salt Lake City, Jeepers Creepers)
Mercer, Mabel (singer--Fly Me to the Moon)
Mercer, Ray (boxing)
Merchant, Natalie (singer)
Mercouri, Melina (actress--Never On Sunday; Gr.)
Meredith, George (author--The Egoist)
Merganthaler, Ottmar (inventor--linotype)
Merimee, Prosper (author--Carmen)
Merkel, Angela (politician; Ger.)
Merkel, Una (The Bank Dick, Destry Rides again)
Merkerson, Epatha (actress)
Merman, Ethel (singer/actress--Annie Oakley)
Merriam, Eve (poet)
Merrill, Bob (composer/lyricist/actor--Carnival, Take Me Along)
Merrill, Dina (actress)
Merrill, Robert (singer/actor--Figaro)
Merrimam, Nan (singer--soprano)
Mersenne, Marin (mathematician)
Merton, Thomas (author--philosophy & meditation)
Meryman, Richard (author--Enter Talking) (co-author--Joan Rivers)
Mesley, Wendy (journalist)
Mesmer, Franz Anton (doctor/hypnotist)
Messi, Lionel (soccer)
Messier, Mark (hockey)
Messing, Debra (actress)
Mesta, Perle (hostess)
Mestrovic, Ivan (sculptor)
Metastasio, Pietro (poet)
Metcalf, Laurie (actress)
Metchnikov, Elie (biologist; Ru.)
Meyer, Debbie (swimmer)
Meyer, Nicholas (author--The Seven-Percent Solution)
Meyer, Richard (architect)
Meyer, Russ (director)
Meyer, Stephenie (author--Twilight)
Meyer, Urban (football coach)
Meyerbeer, Giacomo (composer--L'Africana/e, the Huguenots)

Meyers, Ann (basketball)
Meyers, Ari (actress--Kate & Allie)
Meyers, Seth (actor/comedian--S.N.L./T.V. host--Late Night with Seth Meyers)
Meyers, Stephenie (author/producer--Twilight)
Michael, George (musician--band--Wham)
Michaels, Anne (author)
Michaels, Lorne (producer--S.N.L.)
Michelangelo (architect/sculptor/painter--frescos)
Michele, Lea (singer/actress--Glee)
Michele, Michael (actress--Cleo on E.R.)
Michelin, Andre (industrialist--Michelin Tyre Company)
Michelin, Edouard (industrialist--Michelin Tyre Company)
Michener, James A. (author--Space, Iberia, Bridges at Toko-Ri, Tales of the South Pacific, Texas, Poland)
Middlecoff, Cary (golfer)
Middleton, Velma (singer)
Midler, Bette (Divine Miss "M") (comedian/actress/singer--For the Boys, Scenes from a Mall, The Rose, Diva Las Vegas)
Mielziner, Jo (scene/lighting designer)
Mies van der Rohe, Ludwig (architect; Am.)
Mifune, Toshiro (actor)
Mikan, George (basketball)
Mikita, Stan (hockey)
Milano, Alyssa (actress--Charmed, Who's the Boss)
Miles, Sarah (actress)
Miles, Vera (actress)
Milhaud, Darius (composer)
Milian, Christina (singer)
Milk, Harvey (assassin)
Millan, Cesar (The Dog Whisperer) (dog trainer)
Millar, Kenneth (pseudonym--Ross MacDonald) (author--crime fiction)
Millay, Edna St. Vincent (poet/sonneteer--Aria da Capo)
Miller, Anne (dancer)
Miller, Arthur (essayist/playwright--Willie Loman, The Crucible, All My Sons, After the Fall)

Miller, Cheryl (sportscaster)
Miller, Dennis (author--I Rant Therefore I Am, Bordelo of Blood)
Miller, Henry (painter/author--The Tropic of …) (Anais Nin's life partner)
Miller, Lee (photographer)
Miller, Merle (author--biographer--Truman)
Miller, Mitch (musician--Sing Along with Mitch)
Miller, Nicole (designer)
Miller, Penelope Ann (actress)
Miller, Reggie (basketball)
Miller, Roger (singer--Dang Me)
Miller, Shannon (gymnast)
Miller, Sue (author--The Good Mother)
Miller, Wiley (cartoonist--Non Sequitur)
Millett, Kate (feminist/social critic)
Mills, Enos (homesteader/naturalist/author/lecturer)
Mills, Erie (singer/coloraturist--opera)
Mills, Hayley (actress--Parent Trap)
Milne, Alan Alexander (author--Winnie the Pooh, Now We Are Six, When Were Very Young,   Mr. Pim Passes By, Toad of Toad Hall, The Wrong Sort of Bees)   (autobiography--It's Too Late Now)
Milne, David Brown (painter--snowy scenes)
Milner, Martin (actor--Route 66)
Milsap, Ronnie (singer)
Milstein, Nathan (musician--violin)
Milton, John (poet--elegist--Immortal Hate, Erato, Lycides, On His Blindness)
Mimieux, Yvette (actress--Where the Boys Are)
Mimms, Garnet (singer--Cry Baby)
Minaj, Nicki (rapper--Anaconda)
Minaya, Omar (baseball)
Mineo, Sal (Switchblade Kid) (actor--Exodus/singer--Start Movin, Crime in the Streets)
Miner, Billy (train robber)
Mineta, Norman (politician)
Ming, Yao (basketball)

Mink, Patsy (politician)
Minnelli, Liza (actress/singer--Cabaret, The Act, Arthur, New York; New York) (Vincent's daughter/Lorna Luft's sister, Judy's daughter)
Minnelli, Vincent (director--Gigi) (Liza's father/Judy Garland's husband)
Minogue, Kylie (singer)
Minsky, Howard (impresario--burlesque)
Mintz, Shlomo (musician--violin)
Miracles (musical group--Shop Around)
Miranda, Ernesto (laborer wrongly convicted--Miranda warning)
Miranda, Lin-Manuel (activist/composer/lyricist/singer--Hamilton)
Mirella, Freni (singer--soprano)
Mirer, Richard (Rick) (football)
Miro, Joan (painter--Harlequin's Carnival, The Hunter; Sp.)
Mirren, Helen (Dame) (actress--Excalibur, Cal; Br.)
Mishima, Yukio (author--The Sound of the Waves)
Miss Cleo (nee Youree Dell Harris) (shaman/psychic)
Mitchell, Abbie (singer--opera--Porgy & Bess)
Mitchell, Anais (singer-songwriter--Hadestown)
Mitchell, Cameron (actor--Okinawa)
Mitchell, Joni (singer--Big Yellow Taxi, Amelia)
Mitchell, Kel (actor/comedian--Kenan & Kel) (Kenan Thompson's partner)
Mitchell, Leona (singer--soprano)
Mitchell, Margaret (journalist/author--Gone With the Wind)
Mitchell, William Ormond (author; Can.)
Mitchum, Robert (actor--Macao, G. I. Joe)
Mitropoulis, Dimitri (conductor)
Mitterrand, Francois (politician) (Chirac's predecessor)
Mix, Ron (football)
Mix, Tom (oater)
Miyazaki, Hayao (filmmaker/screenwriter/author/animator--My Neighbor Totoro)
Miyoshi, Ameki (actress)
Mize, Johnny (baseball)
Mizrahi, Isaac (fashion designer)

Mnedeleev, Dmitri (chemist/inventor--periodic table)
Mo'Nique (actress--Precious)
Mocedades (musical group--Eres Tu)
Mochrie, Dottie (golfer)
Modell, Arthur (Art) (business exec./N.F.L. owner--Cleveland Browns)
Modigliani, Amedeo (painter--The Nude Rose)
Modine, Matthew (actor--Streamers, Birdy, Vision Quest)
Modiste (fashion designer; Fr.)
Modugno, Domenico (singer--Volare)
Moe, Tommy (skier)
Moet, Claude (vintner)
Moffo, Anna (diva--soprano)
Mohammed (prophet) (favorite wife--Ayesha, daughter--Fatima, son-in-law--Ali)
Mohede, Sidney (singer--gospel)
Mohr, Jay (comedian/host--Last Comic Standing, Jerry Maguire)
Mohr, Josephus (Josef) (priest/songwriter--Silent Night)
Mohs, Friedrich (mineralogist)
Moi, Daniel Arap (politician--president of Kenya)
Moiseyer, Igor (choreographer)
Mol, Gretchen (model)
Moliere (Jean-Baptiste Poquelin's stage name) (actor/dramatist--Tartuffe, School for Women, The Miser, Le Misanthrope, L'Ecole Des Maris, The Doctor In Spite of Himself)) (Racine's rival)
Molina, Alfred (actor--The Da Vinci Code)
Molina, Rafael Trujilo (dictator--Dominican)
Molinaro, Al (actor)
Moll, Richrd (voice artist/actor--Night Court)
Molnar, Ferenc (playwright--Liliom)
Monae, Janelle (actress/singer)
Monarch, Carole (singer--It's Too Late)
Mondavi, Robert (vintner)
Monday, Rick (baseball)
Mondrian, Piet (artist--Tableau 2)
Monet, Claude (painter--Rouen Cathedral, Vetheuil en Ete, Waterlilies, Haystacks at Giverny, Woman with Parasol,

Cap(e) Martin, Haystack at Giverny, The Woman in the Green Dress, (Camille), Gare Saint-Lazare; Fr.)
Money, Eddie (singer--Two Tickets to Paradise)
Monique (actress--Precious)
Monk, James Arthur (Art) (football)
Monk, Thelonius (musician--bop pioneer/ pianist/ jazz)
Monkeys (musical group)
Monnet, Jean Omer Marie (diplomat/politicial economist--E. Common Market)
Mono, Madeleine (cosmetician)
Monroe, Earl (basketball)
Monroe, James (politician--Founding Father--Era of Good Feeling)
Monroe, Marilyn (Norma Jean Baker's pseudonym) (singer/actress --Bus Stop, Niagara, The Prince and the Showgirl)
Montalban, Ricardo (actor--Sombrero)
Montand, Yves (nee Ivo Levi) (actor--"Z")
Montemezzi, Italo (composer--Lamore dei tre re)
Montesquieu, Charles Loluis de Secondat (judge/scholar/author/philosopher)
Monteverdi, Claudio (composer--opera--L'Orfeo)
Montez, Lola (actress)
Montez, Maria Africa Gracia Vidal (actress)
Montgomerie, Colin (golf)
Montgomery, Bernard Law (Monty/the Spartan General) (Br. Field Marshall in both world wars)
Montgomery, Lucy Maude (author--Anne of Green Gables)
Montgomery, Wes (musician--guitarist)
Monti, Vincenzo (poet)
Montoya, Carlos (guitarist--flamenco)
Montross, Eric (basketball)
Moody Blues (musical group--Go Now, Days of Future Past)
Moody, Hellen (Helen) Wills (tennis)
Moody, Orville (golfer; Am.)
Moody, Ron (actor)
Moody, William Vaugn (playwright/poet--An Ode In Time of Hesitation)
Moog, Robert (inventor--synthesizer)

Moon, Keith (musician--drummer--Who)
Moonves, Leslie (Les) (T.V. exec.--C.B.S.)
Moore, Alan (author--Watchmen)
Moore, Archie (boxer)
Moore, Brian (author--Black Robe)
Moore, Chante (diva)
Moore, Clement Clarke (poet--Twas the Night Before Xmas, Visit From St. Nicholas)
Moore, Demi (actress--G. I. Jane)
Moore, Dickie (actor--Our Gang)
Moore, Dudley (actor--Arthur, Six Weeks, 10)
Moore, Garry (comedian/T.V. personality)
Moore, George (author--Esther Waters)
Moore, Grace (singer--One Night of Love)
Moore, Henry (sculptor)
Moore, Julianne (actress--Still Alice)
Moore, Marianne (poet--To A Steam Roller)
Moore, Maya (basketball)
Moore, Michael (director--Roger & Me, Sicko, Downsize This, Where to Invade Next)
Moore, Roger (actor--007, The Saint)
Moore, Shemar (actor--S.W.A.T.)
Moore, Thomas (poet--Lalla Rookh/singer/songwriter--The Minstrel Boy, The Last Rose of Summer, The Harp That Once Through Tara's Halls)
Moore, Wayetu (author--She Would Be King)
Mora, Jim (football)
Morales, Esai (actor--la Bamba, Bad Boys)
Morales, Evo (politician; Bol.)
Moran, Erin (actress)
Moran, George (radio personality--The Two Black Crows) (Mack's partner)
Moran, Thomas (artist--landscapes)
Moranis, Rick (actor--My Blue Heaven, Ghostbusters)
Morante, Elsa (author--La Storia)
Morath, Inge (photographer)
Moravia, Alberto (author--The Fancy Dress Party, The Conformist)

More, Thomas (Sir) (philosopher/statesman/lawyer/author--Utopia)
Moreau, Jeanne (actress--Fr.)
Morelos, Jose (priest/revolutionary)
Moreno, Omar (baseball)
Moreno, Rita (nee Rosita Alverio) (actress--Popi/singer)
Moretti, Ugo (author)
Moretz, Chloe (actress--Carrie)
Morgan, Alexandra (Alex) (soccer)
Morgan, Henry James (author; Can.)
Morgan, Lorrie (singer--country)
Morgan, Russ (bandleader)
Morgenstern, Erin (author--The Night Circus)
Moriarty, Liane (author--Big Little Lies)
Morini, Erika (actress)
Morissette, Alanis (singer--Alanis Unplugged, Thank U, So-Called Chaos)
Morita, Akio (co-founder--Sony)
Morita, Pat (actor--Karate Kid)
Morley, Christopher (author--Kitty Foyle)
Morley, Robert (actor)
Moro, Aldo (politician; It.)
Morricone, Ennio (composer--The Untouchables)
Morris, Desmond (author--The Naked Ape, the Human Zoo)
Morris, Errol (documentarian/director--The Fog of War, The Thin Blue Line)
Morris, Samuel Kaboo (missionary)
Morrison, Frank (pseudonym--Mickey Spillane) (author--I the Jury/Mike Hammer creator)
Morrison, Shana (singer/songwriter) (Van's daughter)
Morrison, Toni (author/Nobelist--Beloved, Sula, Jazz)
Morrison, Van (singer/songwriter/musician--Into the Mystic, Moondance, Brown Eyed Girl)   (Shana's father)
Morrow, Vic (actor)
Morse, Barry (actor)
Morse, David (actor)
Morse, Robert (actor--Tru)
Morse, Wayne (politician)
Mortensen, Viggo (actor)

Morton, Levi P. (politician)
Mos Def (nee Dante Terrell Smith) (actor/rapper--Dexter)
Moscovitz, Jason (reporter)
Mose, Allison (pianist--jazz)
Mosel, Tad (playwright)
Moses, Anna Mary Robertson Moses (Grandma) (painter--folk/author--My Life's History)
Moses, Daniel David (playwright; Can. native)
Moses, Robert (Master Planner) (city planner--N.Y.)
Mosher, Terry (pseudonym--Aislin) (cartoonist--political)
Mosrat, Samin (chef/author--cookbooks/food columnist)
Moss, Arnoldl (actor/crossword puzzle creator)
Mostel, Samuel Joel (Zero) (actor/singer/comedian--Fiddler on the Roof (Tevye the milkman)
Mota, Manny (baseball)
Mota, Rosa (runner)
Mother Teresa (nee Agnes) (Saint) (missionary--Missionaries of Charity founder)
Motley Crue (musical group--Dr. Feelgood)
Mott, John Raleigh (protestor--Young Legacy)
Mott, Lucretia (reformer/suffragette)
Mott, Nevill (Sr.) (physicist)
Mountbatten, Philip (Prince; Br.) (Edwina's husband)
Mouse, Eeka (musician--raggae)
Moya, Carlos (tennis)
Moynihan, Pat (politician)
Mozart, Wolfgang Amadeus (composer--Cosi Fan Tutte, Rondo alla Turca, Il Re Pastore, Eine Kleine Nachtmusik, L'oca del Cairo, The Magic Flute, Die Zauberflote, Donna Elvira, Serenade (opus), Idomeneo, Fra Gli Amplessi (duet), La Clemenz Di Tito, The Marriage of Figaro (aria--Porgi, amor))
Mr. Mr. (musical group--Broken Wings)
Mr. T (nee Tero) (Laurence Tureaud's pseudonym) (actor--D. C. Cab)
Mraz, Jason (singer/songwriter--I'm Yours)
Mubarak, Hosni (politician--Egypt)
Mudd, Roger (newsman)

Muddy Waters (Mississippi) (singer--Hoochie Coochie Man)
Mueller, Lisel (poet)
Mufune, Toshiro (actor)
Muhammad, Elijah (religious leader)
Muir, David (newsman)
Muir, John (ecologist--Sierra Club/author--Our National Parks)
Muir, Lewis (pianist/composer--ragtime--Mammy Jinny's Jubilee)
Muldaur, Maria (author--I'm A Woman)
Mulgrew, Kate (actress)
Mull, Martin (comedian/actor--Fernwood 2Night/Fernwood Tonight)
Mullally, Megan (actress)
Mulligan, Gerry (saxophonist)
Mulrooney, Brian (politician; Can.)
Mulrooney, Mila (engineer)
Mumford, Thad (writer--T.V.)
Mun (economist--17th Century)
Munch, Edvard (painter--The Scream)
Muni, Paul (actor--Pasteur, The Good Earth, Scarface/Oscar winner I936)
Muniz, Frankie (actor--Malcolm in the Middle)
Munoz, Rie (artist; Alaskan)
Munro, Alice (author)
Munro, Hector Hugh (pseudonym--Saki) (author--The Open Window, Esme, The Chronicles of Clovis)
Munsel, Patrice (diva)
Munson, Ona (actress--Gone With the Wind)
Murdoch, Iris (philosopher/author--The Sandcastle, The Bell, An Accidental Man, Under the Net)
Murdoch, Rupert (media mogul--Australian)
Muresan, Gheorghe (basketball)
Murillo, Bartolome Esteban (painter--Immaculate Conception)
Murkowski, Lisa (politician)
Murphey, John Cullin (cartoonist--Prince Valiant)
Murphy, Audie (war hero/actor--To Hell and Back)
Murphy, Eddie (actor--48 Hours, Coming to America--Akeem)
Murray, Arthur (dancer)

Murray, Bill (actor/comedian)
Murray, James (editor--O. E. D.)
Murray, Ken (a.k.a. Don Court) (actor/comedian/author/T.V. personality)
Murray, Mae (actress--Ziegfeld Follies)
Murray, Ty (rodeo cowboy)
Murrow, Edward Roscoe (newsman--U. S. I. A., See It Now)
Musante, Tony (actor--Toma)
Musburger, Brent (sportscaster)
Musgrave, Thea (composer)
Musial, Stan (#6) (baseball)
Musk, Elon (entrepreneur/engineer/inventor--C.E.O.--Tesla)
Mussina, Mike (baseball)
Mussolini, Benito (journalist/politician--National Fascist Party leader) (Edda's father/ Gian Galeazzo Ciano's father-in-law)
Mussorgsky, Modest Petrovich (composer--Night on Bald Mountain, Pictures of an Exhibition, Bilder Einer Ausstellung, The Great Gate of Kiev, Song of the Flea)
Muzorewa, Abel Tendekayi (ecclesiastic; Zim.)
Mya (nee Mya Marie Harrison) (actress/songwriter/singer--Case of the Ex)
Myers, Deedee (Clinton press sec./politican pundit)
Myers, Mike (actor--Wayne's World)
Myers, Russell (cartoonist--Broomhilda)
Myerson, Bess (actress/Miss America)
Myron (sculptor--Discobolus)

--N--

Na, Ming (actress--E.R.)
Nabokov, Vladimer (author--Pnin, Lolita, Ada, Dar (The Gift), The Eye/ translator--Alice in Wonderland) (auto-biography--Speak Memory)
Nadal, Rafael (tennis)
Nadelman, Elie (sculptor)

Nader, Ralph (consumer advocate/author--Who's Poisoning America/   founder--Public Citizen/ An Unreasonable Man subject)
Nagel, Conrad (actor--The Mysterious Lady)
Nagurski, Bronislau (Bronko) (football)
Nagy, Imre (politician; Hung.)
Naipaul, Vidiadhar Surajprasad (V.S.) (author--A Bend in the River)
Nair, Mira (director--The Name Sake, Mississippi Masala)
Naisbitt, John (columnist--trends)
Naish, Joseph Carrol (actor--Charlie Chan, Sahara)
Nakasone, Yasuhiro (politician; Jap.)
Naldi, Nita (actor--silent movies--A Sainted Devil)
Namath, Joseph William (Joe) (football/actor--C.C. and Company)
Nance, Jack (actor--Twin Peaks, Eraserhead)
Nance, Jim (sportscaster)
Nancherla, Aparna (comedian)
Nano, Luigi (composer)
Napier, John (inventor--logarithms)
Narz, Jack (gameshow host--Dotto)
Nas (musician--rap--Illmatic, If I Ruled the World, I Mic, NY State of Mind)
Nash, Charles (automaker)
Nash, Graham (singer-songwriter)
Nash, Johnny (singer--Stir It Up)
Nash, Ogden (poet--Reflection on Ice Breaking, Llamas, Candy is Dandy, The Turtle,   Free Wheeling, Hard Lines) (Francis Leonard's husband)
Nashe, Thomas (also Nash) (playwright/poet/pamphleteer/satirist--Antipuritan; Br.)
Nashville Teens (musical group)
Naso, Ovidius Publius (Ovid) (poet--The Art of Love, Tristia, Amores, Ars Amatoria,   Heroides)
Nasreddin (Shah; Persia)
Nasser, Gamal Abdel (politician--Pan Arab Movement; Egypt)
Nast, Conde (publisher)

Nast, Thomas (cartoonist--political--Harper Weekly/Tammany
Hall Tiger/author--   Vanity Fair/ G.O.P. elephant
logo creator; Am.)
Nastase, Ilie (tennis)
Nasty Nas (singer--rap)
Nathan, Robert (author/poet)
Natoire, Charles-Joseph (painter) (Francois Le Moyne's
student)
Nava, Gregory (actor--El Norte)
Navarro, Ana (newsperson/strategist)
Navarro, Jaime (baseball)
Navarro, Ramon (actor)
Nazimova, Alla (actress)
Neagle, Anna (actress/singer)
Neal, Fred (Curly) (basketball)
Neal, Larry (scholar/philosopher/author--BAM (Black Arts
Movement)
Neal, Patricia (actress--Hud, A Face in the Crowd)
Neale, Earle (Greasy) (football)
Neale, John Mason (priest/scholar/hymnist--Good King
Wenceslas)
Neale, Tom (actor)
Nealon, Kevin (actor--S.N.L., Weeds)
Nedved, Petr (hockey)
Nee, Ivo (chess master)
Neely, Cam (hockey)
Neeson, Liam (actor--Schindler's List, The Grey, Kinsey,
Taken)
Neff, Hildegarde (actress)
Negri, Pola (actress--Forbidden Paradise, Passion/Madame
Dubarry) (Rudolph Valentino's love)
Nehru, Jawaharlal (India's first P.M.--Non-Alighned
Movement) (Motilal's son/Indira's father)
          (autobiog.--Towards Freedom)
Nehru, Motilal (politician)
Neil, Jordon (screenwriter--The Crying Game)
Neill, Noel (actress--Lois Lane)
Neill, Sam (actor--Horse Whisperer, The Piano; N.Z.)
Neiman, Leroy (artist--Playboy)

Nell, Gwen (actress)
Nelligan, Kate (actress--Eleni)
Nelly (singer--rap--N Dey Say)
Nelson, Ben (politician)
Nelson, Byron (golfer)
Nelson, Eddy (singer)
Nelson, Gaylord (politician--Earth Day)
Nelson, Horatio (naval hero--Battle of Trafalgar)
Nelson, Jimmy (T.V. personality/ventriloquist--Farfel)
Nelson, Judd (actor)
Nelson, Ricky (actor/singer--It's Late)
Nemerov, Howard (poet)
Nen, Robb (baseball--pitcher)
Nena (singer--99 Luftballoons)
Neneh, Cherry (singer--Buffalo Stance)
Nepos, Cornelius (historian)
Neri, Antonio (glassmaker; Br.)
Neri, Philip (Saint) (priest; It.)
Nero (nee Lucius Domitius Ahenobarbus) (ruler of
Rome/Nero-Galba-Otho)
        (Seneca's pupil/Agrippina's son)
Nero, Franco (actor--Camelot; It.)
Nero, Peter (pianist)
Neruda, Pablo (poet--Odes to Common Things; Chilean)
Nerva (Roman emperor--Trajan's predecessor)
Nesmith, Mike (actor/singer--The Monkeys)
Nessen, Ron (politician--media liaison)
Netanyahu, Benjamin (Bibi) (politician; Isr.)
Netti, John (gangster)
Neuwirth, Bebe (actress--Lillith)
Nevers, Ernie (football)
Neville, Aaron (singer--pop)
Nevin, Ethelbert (pianist/composer--Mighty Like a (Lak'A)
Rose, The Rosary)
Nevins, Allan (author/biographer--Grover Cleveland)
Newell, Mike (director--Harry Potter)
Newhart, Bob (actor)
Newhouser, Hal (baseball)
Newley, Anthony (actor)

Newman, Edwin (newscaster/journalist/author)
Newman, Laraine (actress--S.N.L.)
Newman, Paul (actor/director--Wusa, Hombre, Rachel Rachel, Hud, The Sting,   Cool Hand Luke)
Newman, Randy (singer/songwriter/composer--Short People, I Love L.A., Toy Story)
Newsom, Gavin (politician; San Fran.)
Newton, Byron Rufus (journalist/aviator/author--satirical poetry)
Newton, Cam (football)
Newton, Isaac (Sir) (scientist/mathematician/author--Opticks)
Newton, Juice (singer)
Newton, Nate (football)
Newton, Wayne (singer)
Newton-John, Olivia (actress/singer--Let Me Be There, Physical)
Ney, Michel (General--Napoleonic)
Ney, Richard (author--Wall Street Jungle)
Ne-yo (singer--So Sick, Mad)
Ngor, Haing S. (doctor/author--A Cambodian Odyssey/actor--The Killing Fields)
Nhu, Ngo Dinh (politician--Vietnam)
Nhu, Tran Le Xuen (Madame) (Ngo Dinh's wife)
Nichause, Lennie (musician--jazz)
Nichol, Eric (columnist--humour)
Nichols, Anne (producer/playwright/director--Abie's Irish Rose)
Nicholson, Jack (actor--The Two Jakes, Hoffa)
Nicks, Stevie (singer)
Nico (actress/singer--Evita)
Nicol, Lesley (actress--Downtown Abbey)
Nicolas III (born Orsini) (politician)
Nicolson, Adela (poet)
Niedzviecki, Val (author)
Nielsen, Leslie (actor--Forbidden Planet, The Naked Gun)
Nielson, Carl August (composer; Dan.)
Nielson, Sandra (lexicographer/metalexicographer)
Niemeyer, Oscar (architect; Braz.)
Nier, Alfred Otto Carl (physicist)
Nies, Judith (author--Seven Women)

Nieto, Enrique Pena (politician; Mex.)
Nietzsche, Friedrich (philosopher--Eine)
Nikolaidi, Elena (singer--contralto)
Nilsson, Birgit (singer--soprano--Swed.)
Nilsson, Harry (musician/singer/songwriter--Jump into the Fire, One--Three Dog Night)
Nimitz, Chester (Admiral)
Nimoy, Leonard (actor/host--In Search of ...)
Nin, Anais (diarist/author--Winter of Artifice, Delta of Venice, Ladders to Fire, Under the Glass Bell,   Seduction of the Minotaur, Henry & June, Cities of the Interior, Collages,   Little Birds, Children of the Albatross, A Spy in the House of Love)   (Henry Miller's life partner)
Ninn, Rob (baseball)
Nirvana (musical group--In Utero, Come As You Are)
Nitti, Giolitti (The Enforcer) (gangster/politician exiled by Mussolini)
Niven, David (actor--Separate Tables) (autobiography--The Moon's a Balloon)
Nixon, Cynthia (actress--Sex and the City)
Nixon, Marni (singer)
Nixon, Pat (nee Thelma Catherine Ryan) (Richard's wife)
Nixon, Richard (politician)
Nizer, Louis (lawyer--libel/author--My Life in Court)
Noah, Trevor (author--Born A Crime)
Noah, Yannick (tennis)
Nobel, Alfred (inventor--dynamite/Nobel Prize)
Nofziger, Lyn (politician)
Noguchi, Isamu (sculptor)
Nokomis (Hiawatha's grandmother)
Nol, Lon (politician; Cambodian)
Nolan, Christopher (director--The Dark Knight, Inception)
Nolan, Jeannette (actress)
Nolan, Jonathan (co-creator/producer/writer--Westworld)
Nolan, Lloyd (actor)
Nolan, Philip (actor)
Nolan, William (surgeon/author--The Making of a Surgeon)
Nolde, Emil (printmaker/painter--expressionism)

Nolin, Gena Lee (actress--Baywatch)
Noll, Charles Henry (Chuck) (football)
Nolte, Nick (teacher/actor--Jefferson in Paris, Mother Night, Prince of Tides, North Dallas Forty, Warrior, Affliction, Mulholland Falls, Extreme Prejudice)
Nomo, Hideo (baseball--pitcher)
Nono, Luigi (composer)
Noo, Noor (nee Lisa Najceb Halaby) (Queen of Jordon) (author--Leap of Faith)
Noonan, Frederick Joseph (aviator) (Earhart's navigator)
Noonan, Peggy (columnist/author--Reagan's autobiography)
Noonan, Tommy (actor--Gentlemen Prefer Blondes)
Noone, Jimmy/Jimmie (bandleader/musician--clarinetist--jazz)
Noone, Kathleen (actress--Knots Landing)
Noone, Peter (singer--Herman's Hermits, V. H. 1)
Noor, Al-Hussein (Queen of Jordan)
Nordstrom, Elmer (merchant)
Norgay, Tenzing (Sherpa mountaineer)
Noriega, Manuel (politician--Panama)
Norman, Jessye (diva)
Norman, Marsha (author/playwright)
Normand, Mabel (actress)
Norris, Carlos Ray (Chuck) (martial artist/screenwriter/producer/actor--Good Guys Wear Black/author--Black Belt Patriotism: How to Reawaken America)
Norris, Frank (author--The Pit, The Octopus)
Norris, Kathleen (author--Through A Glass Darkly)
North, Jay (actor--Dennis the Menace)
North, Oliver (politician--Watergate)
North, Sheree (actress)
North, Sterling (author--Rascal)
Norton, Eleanor Holmes (politician)
Norwood, Brandy (actor--Moesha)
Noth, Chris (actor--Sex and the City)
Notorious B.I.G. (nee Christopher Wallace) (Biggie Smalls) (singer--Poppa)
Nouri, Michael (actor--Flashdance)
Novak, Robert (journalist) (Evan's partner)

Novarro, Ramon (actor)
Novello, Ivor (composer/actor--The Lodger)
Novotna, Jana (tennis)
Noyes, Alfred (poet--The Highwayman, Drake, The Loom of Years, The Barrel Organ/   playwright--Rada; Br.)
NSync (musical group--Bye, Bye, Bye, God Must Have Spent a Little More Time on You,   Tearin Up My Heart, This I Promise You)
Nu Snooz (musical group)
Nu, U (politician/author--Burma Looks Ahead; Burma)
Nugent, Maude (singer/composer--Sweet Rosie O'Grady)
Nugent, Ted (singer--Cat Scratch Fever/guitarist--rock)
Numa (politician--Romulus's successor)
Nunez de Balboa, Vasco (explorer)
Nunez, Jorge Orta (baseball)
Nunn, Sam (politician)
Nunn, Trevor (director--Cats; Br.)
Nunn, William Goldwyn (Bill) (actor--Radio Raheem)
Nuno, Jaime (composer--Mex. National Anthem)
Nureyev, Rudolf (dancer--ballet/author--I Am a Dancer) (Margot Fonteyn's partner)
Nurmi, Paavo (Flying Finn) (track & field/Olympian)
Nuyen, France (actress)
Nyad, Diana (swimmer)
Nye, Bill (humorist--History of America)
Nye, Carrie (actress)
Nye, Louis (comedian)
Nye, Russell (historian/author)
Nykvist, Sven (photographer/cinematographer)
Nyman, Lena (actress)
Nyro, Laura (songwriter/singer--Wedding Bell Blues, Eli's Coming)

--O--

O'Brien, Conor (author/diplomat)

O'Brien, Dan (decathlete)
O'Brien, Edmund (actor--Dead on Arrival (D.O.A.), 1984)
O'Brien, Edna (author; Ir.)
O'Brien, Larry (basketball)
O'Brien, Pat (actor--Okinawa)
O'Brien, Soledad (newscaster)
O'Brien-Moore, Erin (actress)
O'Casey, Sean (playwright--The Plow and the Stars, The Dublin Trilogy, Juno and the Paycock, Red Roses for Me, The Star Turns Red)
O'Connell, Helen (singer)
O'Connor, Edwin (author)
O'Connor, Renee (actress--Xena Warrior Princess)
O'Connor, Sandra Day (justice--Supreme Court) (Alito's predecessor)
O'Connor, Sinead (singer--Nothing Compares 2 U)
O'Connor, Una (actress)
O'Day, Anita (singer--jazz)
O'Day, Aubrey (singer/songwriter)
O'Dell, Scott (author--children--Island of the Blue Dolphins)
O'Donnell, Chris (actor--Robin of Batman)
O'Donnell, Norah (newsperson)
O'Donnell, Rosie (comedienne)
O'Doul, Francis Joseph (Lefty) (baseball)
O'Dowd, George (Boy George) (singer/composer)
O'Faolain, Sean (author--Come Back to Erin)
O'Flaherty, Liam (author--The Informer)
O'Flynn, Liam (musician--folk)
O'Grady, Sean (boxer)
O'Hair, Madalyn Murray (atheist leader)
O'Hara, Catherine (actress--Home Alone)
O'Hara, John (author--Butterfield 8, Appointment in Samarra, A Rage to Live, Pal Joey, From the Terrace, Ten North Frederick)
O'Hara, Kelli (singer/actress--The King and I)
O'Hara, Maureen (actress)
O'Hare, Denis (actor)
O'Hare, John (author--The Cape Cod Lighter)
O'Higgins, Bernardo (revolutionary leader/politician; Chile)

O'Jays (musical group--Love Train)
O'Keefe, Dan (singer--Good Time Charlie's Got the Blues)
O'Keefe, Dennis (actor)
O'Keefe, Michael (actor--Caddy Shack, The Great Santini)
O'Keefe, Miles (actor--Tarzan)
O'Keeffe, Georgia (Mother of American Modernism) (painter--
Irises, Black Poseas)
O'Kelly, Sean (politician; Ir.)
O'Leary, Hazel (politician)
O'Leary, Michael (politician--Clinton cabinet)
O'Malley, Walter (sports exec./baseball team owner--Dodgers)
O'Neal, Jermaine (basketball)
O'Neal, Patrick (actor)
O'Neal, Ron (actor)
O'Neal, Ryan (actor)
O'Neal, Shaquille (Big Aristotle) (basketball/analyst--Inside the
N.B.A./ rapper--Shaq   Diesel)
O'Neal, Tatum (actress--Paper Moon--Addie Loggins)
O'Neil, John Jordan (Buck) (baseball)
O'Neil, Kitty (Fastest Woman in the World) (stuntwoman/racer)
O'Neil, Roger (newsman)
O'Neill, Ed (actor--Modern Family, Married with Children)
O'Neill, Eugene (playwright--Strange Interlude, Marco Millions,
The Iceman Cometh,   A Moon for the
Misbegotten, Desire Under the Elms, A Touch of the Poet,
Anna Christie,   Ah Wilderness, Hairy Ape, Ile)
O'Neill, Jennifer (actress--Summer of 42)
O'Neill, Oona (Eugene's daughter/married Charlie Chaplin)
O'Neill, Thomas Phillip (Tip) (politician) (James Wright's
successor)
O'Reilly, Bill (author--The No Spin Zone)
O'Shea, Milo (actor--Only the Lonely, Barbarella, Romeo and
Juliet, Mass Appeal)
O'Shea, Tessie (comedian/actress/singer--Two Ton Tessie)
O'Toole, Annette (actress--48 Hours)
O'Toole, Peter (actor--Priam in Troy, Lion in Winter, Becket,
Stunt Man, Lord Jim,   High Spirits,
Good-bye Mr. Chips, Lawrence of Arabia, The Ruling Class)
Oakie, Jack (actor--The Great Dictator)

Oates, John (singer--Hall & Oates--Rich Girl, She's Gone)
Oates, Joyce Carol (author--Wonderland, Them, Bellefleur, Black Water, Tatooed Girl, Grave Digger's Daughter, Cybele, Solstice, The Profane Art, A Garden of Earthly Delights)
Oates, Titus (Titus the Liar) (perjurer--Popish Plot)
Oates, Warren (actor--Bring Me the Head of Alfredo Garcia)
Obama, Barack (No Drama) (politician/author--Dreams from My Father)
Obama, Malia (Barack's daughter)
Obama, Michelle La Vaughn Robinson (lawyer) (Barack's wife)
Obama, Sasha (Barack's daughter)
Obama, Stanley Ann (economic anthropologist) (Barack's mother)
Oberon, Merle (actor)
Obote, Milton (politician; Uganda) (Idi Amin's successor)
Ocasek, Ric (singer) (band--Cars)
Ocean, Billy (singer; Trinidad)
Ochoa, Lorena (golfer)
Ochoa, Severo (biochemist--R.N.A./nobelist; Sp. Am.)
Ochs, Adolph (newspaper publisher)
Ochs, Phil (activist/singer--Love Me I'm A Liberal, The War is Over, I Aint Marching Anymore)
Oculato, Cara (dancer--ballet)
Odets, Clifford (director/playwright--Golden Boy, Country Girl, Awake & Sing, Waiting for Lefty, Night Music, I Can't Sleep)
Odetta (singer--My Eyes Have Seen, Glory, Glory, Cool Water)
Odo, Rene (actress)
Odom, Johnny Lee (Blue Moon) (baseball)
Odom, Lamar (Candy Man) (basketball)
Odom, William Paul (Bill) (aviator)
Odomes, Nate (football)
Odoul, Francis (Lefty) (baseball)
Oersted, Hans Christian (physicist)
Oerter, Alfred A. (discus)

Offenbach, Jacques (musician--cellist/composer--Orpheus In the Underworld)
Ogle, Brent (golfer/sportscaster)
Ohm, Georg (physicist)
Ohno, Apolo Anton (speed skater)
OK Go (musical group)
Okada, Katsuya (politician; Jap.)
Okalik, Paul (politician; Nunavut, Can.)
Olajuwan, Akeem (basketball)
Oland, Ken (actor)
Oland, Warner (actor--Charlie Chan; Swede)
Olav II (The Stout) (King of Norway)
Olav V (King of Norway) (Harald V's father)
Olbermann, Keith (author/commentator--sports)
Oldenburg, Claes (sculptor)
Oldman, Gary (actor; Br.)
Olds, Ransom Eli (inventor--Oldsmobile)
Olerud, John (baseball)
Oles, Bull (violinist)
Olin, Ken (actor--Brothers and Sisters, Thirtysomething) (Patricia Wettig's husband)
Olin, Lena (actress--Chocolat, Havana, Romeo is Bleeding, Enemies; A Love Story)
Oliva, Tony (baseball)
Oliver, Edna May (actress)
Olivier, Laurence (Sir) (actor--Sleuth)
Olmedo, Alex (tennis)
Olmert, Ehud (politician; Isr.)
Olmos, Edward James (actor--Miami Vice, Stand and Deliver)
Olmsted, Frederick Law (architect/landscape designer--Central Park)
Olney, Richard (politician)
Olsen, Ashley (actress--New York Minute)
Olsen, Carl Gustav Sparre (composer/violinist)
Olsen, John Sigvard (Ole) (vaudevillian) (Harold Ogden John's partner)
Olsen, Mary Kate (actress--New York Minute)
Olsen, Merlin (football/announcer/actor)
Olsen, Ole (comedian/actor--Hellzapoppin)

Olsen, Ole (composer/conductor/military musician)
Olsen, Ole (motorcycle racer)
Olsen, Tillie (author--Tell Me a Riddle)
Olshansky, Igor (football)
Olshansky, Mike (actor--Hack)
Olson, Gregg (baseball--pitcher)
Olson, Johnny (announcer--The Price Is Right)
Olson, Nancy (actress--Pollyanna, Sunset Boulevard)
Olson, Theodore (politician)
Omar (a.k.a. Omar Khayyam) (The Astronomer-Poet of
Persia) (poet--A Book of Verses   Underneath the Bough,
Rubaiyat, A Jug of Wine) (translated by Edward Fitzgerald)
Omar (Taliban mullah)
Omarr, Sydney (astrologer)
Omeara, Mark (golfer)
Onassis, Jackie (singer)
Onate, Juan de (explorer; Sp.)
Ondaatje, Michael (author--The English Patient)
Ono, Yoko (artist--neo dada, Wish Tree, Double
Fantasy/musician--Walking on Thin Ice,   Yes I'm a
Witch, Don't Worry Kyoko)
Onsager, Lars (chemist/nobelist)
Oort, Jan (astronomer)
Ophuls, Max (actor--La Ronde)
Opie, Alan (singer--baritone)
Oppenheim, Edward Phillips (author--Slane)
Oppenheimer, J. Robert (scientist/inventor--A Bomb
(Hydrogen Bomb)
Opper, Burr (cartoonist--Happy Hooligan)
Optic, Oliver (William Taylor Adam's pseudonym)
(politician/author)
Ora, Rita (actress/singer--R.I.P.)
Orantes, Manuel (tennis)
Orbach, Jerry (actor--Law & Order)
Orbach, Susie (feminist)
Orbison, Roy (singer--Leah, Pretty Woman, It's Over) (K. D.
Lang's   duet partner--Crying)
Oreck, David (inventor--vacuum cleaner)
Oren, Daniel (conductor--opera)

Orendt, Hannah (political theorist)
Orff, Carl (composer--Carmina Burana, Antigonae)
Origen (theologian--Alexandria)
Orlar (murdered Peter III)
Orlean, Susan (author--The Orchid Thief)
Orlons (musical group--The Wah Watusi)
Orman, Suze (financial advisor)
Ormandy, Eugene (conductor)
Ormond, Julia (actress--Sabrina, The Curious Case of Benjamin Button)
Oronofsky, Darren (actor--Pi)
Orosco, Jesse (baseball)
Orozco, Jose Clemente (muralist--Prometheus, The Epic of American Civilization; Mex.)
Orr, Ben (singer--The Cars)
Orr, Christopher (film critic)
Orr, John Boyd (Lord) (teacher/doctor/biologist/politician)
Orr, Louis (basketball)
Orr, Marion (aviator)
Orr, Robert Gordon (Bobby) (hockey)
Orser, Brian (skater)
Orta, Jorge (Jorge Orta Nunez) (baseball)
Ortega, Daniel (politician--Sandinista leader; Nic.)
Ortiz, Ana (actress--Ugly Betty)
Ortiz, Carlos (boxer)
Orton, Joe (playwright--Loot, Entertaining Mr. Sloane, What the Butler Saw)
Orwell, George (Eric Arthur Blair's pseudonym) (author--Animal Farm, 1984)
Osborn, Paul (playwright--Luther, On Borrowed Time)
Osborne, Joan (singer--One of Us)
Osborne, John James (playwright--Tom Jones, Paper Chase, Look Back in Anger)
Osbourne, Ozzy (musician/singer/songwriter) (Sharon's husband)
Osbourne, Sharon (music manager/suthor/T.V. personality--The Talk) (Ozzie's wife)
Osceola la.k.a. Billy Powell) (Native Chief--Seminole)
Ose, Patrick (musician--hip hop)

Osgood, Charles (newscaster--Kuralt's successor)
Osler, William (Sir) (physician/author--The Principles and Practice of Medicine)
Oslin, K. T. (singer--country--80's Lady)
Osman/Othman (emperor--Ottoman Dynasty founder) (Ertugrul's son)
Osment, Haley Joel (actor--The Sixth Sense)
Osmond, Donny (actor/singer--Hey Girl)
Osmond, Marie (singer/actress/talk show hostess)
Osmond, Rigdon Dees III (Rick) (comedian/actor/T.V. personality/voice artist)
Ossian/Ossin (poet; Gaelic)
Osteen, Joel (televangelist)
Osterberg, James Newell (stage name--Iggy Pop) (singer/songwriter/actor)
Ostertag, Greg (basketball)
Oswald, Lee Harvey (assassin--J. F. K.)
Oteri, Cheri (actress)
Oteri, Willie (singer/songwriter/musician--guitarist)
Otescu, Ion Nonna (composer; Rom.)
Othman/Osman (emperor--Ottoman Dynasty founder)
Otho (H. R. Emperor, Nero-Galba-Otho)
Otis, Amos (baseball)
Otis, Carre (model)
Otis, Elisha Graves (inventor--elevator; Am.)
Otis, Harrison Gray (publisher)
Otis, James (orator--revolutionary)
Otis, William S. (inventor--steam shovel; Am.)
Otto I (Italian Emperor)
Otto II (Red/Rufus) (Holy Roman Emperor)
Otto the Great (King of Germany)
Otto, Kristin (swimmer)
Otto, Miranda (actress--Homeland)
Otway, Thomas (playwright--Venus Preserved)
Oudin, Melanie (tennis)
Ouida (Marie Louise de la Ramee's pseudonym) (author--A Dog of Flanders)
Outkast (musical group--Hey Ya)
Ovett, Steve (track athlete)

Ovid, (nee Ovidius Publius Naso) (poet - Ars Amatoria, Heroides, The Art of Love, Amores,   Tristia)
Ovitz, Michael (talent agent/Disney president)
Owen, Chris (photographer/actor--American Pie)
Owen, Wilfred (poet)
Owens, Alvis Edgar (Buck) (singer--Tall Dark Stranger)
Owens, Gary (announcer--Laugh In)
Owens, Jesse (track--olympian)
Oz, Amos (author--A Tale of Love and Darkness, In the Land of Israel, My Michael)
Oz, Frank (actor--Yoda)
Ozawa, Seiji (conductor)
Ozick, Cynthia (author)

--P--

Paar, Jack (T. V. personality/author--I Kid You Not)
Pabst, Frederick (brewer)
Pabst, Georg Wilhelm (director--Three Penny Opera)
Pachelbel, Johann (composer--Canon in D Major)
Pacino, Al (actor--Sea of Love, Me Natalie/director--Looking for Richard)
Pacquiao, Emmanuel Dapidran (Manny) (boxer)
Paderewski, Ignace (producer)
Paer, Ferdinando (composer--opera/oratorios)
Paganini, Niccolo (composer--24 Caprices for Solo Violin/violinist)
Page, Bettie (model--pin-up)
Page, Ellen (actress--Juno)
Page, Geraldine (actress--Toys in the Attic)
Page, Oran (Hot Lips) (musician--trumpet)
Page, Patricia Kathleen (poet)
Page, Patti (nee Clara Ann Fowler) (singer--Tennessee Waltz)
Page, Thomas Nelson (author--In Ole Virginia, Marse Chan)
Paget, Debra (actress)
Pahlavi, Mohammad Reza (politician--Shah; Iran)
Paige, Elaine (actress/singer--Evita)

Paige, Janis (actress)
Paige, Leroy (Satchel) (baseball/author--Maybe I'll Pitch Forever)
Paige, Rod (politician)
Paine, Albert Begelow (author--Twain's autobiography)
Paine, Thomas (author--Common Sense, Age of Reason, The Rights of Man, The Crisis)
Paisley, Ian (politician-N. Ir.)
Pak, Seri (golfer)
Pakula, Alan (writer/producer/director--All the President's Men)
Palestrina, Giovanni (composer--motet)
Paley, Babe (socialite)
Palin, Bristol (public speaker/reality T.V. personality) (Todd & Sarah's daughter)
Palin, Michael (author/actor--Hemingway's Chair, Monty Python)
Palin, Sarah (politician/author--Going Rogue, America By Heart) (Todd's wife)
Palin, Todd (oil field manager) (Sarah's husband)
Palladio, Andrea (architect)
Palme, Olof (politician; Swed.)
Palmer, Arnold (The King) (golfer)
Palmer, Betsy (actress/T.V. personality--I've Got a Secret)
Palmer, Jim (baseball)
Palmer, Lilli (actress)
Palmer, Peter (actor--L'il Abner)
Paltrow, Gwyneth (actress/ Blythe Danner's daughter)
Panetta, Leon (lawyer/politician--C.I.A. director)
Pankhurst, Sylvia (suffragette)
Pankow, Ira (actor--Mad About You)
Panov, Valery (dancer)
Paolantonio, Sal (newsman--sports)
Paoli, Pasquale (patriot; Corsican)
Paolini, Christopher (author--Eragon)
Paolozzi, Eduardo (sculptor)
Papas, Irene (actress)
Paper Lace (musical group--The Night Chicago Died)
Papini, Giovanna (author--Storia di Cristo)

Papp, Joseph (actor/ producer--Hair, Chorus Line) (founder of N. Y. Public Theater)
Pappas, Ike (nee Icarus Nestor Pappas) (newsman)
Paquin, Anna (actress--True Blood)
Pardo, Don (announcer--S.N.L.)
Pardue, Kip (actor)
Parent, Gail (author)
Parenti, Noel (mime-dancer)
Pareto, Vilredo (author--Mind and Society)
Paretsky, Sara (author)
Parish, Mitchell (singer--country--Stars Fell on Alabama)
Park, Merle (Dame) (teacher/dancer--ballet)
Parker, Alan (director--Evita)
Parker, Bonnie (criminal--Bonnie & Clyde Barrow)
Parker, Brant (cartoonist--Wizard of Id)
Parker, Charlie (Bird) (musician)
Parker, Clarence McKay (Ace) (football)
Parker, Cleo (dancer--Robinson Dance Ensemble)
Parker, Dorothy (author--mystery)
Parker, Eleanor (actress)
Parker, Evan (saxophonist)
Parker, Fess (actor--Davy Crockett)
Parker, Molly (actress)
Parker, Nicole Ari (actress)
Parker, Posey (actress)
Parker, Robert (wine critic)
Parseghian, Ara (football)
Parsons, Estelle (actress)
Parsons, Jim (actor--Big Bang Theory)
Parsons, Louella (gossip columnist)
Part, Arvo (composer)
Partch, Virgil (cartoonist)
Parton, Dolly (actress/singer--Here You Come Again)
Partridge, Eric (lexicographer--slang--The World of Words)
Pascal, Blaise (mathematician/inventor--calculator; Fr.)
Pasdar, Adrian (actor--Near Dark)
Pasha, Mustapha Kemal (Father of the Turks) (politician; First President of Turkey)

Pasolini, Pier Paolo (author/poet/director--Salo, Canterbury Tales)
Pasquale, Don (singer--basso)
Pasternak, Boris (author--Dr. Zhivago)
Pastore, John Orlando (politician)
Pataky, Elsa (model/actress)
Patavinus, Titus (Livy) (historian; Roman)
Patchett, Ann (author--Bel Canto, Run)
Patel, Dev (actor--The Best Exotic Marigold Hotel, Lion)
Pater, Erra (astrologer)
Pater, Walter (author--Marius the Epicurian)
Pathe, Warner (publisher--newsreels)
Patinkin, Mandy (actor--Chicago Hope)
Paton, Alan (author--Too Late the Phalarope)
Patri, Angelo (educator/author)
Patric, Jason (actor--The Alamo)
Patricia Wettig (actress) (Ken Olin's wife)
Patrick, Dan (nee Dan Patrick Pugh) (sportscaster/radio personality, actor)
Patterson, Lorna (actress)
Patterson, Neva (actress)
Patti, Adelina (singer--soprano)
Pattinson, Robert (actor--Twilight)
Patton, George (Gen.) (Old Guts & Glory/Old Man)
Paul, Alice (suffragette)
Paul, Christi (newsperson)
Paul, Les (quitarist/bandleader)
Paul, Ronald Ernest (Ron) (physician/author/politician--small gov't)
Paul, Sean (rapper)
Pauli, Wolfgang (physicist/nobelist)
Pauling, Linus (actor)
Paulsen, Axel (skater)
Paup, Bryce (football)
Pavan, Marisa (actress)
Pavarotti, Luciano (singer--opera--O Sole Mio)
Pavlov, Ivan (scientist)
Pavlova, Anna (dancer--ballet--Swan Lake)
Payne, Freda (actress/singer--Band of Gold)

Payne, John (actor--Miracle on 34th Street/poet/playwright/author--Home, Sweet Home)
Payne, John Howard (author--Home, Sweet Home)
Paz, Octavio (poet--A Hernating Current)
Peaches & Herb (musical group)
Peale, Charles (soldier/scientist/inventor/naturalist/painter--American Rev. portraits)
Peale, Norman Vincent (author--The Power of Positive Thinking)
Peale, Rembrandt (museum keeper/painter--portraits)
Pearce, Alice (actress--Bewitched)
Pearce, Edward Lovett (architect)
Pearce, Guy (actor--Factory Girl)
Pearl Jam (musical group--Ten)
Pearlroth, Norbert (linguist/researcher--Ripley's Believe It Or Not cartoon)
Pearson, Drew (columnist--Washington Merry-go-round)
Pearson, Lester Bowles (politician; Can.)
Peart, Neil (musician--drummer) (band--Rush)
Peary, Robert Edwin (explorer--Arctic)
Peck, Gregory (actor--Moby Dick)
Peel, Emma (actress)
Peel, Robert (Sir) (politician)
Peele, George (translator/poet/playwright--Old Wives Tales)
Peele, Jordan (director--Get Out)
Peeples, Nia (actress)
Peer Gynt's mother (Ase)
Peerce, Jan (singer--opera tenor)
Peet, Amanda (actress--Jack and Jill, Syriana, 2012, Togetherness)
Peete, Calvin (golfer)
Peete, Rodney (football)
Pegg, Simon (comedian/screenwriter/producer/actor--Mission Impossible)
Pei, Ieoh Ming (architect--Louvre Pyramid, R.&R. Hall of Fame, John Hancock Building, Bank of China; Chin.-Am.)
Pei, Mario (linguist)

Pele (nee Edson Arantes do Nascimento) (O Rei do Futebol)
(soccer)
Pell, John (politician)
Pelletier, David (skater)
Pelli, Cesar (architect)
Pelosi, Nancy (politician--Speaker of the House) (Dennis
Hastert's/Ryan's successor/
        Boehner's predecessor)
Pelton, Lestor (inventor--water wheel)
Pemmaraju, Uma (newscaster)
Pena, Alejandro (baseball)
Pena, Federico (politician)
Pena, Tony (baseball)
Pendergrass, Teddy (singer)
Pendleton, Nat (actor)
Peniston, Cece (singer)
Penkovshy, Oleg (spy)
Penn, Christopher (actor)
Penn, Kal (producer/actor--Van Wilder, Harold & Kumar)
Penn, Sean (actor--Dead Man Walking, The Weight of Water,
I Am Sam, Milk)
Pennington, Janice (model--Price is Right)
Pennington, Ty (decorator--Trading Spaces)
Peno, Elizabeth (actress--La Bamba)
Penrose, Roger (scientist--astronomy--black holes)
Penske, Roger (racecar driver)
Penzias, Arno (physicist)
Pep, Willie (boxer)
Pepin the Short (King of the Franks) (Charlemagne's father)
Pepper, Claude (politician)
Pepys, Samuel (diarist--Great Fire of London)
Percy, Walker (author--Love in the Ruins)
Perec, Georges (poet/author/essayist/dramatist--Life: A
User's Manual)
Perelman, Ron (businessman)
Perelman, Simeon/Sidney Joseph (S.J.)
(humorist/screenwriter/author--   The
Road to Miltown, Aches and Pains)
Perelman, Yakov (author; Rus.)

Peres, Shimon (politician--former P. M. of Israel)
Peretti, Elsa (jewelry designer)
Peretti, Frank (author--The Oath)
Peretz, Amir (politician; Isr.)
Perez, Rosie (actress)
Perez, Tom (lawyer/politician--Democratic National Committee)
Pergolesi, Giovanni Battista (musician--violin, organ/composer--La Serva Padrona)
Pericles (statesman) (opponent--Cleon)
Perino, Dana (Press Secretary/political commentator/author)
Perkins, Anthony (actor)
Perkins, Carl (singer/songwriter--country--Stars Fell on Alabama, Blue Suede Shoes)
Perkins, Maxwell (editor)
Perkins, Osgood (actor/writer/director)
Perle, George (composer)
Perlman, Itzhak (violinist)
Perlman, Rhea (actress--Cheers)
Perlman, Ron (actor--Hellboy)
Peron, Eva (politician; Arentina) (Juan's wife)
Peron, Juan (politician--Descamisados leader) (Eva's husband)
Perot, Henry Ross (politician--Reform Party founder/United We Stand America/ businessman--EDS/author--Citizen Perot)
Perrault, Charles (author--Puss in Boots)
Perry, Katy (singer--One of the Boys, Part of Me, Roar)
Perry, Luke (actor)
Perry, Matthew (actor)
Perry, Matthew Calbraith (Commodore)
Perry, Oliver Hazard (Admiral--Battle of Lake Erie)
Perry, Steve (singer--She's Mine)
Perry, Tyler (author--Diary of a Mad Black Woman (Madea))
Perse, St. John (Alex Legis's pseudonym) (diplomat/poet/nobelist; Fr.)
Pershing, John Joseph (Gen.--W.W.I)
Persson, Essy (actress; Swed.)
Pesci, Joe (actor--My Cousin Vinny, Home Alone, Casino)

Peshkov, Aleksei (pseudonym--Maxim Gorki) (author)
Pet Shop Boys (musical group--It's a Sin)
Petain, Henri Philippe (General--Vichy Marshal)
Peter & Gordon (musical duo--I Go To Pieces, Nobody I Know)
Peter II (politician; King of Yugoslavia)
Peter, Nora (pianist)
Peter, Paul & Mary (musical group--Day is Done)
Peters, Bernadette (singer/actress)
Peters, Jean (actress)
Peters, Mike (cartoonist--Mother Goose, Grimm)
Peters, Roberta (singer)
Petersen, Paul (singer--My Dad)
Petersen, William (actor--C. S. I.)
Petersen, Wolfgang (director--Perfect Storm)
Peterson, Adrian (football)
Peterson, Oscar (pianist--jazz)
Petina, Irra (actress/singer)
Petraeus, David (C.I.A. director)
Petrarch (poet--sonnets)
Petri Jr., William (microbiologist/pathologist--petri dish)
Petri, Elio (director)
Petri, Julius (bacteriologist)
Petrie, Anne (writer/broadcaster--C. B. C.)
Petrocelli, Rico (baseball)
Petrosian, Tigran Vartanovich (chess master)
Petrova, Nadia (tennis)
Petrova, Olga (actress)
Petty, Dini (talkshow host)
Petty, Kyle (racecar driver)
Petty, Lori (actress--A League of Their Own, Tank Girl)
Petty, Tom (singer--Free Fallin)
Pfeiffer, Dedee (actress--Cybill)
Pflug, Joann (actress)
Phair, Liz (singer)
Phelps, Michael (swimmer)
Phelps, Richard Frederick (Digger) (basketball--Notre Dame)
Phidias (architect/painter/sculptor--Statue of Zeus)
Philbin, Regis (T. V. personality)

Philby, Kim (spy)
Philip IV (Le Bel) (King of France 1294-1328)
Philips, Emo (comedian)
Phillip, Andy (Handy Andy) (basketball)
Phillippe, Ryan (actor--Crash)
Phillips, Irna (actress/writer--soap opera)
Phillips, Lou Diamond (actor)
Phillips, Pauline (pseudonym--Abigail Van Buren) (Dear Abby) (advice columnist)
Phillips, Sian (actor--I Claudius)
Phillpotts, Eden (author--The Gray Room)
Phish (musical group--Junta)
Phiz (Hablot Knight Browne's pseudonym) (illustrator--Charles Dickens)
Phoenix, Joaquin (producer/musician/actor--Her)
Phyfe, Duncan (furniture maker)
Piaf, Edith (Little Sparrow) (actress/singer-songwriter--La Vie En Rose, Non, Je Ne Regrette Rien)
Piaget, Jean (psychologist)
Piao, Lin (politician--Mao contemporary)
Piast, Mieszko I (politician/dynasty member; Pol.)
Piatigorsky, Gregor (musician--cello)
Piazza, Marguerite (diva)
Piazza, Mike (baseball)
Picasso, Pablo Ruiz (artist--Woman with a Crow, Ma Jolie, She-goat, Mandolin and Guitar, Three Musicians, Les Demoiselles d'Avignon, Dona Maar Seated, Dora Maar Seated, Guernica) (Dora Maar's lover)
Picasso, Paloma (fashion designer)
Pickens, Thomas Boone (oil tycoon/author--The First Billion Is the Hardest)
Pickett, George Edward (Civil War--led Gettysberg charge)
Pickett, Wilson (singer--Mustang Sally)
Pickford, Mary (producer/actress)
Picon, Molly (actress)
Picone, Evan (fashion designer)
Pidgeon, Walter (actor--How Green Was My Valley, Mrs. Miniver)
Pierce, Paul (basketball)

Pierce, Ronald (pseudonym--Ron Ely) (actor--Tarzan)
Piercy, Marge (poet)
Piers, Anthony (author--sci.-fi.)
Pierson Kate (singer--B 52)
Pierson, Frank (director--A Star is Born)
Pike, Zebulon (explorer--Pike's Peak)
Pincay, Laffit Alejandro (jockey)
Pindar (poet--odist) (muse--Erato)
Pine, Chris (actor--Star Trek)
Pinel, Philippe (physician/psychologist--mental illness/moral therapy)
Pinero, Arthur Wing (Sir) (actor/playwright--Mrs. Tanqueray)
Pinkerton, Allan (detective--Lincoln era; Am.)
Pinkett, Jada (actress)
Pinkham, Lydia Estes (businesswoman; Am.)
Pinsent, Leah (actress)
Pinter, Harold (playwright--The Birthday Party)
Pinza, Ezio (singer--opera--South Pacific)
Pinzon, Martin (Captain of the Pinta)
Pioline, Cedric (tennis)
Pious XI (nee Ratti) (Pope)
Pippig, Uta (marathoner)
Pirandello, Luigi (playwright--Six Characters in Search of an Author (Sei Personaggi))
Pirsig, Robert M. (author--Lila)
Pisano, Giovanni (sculptor)
Pisano, Nicola (sculptor)
Piscopo, Joe (actor--S.N.L.)
Pissarro, Camille (painter)
Pitcher, Molly (Mary Hays McCauly's nickname) (activist--American Revolution)
Pitino, Rick (basketball)
Pitman, Isaac (inventor--shorthand)
Pitney, Arthur (software-hardware manufacturer/packaging-mailing provider)   (Walter Bowes partner)
Pitt the Elder, William (The Great Commoner) (politician)
Pitt, Brad (actor--Se7en/Seven)
Pitt, Michael (actor)

Pitts, Zasu (actress)
Pizarro, Francisco (explorer--Lima founder)
Pizzey, Erin (activist--battered women)
Planck, Max (physicist--Quantum Theory)
Plastic (Ono Band)
Plath, Sylvia (poet--Ariel/author--The Bell Jar, Dying is an Art, Ariel)
Plato (philosopher--Academy founder/author--Phaedo, Ion) (Aristotle's teacher)
Platt, Oliver (actor--West Wing, Frost/Nixon)
Platters (musical group--Only You)
Plessis, Louise (composer; S. Afr.)
Pliny (author--Natural History)
Plishka, Paul (singer--basso)
Plumb, Eve (actress--Brady Bunch)
Plummer, Amanda (actress--Agnes of God)
Plummer, Christopher (actor--Cyrano)
Plutarch (author/biographer/moralist--Parallel Lives)
Po, Li (Li Bai) (poet--Tang Dynasty)
Pocahantas (John Rolfe's wife)
Pocklington, Peter (entrepreneur)
Poe, Edgar Allan (poet/author--Gold Bug, Lenore, The Black Cat, The Oblong Box,   The Bells, Ulalume, The Mystery of Marie Roget, To One in Paradise, Memories of Eld, Eldorado, The Premature Burial, To Helen, Al Aaraaf, The Telltale Heart,   The Fall of the House of Usher, Arthur Gordon Pim, Hop-Frog, Israfel, For Annie   Annabel Lee) (John & Frances Allan's adopted son)
Poehler, Amy (comedian)
Pohl, Frederik (author--sci-fi--Black Star Rising)
Pointer Sisters (musical group--I'm So Excited, Neutron Dance)
Pointer, Anita (singer--Pointer Sisters)
Pointer, Bonnie (singer--Pointer Sisters)
Pointer, June (singer--Pointer Sisters)
Pointer, Ruth (singer--Pointer Sisters)
Poitier, Sidney (actor--Mr. Tibbs, Raisin in the Sun) (autobiography--This Life)

Polanski, Roman (director--Tess, The Tenant)
Police (musical group--Roxanne, Every Breath You Take)
(Sting's band)
Polk, James Knox (politician)
Pollack, Sydney (director--Tootsie)
Pollaiuolo, Antonio Del (painter/sculptor/engraver/goldsmith)
(L. Medici's protégé)
Pollard, Michael J. (actor--C. W. Moss in Bonnie & Clyde)
Pollock, Sharon (playwright)
Polo, Marco (explorer/author--Description of the World)
Polo, Theresa Elizabeth (Teri) (actress--Meet the Parents,
Meet the Fockers, The Fosters)
Polyclitus (sculptor--Hera)
Pompeo, Ellen (actress--Gray's Anatomy)
Ponce de Leon, Juan (explorer)
Ponchielli, Amilcare (composer--Cielo e Mar)
Pong, John Rodger (singer--tenor--Turandot)
Pons, Lily (diva--soprano)
Ponselle, Rosa (diva)
Ponti, Carlo (producer) (Sophia Loren's husband)
Pontiac (Native Chief--Ottawa Tribe)
Ponty, Jean Luc (violinist)
Poole, John (playwright--Paul Pry)
Poore, Henry Rankin (painter)
Poortvliet, Rien (painter)
Pope John Paul II (nee Karol Wojtyla)
Pope John XXIII (nee Angelo Giuseppe Roncalli)
Pope Leo X (nee Medici)
Pope Paul (Karol Wojtyla)
Pope Paul II (Sixtus IV predecessor)
Pope Paul VI (author--Ecclessiam Saum)
Pope Pious XI (nee Ratti)
Pope St. Leo I (St. Leo the Great) (negotiated with Attila)
Pope, Alexander (poet--Windsor Forest, Dunciad, Essay on
Man, The Rape of the Lock, Ode On
        Solidtude/translator--Homer--The Iliad)

Popeil, Ron (gadgeteer)

Poquelin, Jean-Baptiste (stage name--Moliere) (actor/dramatist--Don Juan, L'Ecole Des Maris, The Miser, School for Women, Tartuffe, La Misanthrope)
Porfirio, Diaz (director)
Porsena, Lars (Etruscan King)
Porter, Cole (songwriter--Bingo Eli Yale, You Don't Know Paree, I Am Loved, Rosalie, From This Moment On, I Hate Men, Well Did You Evah, Kate, I Love Paris, Let's Do It, Can Can, You're the Top, Be A Clown, DuBarry Was A Lady, So In Love, You've Got That Thing, Katie Went to Haiti, Mexican Hay Ride, Abracadabra, My Heart Belongs to Daddy, Leave It To Me, Born to Dance, Kiss Me Kate, Love for Sale, Gaky Divorce)
Porter, Katherine Anne (author)
Porter, Ross (T. V. personality--C.B.C.)
Porter, William Sydney (pseudonym--O. Henry) (author--short stories/ironic--The Ransom of Red Chief)
Portman, Eric (actor)
Portman, Natalie (actress)
Posey, Buster (baseball)
Post, Charles William (food manufacturer)
Post, Emily (author--etiquette)
Post, Wiley (aviator)
Potok, Chaim (author--My Name is Asher Lev, The Chosen)
Potter, Helen Beatrix (illustrator/natural scientist/conservationist/author--The Tale of Peter Rabbit, Tale of Jemima Puddle-Duck)
Potter, Ned (newsman)
Potter, Stewart (justice--Supreme Court)
Potts, Annie (actress--Young Sheldon, Toy Story (Bo Peep))
Potvin, Denis (hockey)
Poulter, Ian (golfer)
Pound, Ezra Loomis (poet--Noh poetry/imagist--Pisan Cantos; Am.)
Pounder, Carol Christine Hilaria (C.C.H.) (actress--Avatar)
Pounder, Tylo (actor)
Poundstone, Paula (comedian)

Poussin, Nicholas (painter)
Povich, Maury (T. V. personality--A Current Affair)
Powell, Adam Clayton (Jr.) (politician)
Powell, Billy (a.k.a. Osceola) (Native leader--Seminole)
Powell, Colin (Gen.) (Shalikashvili's predecessor)
Powell, William (actor--The Thin Man--Nick Charles)
Power, Tyrone (actor)
Powhatan (Native chief)
Pratt, Edwin John (poet)
Pratt, Mary (painter)
Pratt, William Henry (a.k.a. Boris Karloff) (actor--The Mummy,
The Ape)
Praxiteles (Hermes of) (sculptor--Enos; Gr.)
Preminger, Otto (director--Laura; Am.)
Prentiss, Paula (actress)
Presley, Elvis Aron (musician/singer--Are You Lonesome
Tonight, Don't, Surrender, One   Broken Heart
For Sale, Feel So Bad, If I Can Dream, All That I Am/actor--
Kissin   Cousins)
Pressly, Jaime (actress)
Preston, Kelly (actress)
Preston, Robert (actor--Music Man)
Preval, Rene (politician; Haiti)
Previn, Andre (composer) (Soon Yi's stepfather)
Prevost, Antoine Francois (Abbe) (author)
Priam (King of Troy)
Price, Leontyne (diva--Tosca, Aida)
Price, Ray (singer--country)
Price, T. Rowe (entrepreneur--investment)
Price, Vincent (actor)
Pride, Charley (musician/singer--Is Anybody Goin to San
Antone, Kiss An Angel Good   Mornin)
Priest, Ivy (politician/activist)
Priestley, Jason (actor--Beverly Hills 90210, Bare Naked in
America)
Prima, Louis (actor/songwriter/singer/musician--
trumpeter/bandleader--jazz)
Prince (singer--Raspberry Beret, Let's Go Crazy, Purple Rain)
Prince, Hal (actor)

Principal, Victoria (nee Vicki Ree)
(producer/entrepreneur/author/actress--Dallas)
Prine, John (singer--Bruised Orange)
Pringle, Aileen (actress)
Prinze, Freddie (comedian)
Prior, Matthew (diplomat/poet)
Privalova, Irina (athlete--hurdler)
Probst, Jeff (T.V. personality--Survivor host)
Proft, Pat (comedy writer)
Prokofiev, Sergei (composer--War Sonatas)
Promo, Levi (author)
Prosperi, Franco (filmmaker--Mondo Cane)
Prost, Alain (race car driver)
Protopopov, Oleg (figure skater)
Proust, Marcel (author--Budding Grove, Swann's Way, A La
Recherche Du Temps Perdu   (In Search of
Lost Time), Remembrance of Things Past--Seve)
Prout, Ebenezer (musician/composer)
Prowse, Juliet (dancer)
Prudhomme, Paul (chef)
Pryce, Jonathan (actor)
Pryor, Richard (comedian/actor--The Toy, Dynamite Chicken)
Psy (musician--Gangnam style)
Pucci, Emilio (fashion designer)
Puccini, Giacomo (composer--Vissi d' Arte, Manon Lescaut,
Nessun Dorma, Turandot,   Tosca--Recondita
Armonia) (heroine--Mimi)
Puente, Tito (bandleader/musician--timbales)
Pugh, Dan Patrick (sportscaster/radio personality/actor)
Puig, Manuel (author)
Puig, Yasiel (baseball)
Pulaski, Casimir/Kazimierz (patriot; Pol.)
Pulp (musical group--His 'n Hers)
Purcell, Henry (composer--Dido and Aeneas, Odes and
Welcome Songs)
Purl, Linda (actress)
Purviance, Edna (actress)
Pushkin, Alexander (Aleksandr) (Russian Byron) (poet--
Eugene Onegin)

Pussy Riot (musical group; Rus.)
Putin, Vladimir (politician; Rus.)
Putnam Isreal (Amer. Rev. General)
Putnam, Amelia Earhart (aviator)
Putnam, George Palmer (publisher)
Putnam, Rufus (soldier/pioneer)
Puzo, Mario (author--The Last Don, Omerta, Superman,
Mafia)
Pye, Henry James (poet--Alfred)
Pyle, Denver (actor)
Pyle, Ernie (journalist--Brave Men, Here Is Your War) .
Pyle, Howard (author--Men of Iron)
Pyle, Missy (actress)
Pym, Barbara (author)

--Q--

Qing, Jiang/Chiang Ching (actress) (Mao's wife)
Quadaffi, Muammar el (politician; Libya)
Quaid, Dennis (actor--D.O.A., The Rookie)
Quaid, Randy (actor)
Quant, Mary (fashion designer--Mod)
Quattro (musical group--If You Knew Suzy)
Queeg, Philip Francis (Capt.) (character--Caine Mutiny)
Queen (musical group--Seven Seas of Rhye)
Queen, Ellery (Frederic Dannay & Manfred B. Lee's
pseudonym) (author--mystery)
Queenan, Joe (author)
Queler, Eve (conductor)
Quentin, Crisp (author/cartoonist)
Questel, Mae (actress/vocal artist--Betty Boop)
Quilico, Louis (singer--opera)
Quindlen, Anna (author--One True Thing)
Quinn, Aidan (actor)
Quinn, Aileen (actress--Annie)
Quinn, Anthony (actor--Zorba)
Quinn, Colin (actor--S. N. L.)

Quinn, Gillian (Aidan's daughter)
Quisenberry, Dan (baseball)
Quivers, Robin (author/actress/radio personality)

--R--

R. E. M. (musical group--Man On The Moon, Stand, The One I
Love, Monster, Everybody   Hurts, New
Adventures in Hi-fi, Shining Happy People)
Ra, Sun (born Le Sony'r Ra) (Herman Poole Blount's
pseudonym) (composer)
Raab, Dominic Rennie (politician; Br.)
Raab, Julius (politician; Austria)
Rabanne, Paco (fashion designer)
Rabbitt, Eddie (singer--You and I, Every Which Way But
Loose)
Rabe, David (playwright--Hurlyburly, Streamers, In the Boom
Boom Room)
Rabelais, Francois (author--Pantagruel)
Rabi, Isidor (physicist/nobelist)
Rabin, Leah (activist) (Yitzhak's wife)
Rabin, Yitzhak (politician; Isr.)
Race, Eloi (actor--Time Machine)
Rachins, Alan (actor)
Rachmaninov, Sergei Vassilievich (composer--Etudes
Tableau(x), The Lilacs)
Racine, Jean (John) Baptiste (playwright--Britannicus,
Phaedre, Athalie)
Radclif, Ann (author--gothic)
Rademacher, Ingo (actor)
Rader, Dotson (author)
Radner, Gilda (comedian--Baba Wawa)
Radnor, Josh (actor--How I Met Your Mother)
Rado, James (lyricist--Hair)
Rae, Bob (politician; Can.)
Rae, Charlotte (actress--Facts of Life)
Rae, Chris (singer)

Rae, Corinne Bailey (singer)
Rae, Issa/Jo-Issa (actress/author--Misadventures of Awkward Black Girl/director/   producer/web series creator--Insecure)
Rae, John (explorer--Sc.)
Raeder, Erich (naval officer--W.W. II)
Raeside, Adrian (cartoonist--The Coast)
Raffi (singer--children)
Rahal, Bobby (racecar driver)
Rahman, Omar Abdel (politician--Sheik) (Islamic extremist)
Rai, Aishwarya (actress--Bollywood)
Raimi, Sam (actor/director--Spiderman/producer--The Evil Dead)
Rainer, Luise (actress--The Good Earth; Austrian)
Raines, Ella (actress--Phantom Lady, Hail the Conquering Hero)
Raines, Tim (baseball)
Rainey, Ma (singer--blues)
Rainier (family name--Grimaldi) (Prince of Monaco)
Rains, William Claude (actor--Four Daughters)
Raisa, Rosa (singer--opera--soprano)
Raisman, Aly (gymnast)
Raitt, Bonnie (singer--I Can't Make You Love Me, The Luck of the Draw, Nick of Time,   Something to Talk About)
Raitt, John (actor/singer)
Raji, Busari (B.J.) (football)
Rall, Ted (cartoonist--political)
Ralo (nee Terrell Davis) (singer--Can't Lie)
Ralston, Dennis (tennis)
Ralston, Esther (actress)
Ralston, Vera (actress)
Rameau, Jean-Philippi (composer--Les Indes Galantes)
Ramirez, Marisa (actress--General Hospital)
Ramirez, Raul (tennis)
Ramis, Harold (director/actor--Ghost Busters, Stripes)
Ramon, Razor (wrestler)
Ramone, Dee Dee (musician--bassist)
Ramones (musical group--I Wanna Be Sedated)

Rampal, Jean-Pierre (musician--flute)
Ramsay, Gordon (chef/T.V. personality)
Ramses I (Pharoah) (King of Karnak) (successor--Seti, Exodus pharoah)
Ramsey Lewis Trio (musical group)
Ramsey, Hec (actor)
Rand, Ayn (politician--libertarian/objectivist/author--Fountainhead, Anthem, We the Living)
Rand, Sally (Helen Gould Beck's stage name) (actress--Fandango/dancer--fan; Am.)
Randall, Ethan (a.k.a. Ethan Embry) (actor)
Randall, Tony (actor--Odd Couple, Dr. Lao)
Randi, James (The Amazing Randi) (magician)
Rank, Otto (Dr.) (psychologist--Freud critic)
Rankin, Ian (author--Inspector Rebus)
Ransom, John Crowe (poet/author)
Rao, Pamulaparti Venkata Narashimha (India P. M.)
Rao, Raja (author--The Serpent and the Rope, Kanthapura)
Rapaport, Michael (actor--Poetic Justice)
Rapee, Erno (conductor)
Raphael, Raffello (artist--Triumph of Galatea)
Rashad, Ahmad (sportscaster)
Rashad, Phylicia (actress--Cosby Show, Creed)
Rashi (Jewish scholar)
Rask, Ramus Christian (philosopher/philologist; Dan.)
Raskin, Ellen (author--The Westing Game)
Raspe, Rudolf Erich (librarian/scientist/author--Baron Munchausen's Tales)
Rasputin, Grigori (Mad Monk) (mystic)
Rathbone, Basil (actor)
Ratt (musical group--Infestations)
Rattigan, Terence (playwright--Separate Tables)
Rau, Doug (baseball)
Rau, Johannes (politician; Ger.)
Rau, Santha Rama (author--This is India)
Raul, Julia (actress)
Ravel, Edeet (author--The Wall of Light)

Ravel, Maurice (composer--La Valse, Menuet Antique, Gaspard de la Nuit, Tzigane, Bolero,   Ma Mere L'Oye, L'Heure Espagnole)
Raver, Kim (actress--24)
Rawls, Lou (singer--Lady Love, Love is a Hurtin Thing)
Ray, Aldo (actor--Battle Cry)
Ray, Gene Anthony (actor--Fame)
Ray, Man (artist--dada--litho/photography)
Ray, Satyajit (author--The Apu Trilogy)
Rayburn, Gene (T. V. personality)
Rayburn, Sam (politician--L. B. J.'s mentor)
Raye, Collin (singer)
Raye, Martha (comedienne/actress--Pippin, Hellzapoppin)
Raymond, Alex (cartoonist--Flash Gordon)
Raymond, Jennie (actress--The Associates)
Raymond, Jim (cartoonist--Blondie)
Rea, Gardner (cartoonist)
Rea, Stephen (actor--Crying Game, End of the Affair, The Butcher Boy, Still Crazy, Bloom,   In Dreams, Interview With the Vampire)
Read, Piers Paul (author--Alive)
Reade, Charles (author--The Cloister & the Hearth, Peg Woffington, Griffith   Gaunt, Hard Cash; Br.)
Reagan, Nancy (actress) (Ronald's wife)
Reagan, Patricia (Patti) (actress/author) (Ronald & Nancy's daughter)
Reagan, Ronald (The Gipper/Dutch) (politician/author--An American Life/   T.V. host--Death Valley Days)
Reagle, Merl (crossword constructor)
Reali, Tony (T.V. sportscaster--Around the Horn)
Reaney, James (author--gothic--Donnelly Trilogy)
Rebozo, Charles (Bebe) (businessman) (Nixon's friend)
Red Hot Chili Peppers (musical group--Out in L.A.)
Red Jacket (Wolf clan chief/orator)
Redbone, Leon (musician/singer)
Redding, Otis (singer--soul)
Reddy, Helen (singer--Delta Dawn, Angie Baby, I Am Woman)

Redford, Robert (actor--A River Runs Through It, All is Lost, The Sting)
Redgrave, Corin (actor)
Redgrave, Lynn (actress)
Redgrave, Michael (Sir) (actor--The Captive Heart) (Rachel Kempson's husband)
Redgrave, Vanessa (actress--Agatha)
Redi, Francesco (physician/naturalist)
Redon, Odilon (painter--pre-surrealist; Fr.)
Reece, Gabrielle (volleyball/model)
Reed, Carol (director--Oliver, The Third Man)
Reed, Donna (actress)
Reed, Jerry (singer--Amos Moses)
Reed, Lou (songwriter/singer--Velvet Underground)
Reed, Oliver (actor)
Reed, Rex (critic)
Reed, Walter (Surgeon General)
Reed, Whitelaw (journalist)
Reel Big Fish (musical group--Sell Out)
Rees, Dee (director--Mudbound)
Rees, Jed (actor--Chris Isaac Show)
Rees, Martin (astronomer; Br.)
Rees, Roger (actor--Cheers, Nicholas Nickleby)
Reese, Della (actress/singer--Don't You Know)
Reese, Harold (Peewee) (Little Colonel) (baseball)
Reese, Harry (candy maker)
Reese, Lizette Woodworth (poet--Tears)
Reese, Sarah (singer--soprano)
Reeve, Christopher (actor--Somewhere in Time, The Bostonian/author--Still Me)
Reeves, Del (singer--country)
Reeves, George (actor--Gone with the Wind)
Reeves, Keanu (actor--The Matrix-Neo, John Wick)
Reeves, Rosser (advertising exec./author--Popo)
Reeves, Steve (actor--Hercules)
Regan, Donald T. (politician)
Rehan, Ada (actress)
Rehm, Diane (radio host--N.P.R.)

Rehnquist, William H. (justice--Supreme Court) (Burger's successor)
Reich, Wilhelm (psychoanalyst)
Reichl, Ruth (food writer)
Reid, Beryl (actress)
Reid, Bill (sculptor; Scot.-Haida)
Reid, Fiona (actress)
Reid, Forrest (author--Spring Song)
Reid, Harry (politician)
Reid, Kate (actress)
Reid, Ogden (politician)
Reid, Stephen (author/bankrobber; Can.)
Reid, Tara (actress--American Pie, The Big Lebowski)
Reid, Tim (actor--W.K.R.P. in Cincinnati)
Reid, Whitelaw (journalist)
Reifenstahl, Leni (filmmaker)
Reilly, Charles Nelson (comedian)
Reiner, Carl (actor/director)
Reiner, Fritz (conductor)
Reiner, Rob (actor/director--Stand By Me)
Reinking, Ann (actress/dancer--Pippin)
Reiser, Paul (actor--Mad About You)
Reiss, Winold (painter)
Reitman, Ivan (producer/director--Ghostbusters, Legal Eagles)
Rell, Jodi (politician)
Remarque, Erich Maria (author--Arch of Triumph, All Quiet on the Western Front)
Rembrandt (Rembrandt Harmenszoon Van Rijn) (painter--Lady with a Fan, Aristotle, The Rape of Ganymede, The Rape of Europa)
Remick, Lee (actress--Days of Wine and Roses)
Remington, Frederic (artist)
Remini, Leah (actress)
Remsen, Ira (chemist--discovered saccharin)
Renaldo, Duncan Renault (actor)
Renan, Joselph Ernest (philosopher/historian/author--La Vie de Jesus)
Renault, Louis (automaker)

Rendell, Ruth (Barbara Vine's pseudonym) (author--crime--Inspector Wexford, Kissing the Gunner's Daughter)
Renee, Jean Marie (dancer)
Reni, Guido (painter--Labors of Hercules, Massacre of the Innocents, Aurora, Mary Magdalene)
Renner, Jeremy (actor--North Country)
Rennie, Michael (actor--The Day the Earth Stood Still)
Reno, Janet (politician)
Reno, Jean (actress)
Reno, Jesse (General--Civil War)
Renoir, Jean (director--Elena)
Renoir, Pierre-Auguste (painter--La Loge, La Grenouillere, Dance in the Country, Musee de Orsay, Girl with a Hoop, The Umbrella, Dance at Bougival, The Bathers)
Repplier, Agnes (essayist)
Resnais, Alain (director)
Resnik, Judith (astronaut)
Resnik, Regina (singer--soprano)
Respighi, Ottorino (composer--The Pines of Rome)
Reston, James (journalist)
Retton, Mary Lou (gymnast)
Reuther, Walter (labour leader--U.A.W.)
Revere, Paul & the Raiders (musical group--Let Me)
Revere, Paul (patriot)
Rey, Alvino (Alvin McBurney's pseudonym) (bandleader--jazz)
Rey, Hans Augusto (HA) (author--Curious George)
Rey, Margret (author--Curious George)
Reyes, Alfonso (author/diplomat)
Reyes, Felipe (basketball)
Reyes, Judy (actress--Scrubs, Devious Maids)
Reynolds, Allie (baseball)
Reynolds, Burt (actor--Rent a Cop, Gator)
Reynolds, Debbie (film historian/businesswoman/humanitarian/singer/actress)
Reynolds, Joshua (Sir) (portrait artist)
Reynolds, Ryan (actor)
Reynolds, Sheri (author--The Rapture of Canaan)
Reznor, Trent (singer--Nine Inch Blades)

Rhames, Ving (actor--Mission Impossible)
Rhea, Caroline (comedian)
Rhee, Syngman (a.k.a. Rhee Syng-man) (politician--Korea)
Rhimes, Shonda (author/writer/producer--Grey's Anatomy,
Scandal)
Rhine, Joseph (Dr.) (author, parapsychologist--E.S.P.)
Rhodes, Cecil John (colonial leader/diamond
baron/scholarships; Br.)
Rhodes, Hari (actor--Daktari)
Rhodes, James Lemar (Dusty) (baseball)
Rhu, Madlyn (actress)
Rhymes, Busta (musiscian--rap--Pass the Courvoisier)
Rhymes, Leanne (singer)
Rhys, Jean (author--Wide Sargasso Sea)
Rhys, Matthew (nee Matthew Rhys Evans) (actor--The
Americans)
Rhys-Davies, John (actor)
Riain, Liam Po (a.k.a. William Patrick Ryan)
(journalist/historian/author--The Plough and the Cross,
        The Pope's Green Island; Ir.)
Riba, Kelly (actress/Regis co-host)
Ribera, Jusepe de (a.k.a. Lo Spagnoletto) (painter)
Ribisi, Giovanni (actor--Lost in Translation)
Ric-A-Che (musician--rap)
Ricci, Christina (actress--Lizzie Borden, Monster, Still Alive)
Ricci, Nino (author--Lives of the Saints)
Ricci, Paolo (author--Lives of the Saints)
Rice, Anne (author--Lasher, The Vampire Lestat, The
Witching Hour, The Queen of the   Damned)
Rice, Elmer (playwright)
Rice, Henry Grantland (sportwriter)
Rice, Tim (lyricist--Evita, Aida, Chess)
Rich, Adam (actor)
Rich, Bernard (buddy) (bandleader/musician--trumpet)
Richards, Ann (politician)
Richards, Ariana (actress--Jurassic Park)
Richards, Denise (actress)
Richards, Renee (tennis)
Richardson, Elliot (politician)

Richardson, Gillian (author--Pamela)
Richardson, Ian William (actor)
Richardson, Joely (actress) (Vanessa Redgrave's daughter)
Richardson, Natasha (actress)
Richardson, Sally (writer/director/actress)
Richardson, Samuel (author--Pamela)
Richie, Lionel (singer--You Are, Endless Love)
Richmond, Mitch (baseball)
Rickard, Tex (boxing promoter/founder--New York Rangers/builder--Madison Square Gardens, N.Y.)
Rickenbacker, Edward Vernon (Eddie) (fighter ace--94th Squadron/ race car driver)
Rickey, Branch (baseball)
Rickles, Don (actor/comedian)
Rickman, Alan (actor--Harry Potter)
Rickover, Hyman (Hys) (Admiral)
Rida, Flo (singer--rap)
Riddle, Samuel D. (businessman/racehorse owner--Man of War, War Admiral)
Ridge, Thomas (politician--Homeland Security)
Ridte, Lola (poet)
Riefenstahl, Leni (filmmaker)
Rifkin, Ron (actor)
Rigby, Cathy (actress--Pan)
Rigg, Diana (actress--The Avengers, Rebecca)
Riggs, Bobby (tennis)
Rihanna (singer--S.O.S., If It's Lovin That You Want, Te Amo, Umbrella, Disturbia, Work (ANTI)
Riis, Jacob (journalist/author--How the Other Half Lives, Children of the Poor)
Rijo, Jose (baseball)
Riley, Bridget (artist--op art)
Riley, James Whitcomb (author/poet--Ere I Went Mad, Little Orphan Annie, When the Frost is on the Punkin)
Riley, Patrick James (basketball)

Rilke, Ranier Maria (poet--New Poems, Duino Elegies, The Sonnets to Orpheus, Letters to a Young Poet)
Rimbaud, Arthur (poet--Une Saison En Enfer)
Rimes, LeAnn (singer--How Do I Live)
Rimsky-Korsakov, Nikolai (composer--Le Coq d'Or, The Tzar's Bride, The Tale of Tsar's Salton)
Rinehart, Mary Roberts (author--Tish)
Ringling, Albert (circus owner)
Ringling, Alfred (circus owner)
Ringling, August (circus owner)
Ringling, Charles (circus owner)
Ringling, Henry (circus owner)
Ringling, John (circus owner)
Ringling, Otto (circus owner)
Ringwald, Molly (actress--Pretty in Pink)
Riopelle, Jean-Paul (artist)
Rios Marcelo (tennis)
Rios, Rosie (politician)
Riperton, Minnie (singer)
Ripley, Robert (cartoonist/founder--New York's Odditorium)
Rita, Curly Joe (actor/comedian--Three Stooges)
Ritchard, Cyril (director/actor--Captain Hook)
Ritchie, Guy (singer/director--Swept Away)
Ritchie, John Simon (Sid Vicious's birth name) (Sly) (musician--Sex Pistols)
Ritchie, Robert James (Bob) (pseudonym--Kid Rock) (singer/songwriter--All Summer Long)
Ritt, Martin (filmmaker/director--Sounder, Norma Rae, Hud, The Great White Hope, The Long, Hot Summer)
Ritter, Erika (comedienne--Can.)
Ritter, John (actor--Three's Company)
Ritter, Tex (singer--country)
Ritter, Thelma (author--Birdman of Alcatraz)
Ritts, Herb (photographer--fashion)
Rivera, Chita (dancer/singer)
Rivera, Diego (artist--muralist)
Rivera, Naya (actress--Glee)

Rivers, Joan (comedian/author--Enter Talking) (co-author--
Richard Meryman)
Rixey, Eppa (baseball)
Rizzuto, Phil (baseball)
Roach, Hal (actor/director/producer--Our Gang/Little Rascals)
Robards, Jason (actor--A Moon for the Misbegotten)
Robb, Charles (politician; Virginia)
Robb, Inez (columnist)
Robb, Lynda Bird (nee Johnson) (Lyndon's daughter)
Robbe-Grillet, Alain (author)
Robbia, Luca Della (sculptor)
Robbie, Margot (actress--Itanya)
Robbins, Harold (author--The Betsy)
Robbins, Jerome (choreographer; Am.)
Robbins, Marty (singer/songwriter--country--El Paso)
Robbins, Timothy Francis (activist/actor--The Shawshank
Redemption/director/   producer/screenwriter--Bob
Roberts)
Roberts, Cokie (newswoman)
Roberts, Eric (actor--Star 80)
Roberts, Jane (author--Seth Speaks)
Roberts, John (justice)
Roberts, Julia (actress--Notting Hill)
Roberts, Leland Stanford (Lee) (composer--Smiles)
(Callahan's partner)
Roberts, Nora (author)
Roberts, Oral (evangelist)
Roberts, Pernell (actor--Mission Impossible)
Roberts, Rachel (actress)
Roberts, Robin (T. V. personality--Good Morning America)
Roberts, Tanya (producer/actress--Charlie's Angels)
Roberts, Tony (actor)
Robertson, Anna Mary (Grandma Moses) (painter--folk/author-
-My Life's History)
Robertson, Cliff (actor--Charly)
Robertson, Johnstone Frobes (actor/theater manager)
Robeson, Paul (singer--basso/actor--Emperor Jones/activist)
Robin, Leo (songwriter)
Robinson, Bill (Bojangles) (actor/dancer--soft shoe)

Robinson, David (Admiral) (basketball)
Robinson, Edan (author; Haisla native)
Robinson, Edward G. (actor--I Am the Law, Bullets or Ballots)
Robinson, Edwin Arlington (poet)
Robinson, Henry Crabb (diarist)
Robinson, Michelle (lawyer) (Barack Obama's wife)
Robinson, Paul (cartoonist--Etta Kett)
Roblin, Rodmond (politician--Manitoba Premier)
Robson, Mark (director--Earthquake)
Robustelli, Andy (football)
Robyn (singer--pop--Dancing On My Own)
Roca, Renee (ice dancer)
Rocca, Mo (newsman)
Rochon, Lela (actress--Waiting to Exhale)
Rock, Chris (comedian)
Rockne, Knute (football)
Rockwell, Kent (artist)
Rockwell, Norman (artist)
Rockwell, Sam (actor)
Roddenberry, Gene (philosopher/screenwriter/producer)
Roderick (King; Visigoth)
Rodewalt, Vance (cartoonist--Chubb & Chauncey)
Rodgers, Richard (composer--Kiss Me Kate, Pal Joey, Soon, Isn't It Romantic, Edelweiss)   (lyricist--Oscar Hammerstein/Lorenz Hart)
Rodin, Francois Auguste (sculptor--The Kiss, The Burgher of Calais, The Gates of Hell,   The Broken Nose, Adam)
Rodino, Peter (politician--chair of Nixon impeachment)
Rodman, Dennis (basketball)
Rodnina, Irina (figure skater)
Rodriguez, Gina (actress--Jane the Virgin)
Rodzinski, Artur (conductor)
Roe, Allison (marathoner)
Roe, Preacher (baseball)
Roe, Tommy (singer-songwriter--Sheila)
Roebling, John (engineer--Brooklyn Bridge)
Roeg, Nicolas (director--The Man Who Fell to Earth, Walkabout, Castaway)

Roeper, Richard (film critic--At the Movies) (Siskel's/Ebert's partner)
Rogan, Ella (singer)
Rogan, Joe (actor)
Rogen, Seth (actor--Knocked Up)
Roger, Max (composer)
Rogers St. John, Adela (journalist/author/screenwriter)
Rogers, Desiree (politician)
Rogers, Fred (actor--Mr. Rogers' Neighbourhood)
Rogers, Ginger (dancer/singer--Embraceable You)
Rogers, Kenny (singer--Lady, She Believes in Me)
Rogers, Mimi (actress)Rogers, Roy (nee Leonard Slye) (actor/singer--country)
Rogers, Stan (singer)
Roget, Peter Mark (doctor/inventor/author--Thesaurus)
Roh, Moo-hyun (politician; S. Korea)
Rohmer, Eric (Jean Marie Maurice Scherer's pseudonym) (director/screenwriter--A Tale of Winter)
Rohmer, Sax (Arthur Henry Ward's pseudonym) (poet/songwriter/author--Dr. Fu Manchu)
Rojas, Octavio Victor (Cookie) (baseball)
Roker, Roxie (actress)
Rolen, Scott (baseball)
Rolfe, John (colonist) (Pocahantas's husband)
Rolle, Esther (actress--Good Times)
Rolling Stones (musical group--Angie, Tattoo You, Their Satanic Majesties Request, Brown Sugar, Gimme Shelter, Yesterday's Papers, Get Your Yayas Out)
Rollins, Sonny (musician--jazz)
Rollo (Rolf the Ganger/Gaange) (Viking chieftain)
Rolvaag, Ole (author)
Roman, Ruth (actress) (Andrea Doria survivor)
Rombauer, Irma (author--Joy of Cooking)
Romberg, Sigmund (composer--operettas--Rosalie, One Alone)
Rome, Harold (composer/lyricist--Fanny) (Tin Pan Alley member)
Romeo, Lil (singer--Honey)
Romero, Cesar (actor--The Joker)

Romero, George (director--Creepshow)
Rommel, Erwin (General)
Romney, Ann (Mitt's wife)
Romney, Mitt (politician)
Ronan, Saoirse (actress--Lady Bird)
Roncalli, Angelo Giuseppe (Pope John XXIII)
Ronettes (musical group--Be My Baby)
Ronny & the Daytonas (musical group--G.T.O.)
Ronstadt, Linda (singer--Ooh, Baby Baby, Its So Easy, Poor Poor Pitiful Me)
Rooke, Leon (author--Shakespeare's Dog)
Rooney, Andy (60 minutes commentator)
Rooney, Art (football/owner--Pittsburgh Steelers)
Rooney, Mickey (actor--Babes in Arms)
Roosa, Stuart (astronaut)
Roosevelt, Franklin Delano (politician; Am.) (dog--Fala)
Roosevelt, Quentin (pilot) (Theodore's son)
Roosevelt, Sara Ann Delano (F. D. R.'s mother)
Roosevelt, Theodore (Teddy) (Hero of San Juan Hill) (politician)
Root, Elihu (jurist/statesman/Nobelist; Am.)
Roper, Elmo (polster)
Rorem, Ned (critic/musician/composer--Air Music, Bertha, Miss Julie, Our Town)
Ros, Edmundo (bandleader)
Rosar, Buddy (baseball)
Rose, Anika Noni (singer/actress)
Rose, Billy (William Samuel Rosenberg's pseudonym) (producer/director/lyricist)
Rose, Charlie (talk show host)
Rose, Pete (baseball)
Rose, Tokyo (Iva Toguri's pseudonym) (Japanese propaganda broadcaster)
Rosen, Al (baseball)
Rosen, Jacky (politician)
Rosen, Nathan (physicist--wormholes)
Rosenberg, William Samuel (pseudonym--Billy Rose) (producer/director/lyricist)
Rosetti, Francesco Antonio (composer)

Rosi, Francesco (director--Christ Stopped at Eboli)
Ross, Betsy (seamstress--flag)
Ross, Diana (singer--Endless Love, Last Time I Saw Him/actress--Mahogany)
Ross, Elinor (singer--soprano)
Ross, Harold (editor--New Yorker)
Ross, Katharine (actress--Stepford Wives)
Ross, Lanny (pianist/singer/songwriter)
Ross, Marion (actress)
Ross, Sinclair (author--As For Me and My House)
Rosse, Steven (media exec.)
Rossellini, Isabella (actress)
Rossetti, Christina (poet--Goblin Market)
Rossetti, Dante Gabriel (translater/illustrator/poet--Ecce Ancilla Domini/painter--Beata Beatrix)
Rossi, Aldo (architect; It.)
Rossi, Bruno (physicist)
Rossi, Gaetano (composer--librettist)
Rossi, Paolo (soccer)
Rossi, Steve (comedian)
Rossini, Gioacchino (composer--Barber of Seville--Una Voce Poco Fa, The Thieving Magpie, Le Comte Ory, Tancredi, William Tell Overture, Le Cenerentola)
Rossner, Judith (author--Mr. Goodbar)
Rostand, Edmond (poet/dramatist--Cyrano de Bergerac)
Rosten, Leo (author--The Joys of Yiddish)
Rostin, Norman (poet/playwright/author--Under the Boardwalk)
Rostov, Mara (author--Eroica)
Rostropovich, Slava (conductor/musician--cellist)
Rota, Nino (actor/composer--The Godfather)
Rote, Kyle (football)
Rote, Tobin (football)
Roth, David Lee (singer--Just A Gigolo, Mad Dog)
Roth, Eli (director--Hostel)
Roth, Henry (author)
Roth, Lillian (actress)
Roth, Mark (bowler)

Roth, Philip (author--Goodbye Columbus, My Life as a Man, The Anatomy Lesson,   The Human Stain, Letting Go, Zuckerman Unbound, American Pastoral,   Portnoy's Complaint, Our Gang)
Roth, Tim (actor; Br.)
Roth, William (politician)
Rothenberg, Stu (political analyst)
Rothko, Mark (artist--abstract expressionist--Number 10)
Rouhani, Hassan (politician; Iran)
Rourke, Mickey (actor--The Wrestler)
Rouse, Ervin T. (fiddler/songwriter--The Orange Blossom Special)
Rousey, Ronda (M.M.A. fighter/actress)
Roush, Edd (baseball)
Rousseau, Henri (painter--oil--Sleeping Gypsy, The Snake Charmer)
Rousseau, Jean-Jacques (author--Emile)
Roussel, Albert (composer; Fr.)
Rove, Karl (politician)
Rowan, Daniel Hale (Dan) (comedian--Laugh In) (Dick Martin's partner)
Rowan, Rena (fashion designer/co-creater--Jones of New York)
Rowe, Lynwood Thomas (School Boy) baseball)
Rowe, Nicholas (playwright/poet--Lady Jane Grey, Tamerlane)
Rowlands, Gena (actress--Gloria, Another Woman)
Rowling, Joane K. (Jo) (author--Harry Potter/ screen writerFantastic Beasts and Where   to Find Them)
Roy, Gabrielle (author)
Royce, Henry (automaker)
Royko, Mike (columnist)
Royle, Selena (actress)
Rozelle, Pete (football--commissioner)
Ruark, Robert (author--Uhuru, Something of Value, Poor No More)
Rubens, Peter Paul (artist--The Lion Hunt, Daniel in the Lion's Den)
Rubes, Jan (T.V. host/singer--opera)

Rubik, Erno (inventor--cube; Hung.)
Rubin, Benny (actor)
Rubin, James (politician)
Rubinstein, Anton (musician--pianist)
Rubinstein, Artur (musician--pianist)
Rubinstein, Helena (beautician/makeup pioneer)
Rubio, Marco (politician/author--An American Son)
Ruby, Harry (lyricist--Who's Sorry Now) (Bert Kalmar's partner)
Rucker, Darius (musician)
Rudd, Hughes (newsman/journalist)
Rudd, Kevin (politician; Australia)
Rudd, Paul (writer/producer/comedian/actor--Ant-Man)
Rudi, Joe (baseball)
Rudner, Rita (actress)
Rudnick, Paul (author/screenwriter/assayist/playwright--I The Hamlet)
Rudolph, Wilma (track athlete--sprinter)
Ruehl, Mercedes (actress)
Rufalo, Mark (actor)
Ruiz, John (The Quietman) (boxer)
Ruiz, Rosie (runner)
Rule, Ann (author--crime)
Rule, Ja (singer--rap)
Rumsfeld, Donald (politician/businessman--Searle)
Run D.M.C. (musical group--hip-hop--You Be Illin)
Runyon, Alfred Damon (newspaperman/author--short stories)
Rupp, Adolph (The Baron) (basketball--Wildcats coach)
Rusen, Robert (author--Nowhere Man-Final Days of John Lennon)
Rush, Geoffrey (actor)
Rushdie, Salman (author--Joseph Anton: A Memoir)
Ruskin, John (author--Unto This Last)
Russ, Tim (actor--Star Trek)
Russe, Charlotte (fashion designer)
Russel, Leon (singer/songwriter)
Russel, Lillian (Hour Glass Figure) (singer/actress)
Russell, Bertrand (mathematician/philosopher/activist)
Russell, Cazzie Lee (basketball)

Russell, Jane (actress--The Las Vegas Story)
Russell, Keri (actress--Felicity)
Russell, Kurt (actor)
Russell, Lillian (actress/singer)
Russell, Mark (satirist--politics)
Russell, Rosalind (actress--Never Wave at a Wac, Auntie Mame)
Russert, Tim (newsman/T. V. host--Meet the Press)
Russo, Rene Marie (actress--One Good Cop, Tin Cup)
Russo, Richard (author)
Rutger, Hauer (actor--Blade Runner)
Ruth, George Herman (Babe) (Sultan of Swat/#3) (baseball)
Rutherford, Ernest (physicist)
Rutherford, Therese Ann (actress)
Rutledge, Ann (Abraham Lincoln's love)
Rutledge, John (judge--Supreme Court Chief Justice)
Ruttan, Susan (actress--L. A. Law)
Ryan, Cornelius (author--A Bridge Too Far)
Ryan, Irene (actress)
Ryan, Jeri (actress--Star Trek, Voyager)
Ryan, Matt (football)
Ryan, Meg (nee Margaret Hyra) (actress--You've Got Mail)
Ryan, Nolan (baseball)
Ryan, Robert (director--The Setup)
Ryan, William Patrick (a.k.a. Liam Po Riain) (author; Ir.)
Rydell, Bobby (born Robert Louis Ridarelli) (singer--Bye Bye Birdie, Wild One, I've Got   Bonnie)
Ryder, Albert Pinkham (painter--Death on a Pale Horse, Jonah)
Ryder, Winona (actress--Mermaids, Heathers, Edward Scissorhands, Stranger Things)
Ryga, George (playwright--Ecstacy of Rita Joe)
Ryun, Jim (runner--miler/politician)

--S--

S Club 7 (musical group) (Tina Barrett's band)

Saab, Elie (fashion designer)
Saarinen, Eero (architect--T.W.A. terminal, Gateway Arch) (Eliel's son)
Saarinen, Eliel Gottlieb (architect; Am.) (Eero's father)
Saberhagen, Bret (baseball)
Sabia, Laura (feminist)
Sabin, Albert Bruce (Dr.) (inventor--polio vaccine)
Sabo, Chris (baseball)
Sabu (actor--A Tiger Walks, Thief of Bagdad)
Sacagawea (interpreter/guide--Lewis & Clark expedition)
Sacco, Nicola (anarchist) (Vanzetti's partner)
Sacher, Franz (confectioner--tortes)
Sachs, Andrew (actor)
Sachs, Hans (poet/playwright/composer/singer; Ger.)
Sachs, Nelly (author)
Sacks, Oliver (author--The Man Who Mistook His Wife for a Hat)
Sadaka, Neil (singer)
Sadat, Anwar (politician; Egyptian)
Sade (songwriter/singer--Smooth Operator, No Ordinary Love, The Sweetest Taboo, Soldier of Love, Is It A Crime)
Sadi (poet--Garden of Roses; Persian)
Sadler, Barry (Sgt.) (singer--Ballad of the Green Beret)
Safer, Morley (newsman--60 Minutes)
Safin, Marat (tennis)
Safire, William (columnist--On Language)
Sagal, Katey (actress--Married with Children, Sons of Anarchy)
Sagan, Carl (astronomer/author--Cosmos, The Dragons of Eden, Pale Blue Dot)
Sagan, Francoise (author--A Certain Smile)
Sager, Carol Bayer (lyricist)
Saget, Bob (actor/narrator--How I Met Your Mother)
Sahl, Morton Lyon (Mort) (actor/comedian--Sing A Song of Watergate)
Sailer, Toni (skier)
Sain, Johnny Franklin (baseball)
Saint, Eva Marie (actress)

Saint-Saens, Charles Camille (composer--Carnival of The Animals, Urbs Roma in F,   Le Cygne/The Swan)
Saito, Minoru Makoto (Admiral; Jap.)
Sajak, Pat (T. V. game show host)
Sakharov, Andrei (author)
Saki (H. H. Munro's pseudonym) (author--The Open Window, The Chronicles of Clovis,   Esme, The Square Egg)
Saks, Gene (director--The Odd Couple)
Salamanca, J. R. (author--Lilith)
Salazar, Alberto (marathoner)
Salazar, Ken (politician)
Salazar, Rosa Bianca (actress--Maze Runner)
Saldana, Zoe (actress)
Sale, Jamie (skater)
Salem, Horace (merchant; N.Y.)
Salieri, Antonio (musician/composer) (Mozart's rival/prisoner) (Schubert's teacher)
Salinger, Jerome David (author--Esme, The Catcher in the Rye, Nine Stories, The Laughing   Man)
Salk, Jonas (researcher/virologist--polio vaccine)
Salmi, Albert (actor)
Salonen, Esa-Pekka (conductor)
Salonga, Lea (actress--Miss Saigon)
Salten, Felix (author--Bambi)
Salt-n-Pepa (musical group--Let's Talk About Sex, Swoop)
Samms, Emma (nee Emma Samuelson) (actress--Dynasty)
San Giacoma, Laura (actress)
Sanchez, Manuel Laureano Rodrigues (Manolete) (matador)
Sanchez, Oscar Arias (politician/Nobelist--peace; Costa Rica)
Sand, George (Amandine Aurore Lucie Dupin Dudevant's pseudonym) (author--Lelia,   Elle et Lui)
Sandage, Allan (scientist--quasar codiscoverer)
Sandberg, Ryne (baseball)
Sandberg, Sheryl (author--Lean In)
Sandburg, Carl (editor/author/poet--Chicago Poems, Gypsy Mother, Always   the Younger Stranger, The People-Yes)
Sande, Earl (jockey)

Sanders, Alexander (Sir) (producer)
Sanders, Bernard (politician)
Sanders, Deion (Prime Time) (football)
Sanders, George (actor) (Magna and Zsa Zsa's husband)
Sandler, Adam (actor--Big Daddy, Spanglish, Mr. Deeds,
Opera Man)
Sandoval Pablo (baseball)
Sandoval, Arturo (musician--jazz)
Sands, Diana (actress)
Sands, Diane (politician)
Sands, Evie (singer)
Sands, Thomas Adrian (Tommy) (actor/singer)
Sanford, Isabel (actress--The Jeffersons)
Sanger, Margaret Higgins (birth control pioneer)
Sanjay, Gupta (newsman--C.N.N.)
Santa Ana, Antonio Lopez (politician; Mex.) (deposed by
Alvarez)
Santamaria, Ramon (Mongo) (musicin--percussionist--jazz)
Santana, Carlos (quitarist/songwriter--Maria, Maria, Evil Ways,
Oye Como Va)
Sante, Luc (author--Low Life)
Santee, David (skater)
Santiago, Benito (baseball)
Santoni, Reni (actor)
Saperstein, Abe (basketball/Harlem Globetrotters' founder)
Sapp, Warren (football)
Sappho (poet) (Erinna's contemporary)
Sara, Mia (Sarapocciell) (actress--Ferris Bueller's Day Off)
Saragat, Giuseppe (politician; It.)
Saramago, Jose (author)
Sarandon, Chris (actor)
Sarandon, Susan (actress)
Sarazen, Gene (golfer)
Sardou, Victorien (playwright--A Scrap of Paper, La Tosca)
Sarg, Tony (puppeteer)
Sargent, John Singer (painter--Madame X, Lake O'Hara)
Sargent, Richard (Dick) (actor--Bewitched)
Sargon (Assyrian/Mesopotamian/ Sumer ruler)

Sarkozy, Nicholas (politician--French President) (Carla Bruni's husband)
Sarnoff, David (businessman--R.C.A.)
Saroyan, William S. (author/playwright--Time of Your Life, My Name is Aram)
Sarton, May (nee Eleanor Marie) (author--As We Are Now)
Sartre, Jean-Paul (essayist--Being and Nothingness/ author/-- Nausea/playwright--Dirty Hands, The Flies, No Exit; Huis Clos)
Sassoon, Siegfried (author/poet)
Sastre, Ines (model)
Sater (early Pope)
Sather, Glen (hockey)
Satie, Erik (composer--Velvet Gentlemen, Gymnopedies, 3 Pieces in the Shape of a Pear,   Socrates, Vexation, Mercure)
Sato, Eisaku (politician)
Sato, Yasuo (diplomat)
Satrap (governor--Ancient Persia)
Saud, Abdul Aziz Ibn (Arabian king)
Saud, Muhammed Ibn (First Saudi Emir)
Saul, John Ralston (author--Voltaire's Bastards)
Saunders, Merl (musician--jazz)
Sauyles, John (writer/director--Lone Star)
Savage, John (actor)
Savalas, Telly (actor--Kojak)
Savant, Marilyn Vos (I. Q. recordholder)
Savard, Dini (hockey)
Saverin, Eduardo (co-founder--Facebook)
Sawyer, Diane (T. V. personality)
Sawyer, Forrest (newsman)
Sax, Adolphe (inventor--sax)
Saxe, Maurice de (Comte de) (General/Marshall of France; Napoleonic)
Sayas, Bidu (singer)
Sayer, Gale (football)
Sayer, Leo (singer--More Than I Can Say, When I Need You, You Make Me Feel Like Dancing)

Sayers, Dorothy (author--mystery--The Nine Tailors, Strong Poison, Whose Body--Lord Peter   Wimsey)
Sayers, Henry J. (composer--Ta-ra-ra Boom-de-aye)
Sayles, John (director--Eight Men Out)
Scacchi, Greta (actress)
Scaggs, Boz (singer--Lido Shuffle, Lowdown)
Scala, Gia (actress)
Scalia, Antonin (Supreme Court justice) (Gorsuch's predecessor)
Scalia, Jack (actor--Wolf)
Scaria, Emil (singer--bass baritone)
Scarlatti, Alessandro (composer)
Scarlatti, Domenico (composer)
Scarne, John (author--poker)
Scarry, Richard (author--children)
Schary, Isadore (Dore) (director/producer/playwright)
Schell, Maria (actress)
Schell, Maximilian (actor--Judgement at Nuremberg)
Schenk, Adrianus (Ard) (speed skater)
Schenk, Otoo (actor/director--opera/theater)
Schenkel, Chris (sportscaster)
Scherer, Jean Marie Maurice (pseudonym--Eric Rohmer) (director/screenwriter--Tale of Winter)
Schiaparelli, Elsa (couturier/modiste)
Schiele, Egon (painter)
Schiffer, Claudia (model)
Schifrin, Lalo (conductor/composer--Mission Impossible)
Schiller, Johann Christoph (Friedrich von) (poet--Ode to Joy)
Schilling, Curt (baseball)
Schindler, Oskar (industrialist--saved Jews--Schindler's List)
Schisgal, Murray (playwright--Luv)
Schlesinger, Joseph (reporter)
Schliemann, Heinrich (archaeologist)
Schmidt, Helmut (politician) (Helmut Kohl's predecessor)
Schmitt, Harrison (astronaut)
Schnabel, Artur (pianist)
Schnabel, Stefan (actor)
Schneider, Rob (director)
Schneider, Romy (actor)

Schoemperlen, Diane (author)
Schoenberg, Arnold (composer--Ode to Napoleon, Moses &
(und) Aaron (Aron))
Schon, Neal (musician--guitarist--Santana)
Schopfer, Jean (pseudonym--Claude Anet) (author)
Schott, Marge (baseball--Reds owner)
Schreck, Max (actor--Nosferatu)
Schreiber, Liev (actor)
Schrodinger, Erwin (physicist)
Schroeder, Patricia (politician)
Schubert, Franz (composer--The Unfinished Symphony,
Gretchen Am Spinnrade, Lied, Art Song,   Octet in
F Major, Symphony in B Minor, Ava Maria, The Erlking, Trout
Quintet)
Schulz, Charles Monroe (Sparky) (cartoonist--Peanuts, Li'l
Folks)
Schumacher, Joel (writer/producer)
Schumacher, Ralf (racecar driver)
Schuman, Jean-Baptiste Nicolas Robert (politician)
Schumann, Clara (composer/pianist)
Schumann, Robert (composer--Lie der Kreis, Spring,
Kinderszenen)
Schurz, Carl (statesman/reformer)
Schwarzenegger, Arnold Alois (actor--Conan, Red
Heart/bodybuilder/politician)
Scicolone, Anna Maria Villani (Romano Mussolini's wife/Sofia
Loren's sister)
Sciorra, Annabella (actress--Sopranos)
Scipio (Gen.) (Punic Wars leader)
Scolari, Peter (actor)
Scop, Berengarthe (poet/storyteller)
Scopas/Skopas (sculptor/architect)
Scorsese, Martin (director--The Departed/screenwriter--Mean
Streets/producer/   actor/film historian)
Scott, Adam (comedian/producer/actor--Parks & Recreation)
Scott, Anthony Oliver (A.O.) (T. V. personality--At The Movies)
Scott, Dred (slave)
Scott, Glenn (actor--The Right Stuff)
Scott, Jerry (cartoonist--Zits, Baby Blues)

Scott, Mike (baseball)
Scott, Paul (author--The Raj Quartet)
Scott, Randolph (actor--oaters)
Scott, Ridley (Rid) (director)
Scott, Seann William (producer/actor/comedian--American Pie)
Scott, Steve (athlete--miler)
Scott, Walter (Sir) (author--Kenilworth, Waverley, Ivanhoe)
Scott, Willard (weatherman)
Scott, Winfield (Old Fuss and Feathers) (Major General)
Scott-Heron, Gil (poet/musician--rap)
Scotto, Renata (singer--soprano)
Scowcroft, Brent (Gen.) (politician)
Scriabin, Alexander (composer--etudes)
Scruggs, Earl (musician--banjo--bluegrass) (Lester Flatt's partner)
Scully, Vin (sportscaster)
Scurry, Briana (soccer)
Seale, Bobby (author--A Lonely Rage/activist) (Chicago Seven gangster/Black Panther)
Seamans, Ike (newsman/actor/model/commercial spokesman)
Seaton, Ernest (author)
Seau, Junior (football--Chargers)
Seaver, Tom (baseball)
Seberg, Jean (actress--Saint Joan)
Sebold, Alice (author--The Lovely Bones)
Secada, Jon (singer--Just Another Day, If You Go)
Secondat, Charles Louis de (Montesquieu) (judge/scholar/author/philosopher)
Sedaka, Neil (singer--Laughter in the Rain, Oh Carol)
Sedaris, Amy (humorist/comedian/author/actress--Stranger's with Candy)
Sedaris, David (author--Me Talk Pretty One Day)
Sedgman, Frank (tennis)
Sedgwick, Anne (author--Tante)
Sedgwick, Edith Minturn (Edie) (Girl of the Year/It Girl) (Warhol's actress)
Sedgwick, Kyra (actress--The Closer)
Seeger, Alan (poet)

Seeger, Pete (singer--Turn, Turn, Turn)
Seehorn, Rhea (actress--Better Call Saul)
Seeley, Blossom (actress--silents)
Segal, Erich (author--Love Story, Oliver's Story)
Segal, George (actor--Blume in Love)
Segal, George (sculptor; Am.)
Segal, Hugh (pundit)
Segar, Elzie Crisler (cartoonist--Popeye/Thimble Theater)
Seger, Bob (singer--Like A Rock, Night Moves, Hollywood Nights, Turn the Page)   (band--Silver Bullet Band)
Segovia, Andres (guitarist)
Seixas, Vic (tennis)
Seko, Mobutu Sese (politician; Zaire)
Sela, Owen (author--An Exchange of Eagles)
Selassie, Haile (born Ras Tafari--Rastafarian messiah) (politician--Eth.)
Sele, Aaron (baseball)
Selena (singer--Dreaming of You, Always Mineummmmmmmmmmmmmmmmmmm; Mex.)
Seles, Monica (tennis)
Selig, Allan Huber (Bud) (baseball--commissioner)
Selig, Keri (producer)
Seljuk (Turkish dynasty founder)
Selkirk, Alexander (author--Robinson Crusoe)
Sellecca, Connie (actress/model)
Sellect, Tom (actor--Her Alibi)
Sellers, Peter (actor--There's a Girl In My Soup, The Pink Panther, The Trail of the   Pink Panther)
Selye, Hans (Dr.) (stress pioneer)
Sendak, Maurice (author--Where the Wild Things Are)
Seneca (author--Epistulae Morales, De Ira) (Nero's tutor/ Claudias's exiler)
Sennett, Mack (filmmaker--The Bather/producer--creator of Keystone Cops)
Serious, Yahoo (nee Greg Pead) (composer/director/actor-- Young Einstein)
Serkin, Peter (pianist)
Serkin, Rudolf (pianist) (Peter's father)

Sermon, Erick (musician--hip hop)
Serra, Junipero (missionary)
Serra, Richard (sculptor--Tilted Arc)
Sert, Jose Luis (architect--Miro Museum; Sp.)
Sert, Jose Maria (painter--muralist; Sp.)
Sertis, Marina (actress--Star Trek--Troi)
Sesno, Frank (newsman)
Sessions, Roger (composer)
Seth, Vikram (author)
Seti, Menmaatre (Egyptian pharaoh)
Seton, Anya (author)
Seton, Ernest Thompson (author--Dragonwyck)
Seurat, Georges (painter--pointilist--Une Baignade; Fr.)
Seus(s), Dr. (nee Theodore Seuss Geisel) (author--Gertrude McFuzz, The Sneetches, The 500 Fingers of Dr. T)
Seus, Alan (actor/comedian--Laugh-In)
Sevareid, Eric (newscaster)
Severini, Gino (painter)
Severino, Luis (baseball)
Sevigny, Chloe (actress--adult films)
Sewall, Samuel (printer/businessman/judge--Salem witch trials)
Sewell, Anna (author--Black Beauty)
Sex Pistols (musical group--EMI)
Sexton, Anne (poet)
Sextus (poet)
Seyfried, Amanda (singer-songwriter/actress--Mean Girls, Mamma Mia)
Shackleton, Ernest (explorer)
Shade, Ellen (singer--soprano)
Shadwell, Thomas (author--wit)
Shaffer, Paul (bandleader)
Shaffer, Peter Levin (playwright--Equus, Amadeus; Br.)
Shaheen, Jeanne (politician)
Shahn, Ben (artist--Federal Art Project)
Shaked, Tal (chess master)

Shakespeare, William (Bard of Avon) (actor/author/playwright/poet--The Rape of Lucrece) (Anne Hathaway's husband)
Shakira (singer/songwriter)
Shakur, Tupac Amaru (singer--rap--All Eyez on Me)
Shalala, Donna (politician)
Shales, Tom (T. V. critic)
Shalhoub, Tony (actor)
Shalikashvili, John (Gen.) (Colin Powell's successor)
Shalit, Gene (critic)
Shamir, Shimon (politician; Isreali)
Shane, Rita (singer--soprano)
Shankar, Ravi (composer/musician--sitar--raga; Ind.) (Beatles tutor)
Shannon, Del (singer--Runaway)
Shannon, Molly (comedian--S.N.L.)
Shapiro, Ari (radio journalist)
Shapiro, Artie (musician--bassist--jazz)
Shapiro, Karl (poet)
Sharen, Mona (columnist--politics)
Sharif, Omar (actor--Capt. Nemo, The Tamarend Seed, Dr. Zhivago, Che)
Sharon, Ariel (politician--Israeli)
Sharp, Becky (musician--punk rock)
Sharp, Deedre (Deedee) (singer--Mashed Potato Time)
Sharpton, Al (politician)
Shasaku, Endo (author--Christian; Jap.)
Shastri, Lal Bahadur (politician) (Nehru's successor)
Shatner, William (actor--Tek War, T.J. Hooker/T.V. host--Rescue 911)
Shavers, Earnie Dee (boxer)
Shaw, Artie (musician--clarinet/bandleader--They Say)
Shaw, Bernard (newscaster--C.N.N.)
Shaw, David T. (electrical engineer)
Shaw, George Bernard (playwright--Pygmalian, Arms and the Man, Major Barbara, Man and Superman, Caesar and Cleopatra, Great Catherine) (Fabian Society founder)
Shaw, Irwin (author--Rich Man, Poor Man, The Young Lions)

Shaw, Marlena (singer)
Shawn, Dick (actor--The Producers)
Shawn, Ted (dancer)
Shawn, Wallace (Wally) (actor/playwright--My Dinner with Andre)
Shawn, William (editor--New Yorker)
Shea, John (skater)
Shea, William (lawyer)
Shean, Al (comedian) (Ed Gallager's partner)
Shearer, Harry (radio personality--Public Radio, Le Show)
Shearer, Moira (actress/dancer--ballet)
Shearer, Norma (actress--The Divorcee)
Shearn, Edith (actress) (Warner Olandt's wife)
Sheedy, Ally (actress--St. Elmo's Fire, Breakfast Club)
Sheehan, Neil (author)
Sheehan, Patty (golfer)
Sheehan, Susan (author)
Sheehy, Gail (journalist/author--Passages)
Sheen, Charlie (actor--Lucas)
Sheen, Martin (nee Ramon Estevez) (actor/director)
Shehan, Lawrence Joseph (Roman Catholic Cardinal)
Shelby, Richard (politician--Alabama senator)
Sheldon, Sidney (author--Bloodline)
Shelley, Mary (author--Frankenstein, Modern Prometheus)
Shelley, Percy Bysshe (poet--elegist--Oh Weep for Adonais, Alastor/The Spirit of Solitude,   To A Skylark) (muse--Erato)
Shem-Tov, Baal (mystic healer--Hasidic Judaism)
Shepard, Alan (astronaut)
Shepard, Dax (actor--Without a Paddle)
Shepard, Sam (author--A Lie of the Mind)
Shepherd, Cybill (actress/model)
Shepherd, Sherri (comedian/actress/T.V. personality--The View)
Sheraton, Mimi (food critic)
Sheridan, Ann (The Oomph Girl) (actress)
Sheridan, Richard Brinsley (satirist/poet/playwright--The Rivals)
Sherman, Alexander (Allie) (football)

Sherman, Allan (author/comedian)
Sherman, Bobby (singer)
Sherman, Nat (tobacconist)
Sherwood, Robert E. (playwright--There Shall Be No Night,
The Petrified Forest)
Shicoff, Neil (singer--tenor)
Shields, Brook (actress--The Blue Lagoon)
Shields, Carol (author--The Stone Diaries)
Shilts, Randy (journalist/author--And the Band Played On)
Shire, Talia (actress--Rocky, Rad)
Shisgal, Murray (author--Luv)
Shishigina, Olga (gymnast)
Shoenberg, Arnold (composer)
Sholokhov, Mikhail (author--And Quiet Flows the Don)
Shor, Bernard Toots (restauranteur)
Shore, Dinah (singer--Buttons and Bows)
Shore, Pauly (actor--Bio Dome)
Shorter, Frank Charles (runner)
Shostakovich, Dmitri (composer--Bibi Yar)
Shreve, Anita (author--The Pilot's Wife)
Shriver, Eunice (nee Kennedy) (Special Olympics founder)
Shriver, Pam (tennis)
Shriver, Sargent (politician/Peace Corps director)
Shroyer, Sonny (actor--Enos Strate on Dukes of Hazard)
Shue, Andrew (actor)
Shue, Elisabeth (actress--Leaving Las Vegas, Gracie,
Adventures in Babysitting)
Shultz, George (politician--Reagan's Sec. of State)
Shute, Nevil (author--A Town Like Alice, On the Beach)
Shyamalan, Manoj Nelliyttu (M. Night) (writer/director--Sixth
Sense)
Sia (singer--Cheap Thrills, Chandelier)
Sibelius, Jean (composer--Valse Triste, Finlandia; Finn.)
Siegel, Jerry (cartoonist--Superman)
Siegel, Robert (newsman/radio journalist--All Things
Considered)
Siegmeister, Elie (composer--Ozark Set)
Siemaszko, Casey (actor)
Siepi, Cesare (singer--basso)

Sigler, Jamie-Lynn (actress)
Signe, Hasso (composer/author/actress)
Signoret, Simone (actress--Games)
Sik, Ota (Dr.) (reformer)
Sikorsky, Igor (inventor--helicopter)
Sill, Edward Rowland (poet--Opportunity)

Sillitoe, Alan (author; Br.)
Sills, Beverly (diva)
Sills, Milton (actor)
Silva, Anibal (politician; Port.)
Silver, Horace (musician--piano)
Silver, Nate (statistician)
Silver, Ron (actor)
Silverstein, Shel (activist/singer--Boy Named
Sue/songwriter/musician/composer/poet --
        Where the Sidewalk Ends/illustrator--children's)
Silverstone, Alicia (actress--Clueless)
Silverstone, Ben (actor)
Sim, Alastair (actor--London Belongs to Me)
Simenon, George (author--Maigret)
Simmons, Gene (musician--Kiss)
Simmons, Jean (actress-Desiree)
Simon & Garfundel (musical duo--I Am Rock, The Sound of
Silence)
Simon, Carly (singer/songwriter--Jesse)
Simon, Edie (nee Brickell) (singer-songwriter) (Paul's wife)
Simon, Neil (Doc) (playwright--Chapter Two, Plaza Suite,
Brighton Beach Memoirs,   Last of the
Red Hot Lovers, Lost In Yonkers)
Simon, Paul (musician/composer--The Capeman, A Most
Peculiar Man, Cecilia, I Am Rock,   Obvious Child) (Edie
Brickell's husband)
Simon, Scott (newsman--NPR (National Public Radio)
Simonds, Merilyn (actress--The Lion in the Room Next Door)
Simone, Nina (Eunice Kathleen Wayman's pseudonym)
(singer--I Love You Porgy,   I Put A Spell
on You, Feeling Good)
Simoneau, Yves (director--Memphis)

Simpson, Adele (designer)
Simpson, Ashlee (singer--Pieces of Me)
Simpson, Mona (author)
Sims, John Haley (Zoot) (musician--sax--jazz)
Sims, William (Admiral--W.W. I)
Sin, Jaime (archbishop--Philippines)
Sinatra, Frank (singer--How Little We Know, Meet Me At the Copa, New York, New York, Nice'n Easy/actor--Suddenly, Ocean's Eleven, None But the Brave, Duets) (bio.--My Way)
Sinatra, Nancy (singer)
Sinatra, Tina (producer/singer/actress)
Sinclair, Upton (author--Wide is the Gate, The Jungle, There Will Be Blood, Oil!)
Singer, Isaac Bashevis (author--Shosha) (Yentl subject)
Singer, Isaac Merrett (actor/entrepreneur/inventor--sewing machine)
Singer, Lori (actress--Foot Loose)
Singer, Marc (actor)
Singh, Manmohan (politician; India)
Sinise, Gary (actor/director--Of Mice and Men, Forest Gump, Truman, George Wallace)
Sipe, Brian (football)
Sirtis, Boz (singer--country--Low Down)
Siskel, Eugene (Gene) (journalist/film critic) (Roeper's/Ebert's partner)
Sisler, George (baseball)
Sisqo (singer--rap--Thong Song)
Sister Aimee (evangelist--Foursquare Church)
Sister Sledge (musical group--We Are Family)
Sisto, Jeremy (actor)
Sitwell, Edith (Dame) (biographer/critic/poet--Clown's House, Still Falls The Rain/ author--The Outcasts)
Sixpence None the Richer (musical group--Kiss Me)
Skaggs, Cornelia Otis (psychologist)
Skaggs, Ricky (musician)
Skald (poet--medieval; Icelandic)
Skelton, Edna (nee Stillwell) (writer--Red Skelton Show)

Skelton, Richard (Red) (actor/comedian)
Skerritt, Tom (actor)
Skinner, Corneilia (author/actress) (Otis's daughter)
Skinner, Marina (actress--plays Troi in Star Trek)
Skinner, Otis (actor) (Cornelia's father)
Skipworth, Alison (actress)
Skoda, Emil Ritter von (engineer/industrialist)
Skvorecky, Josef (author)
Skye, Ione (actress--Say Anything)
Slade (musical group; Br.)
Slade, Bernard (playwright--Same Time Next Year)
Slade, Jack (gunslinger/Pony Express operator/Overland
Express wagonmaster)
Slash (guitarist--Guns & Roses)
Slater, Christian (actor--The Name of the Rose)
Slater, Helen (author)
Slaughter, Enos (Country) (baseball)
Slaughter, Karin (author--Grant County)
Slayton, Donald Kent (Deke) (aeronautical engineer/test pilot)
Sledge, Percy (singer--When a Man Loves a Woman)
Slezak, Erika (actress--One Life to Live)
Slick, Grace (singer/songwriter)
Sliwa, Curtis (activist--Guardian Angels founder)
Sloan, Alfred (G. M. Gen. Mgr.)
Sloan, John (painter--McSorley's Bar; Backyards, Greenwich
Village/Ashcanist)
Sloan, Tod (jockey)
Sloane, Everett (actor--Citizen Kane)
Sloane, Hans (Sir) (physician/botanist)
Sloane, Lindsay (actress)
Slocum, Henry W. (Gen.--Civil War)
Slosberg, Pete (brewer)
Slutskaya, Irina (figure skater)
Slye, Leonard (Roy Rogers' birth name) (singer/actor--
country)
Small, Millie (singer--My Boy Lollipop)
Smalls, Charlie (composer--The Wiz)
Smart, Elizabeth (author--By Grand Central Station I Sat
Down and Wept)

Smashnova, Anna (tennis)
Smeal, Eleanor (feminist)
Smetana, Bedrich (composer--The Bartered Bride)
Smirnoff, Yakov (comedian)
Smith, Adam (economist/author--Wealth of Nations)
Smith, Al (co-cartoonist with Bud Fisher--Mutt & Jeff)
Smith, Alfred (Al) (statesman) (autobiography--Up To Now)
Smith, Bessie (Elizabeth) (singer--blues)
Smith, Betty (author--A Tree Grows in Brooklyn)
Smith, Bob (Buffalo Bob) (actor--Howdy Doody)
Smith, Bubba (football)
Smith, Chris (musician--Ballin'the Jack)
Smith, Dean (basketball)
Smith, Dodie (author--101 Dalmations)
Smith, Edward Elmer (Doc) (author--sci-fi.--Lensman, Skylark)
Smith, Helen Sobel (bridge expert) (Charles Goren's partner)
Smith, Hendrick (author--Who Stole the American Dream)
Smith, Ian (politician; Rhodesia)
Smith, Jaden (actor) (Will's son)
Smith, James Todd (a.k.a. LL Cool J) (singer--rap--Going
Back to Cali)
Smith, Joseph (religious leader--Mormon--polygamist)
Smith, Kate (singer--God Bless America)
Smith, Keely (singer--Louis Prima Band)
Smith, Kurtwood (actor--That 70's Show)
Smith, Liz (columnist--gossip)
Smith, Lois (dancer--ballet)
Smith, Louisa (Lula Vollmer's pseudonym) (playwright--Sun-
up)
Smith, Margaret (Maggie) (Dame) (actress--Downton Abbey)
Smith, Otis (basketball)
Smith, Ozzie (baseball)
Smith, Patricia Lee (Patti) (poet/singer/songwriter)
Smith, Paul (fashion designer)
Smith, Reginald (Reggie) (baseball)
Smith, Robyn (jockey) Fred Astaire's wife)
Smith, Shepard (Shep) (news anchor/managing editor--Fox
News)
Smith, Stan (tennis)

Smith, Walter Bedell (Beetle) (General)
Smith, Will (actor--Men In Black, Shark Tale, I Am Legend, I Robot)
Smiths (musical group--Meat is Murder)
Smits, Jimmy (actor--N.Y.P.D. Blue)
Smits, Rik (Dunkin Dutchman) (basketball)
Smollett, Tobias George (author/poet; Scot.)
Smoot, Reed (politician) (Hawley's colleague)
Smullyan, Raymond (author--logic puzzles)
Smuts, Jan (politician; S. African P. M.--Holism Theory)
Smyth, Des (golfer)
Smyth, Patty (musician--rock) (John McEnroe's wife)
Smyth, Tommy (commentator--E.S.P.N.)
Smythe, Reginald (cartoonist--Andy Capp)
Snead, J. C. (golfer)
Snead, Sam (Sammy) (golfer/author--Golf Begins at Forty)
Snee, Chris (football)
Snell, Peter (runner; N.Z.)
Sneva, Tom (race car driver)
Snicket, Lemony (nee Daniel Handler) (author--children's)
Snider, Daniel (Dee) (actor/radio personality/singer-songwriter) (band--Twisted Sister)
Snider, Duke (baseball)
Snipes, Wesley (actor--Boiling Point, The Fan)
Snoop Dogg (singer/songwriter--rap/actor)
Snow, Charles Percy (Sir/Lord) (author--Strangers and Brothers, The Affair)
Snow, Clarence Eugene (singer-songwriter/musician)
Snow, Edgar (author--Red Star Over China)
Snow, Phoebe (nee Phoebe Ann Laub) (singer-songwriter/musician--guitar)
Snowe, Olympia (politician; Maine)
Snyder, Gary (poet--Beat)
Snyder, Tom (talk show host--Tomorrow)
Sobel, Dava (author--Galileo's Daughter)
Sobel, Helen (a.k.a. Helen Sobel Smith) (bridge expert) (Charles Goren's partner)
Sobieski, Leelee (actress--Deep Impact, Joan of Arc)
Sobol, Donald J. (author--Encyclopedia Brown, Longitude)

Socrates (sculptor/philosopher)
Soetoro, Lolo (Obama's stepfather)
Sofer, Rena (actress)
Soglow, Otto (cartoonist--The Little King)
Sohn, Sonja (actress--The Wire)
Sokoloff, Marla (actress)
Sokolova, Erena (figure skater)
Sol Estes, Billy (businessman)
Solon (statesman, poet, lawmaker--Athenian/Thesmothete)
Solow, Robert Merton (economist)
Solti, Georg (Sir) (conductor)
Solzhenitsyn, Alexander (author--The Gulag Archipelago)
Somerhalder, Ian (actor)
Somers, Brett (actress/comedian--Odd Couple)
Somers, Suzanne (actress)
Somes, Michael (dancer--ballet)
Sommer, Elke (actress)
Sommer, Joanie (singer--Johnny Get Angry)
Sondheim, Stephen (lyricist--Not While I'm Around, A Funny
Thing Happened on the Way   to the Forum,
Passion, Maria, Marry Me A Little, A Little Night Music, We're
                  Gonna Be All Right, A Boy Like That,
Anyone Can Whistle, Send in the Clowns)
Song, Aree (golfer)
Sonny & Cher (musical duo--What Now My Love)
Sontag, Susan (author--Illness as Metaphor, The Volcano
Lover, Under the Sign of Saturn,   The Benefactor)
Soo, Jack (actor--Barney Miller)
Soo, Phillipa (actress/singer--Hamilton)
Sophocles (Attic Bee) (playwright--Ajax, Electra/poet)
Sorbo, Kevin (actor--Hercules)
Sorel, Edward (cartoonist)
Sorel, George (philosopher; Fr.)
Sorensen, Theodore C. (author--Kennedy)
Sorenstam, Annika (golfer)
Sorenstam, Charlotta (golfer)
Sorkin, Aaron (actor)
Soros, George (financier/philanthropist)
Sorvino, Mira (actress--Mighty Aphrodite)

Sosa, Jose (baseball)
Sosa, Sammy (baseball)
Soter (Soterus) (religious leader--Pope)
Sothern, Ann (actress--Maisie, Private Secretary)
Soto, Rosana (actress)
Sotomayor, Sonia Maria (Supreme Court justice)
Souez, Ina (singer)
Soul, David (actor--Starsky and Hutch/singer/director)
Soule, Olan (actor--Captain Midnight, Dragnet)
Sousa, John Philip (March King) (composer--Hands Across the Seal, El Capitan, Semper Fidelis)
Souter, David (justice)
Southey, Robert (poet)
Spaak, Paul Henri Charles (politician; Bel.)
Spacek, Sissy (actress--In the Bedroom, Raggedy Man, Violets Are Blue)
Spacey, Kevin (actor--The Ref, House of Cards)
Spade, David (actor)
Spader, James Todd (actor--The Black List, Stargate, Crash)
Spagnoletto, Lo (a.k.a. Jusepe de Ribera) (painter)
Spahn, Warren (baseball)
Spano, Joe (actor--Hill Street Blues)
Spano, Vincent (actor--Alive)
Spark, Muriel (author)
Sparks, Jordin (singer--No Air)
Sparks, Ned (actor)
Sparrow, Ruby (basketball)
Sparv, Camilla (actress)
Spassky, Boris (chess master)
Speaker, Tris (baseball)
Spears, Britney (singer--I Am A Slave 4 You)
Specter, Arlen (politician--Penn.)
Spector, Phil (record producer--The Crystals)
Spector, Ronnie (singer--The Ronettes)
Spee, Maximilian Graf von (Admiral) (ship--Scharnhorst)
Speer, Albert (architect/Nazi organize/author--Inside the Third Reich, Spandau the Secret Diaries)
Spelling, Aaron (producer)

Spelling, Tori (actress)
Spence, Basil (architect--Coventry Cathedral)
Spence, Michael (economist/nobelist)
Spencer, Diana (Princess of Wales)
Spender, Stephen (poet/author/essayist)
Spener, Philipp Jakob (theologian--Lutheran)
Spenser, Edmund (poet--sonnets--The Fairie Queene,
Astrophel; Br.)
Sperry, Elmer (inventor--gyrocompass)
Spessivtsevak, Olga (dancer--ballet)
Spewach, Bella (author--Kiss Me Kate)
Speyer, Joseph (banker)
Spicer, Sean (politician)
Spiegel, Evan (entrepreneur--co-founder--Snapchat)
Spiegelman, Art (author--Maus)
Spielberg, Steven (writer/director)
Spillane, Mickey (Frank Morrison's pseudonym) (author--I the
Jury/Mike Hammer creator)
Spinal Tap (musical group--These Go To Eleven)
Spiner, Brent (actor)
Spinks, Leon (boxer)
Spinoza, Baruch (philosopher/author--Ethics)
Spirit of the West (musical group--Home for a Rest)
Spirlea, Irina (tennis)
Spitz, Mark (swimmer)
Spitzer, Eliot (politician)
Spode, Joshiah (potter--chinawear; Br.)
Spohr, Arnold (director--ballet)
Spohr, Louis (musician--violin/composer--Nonet in F
Major/inventor--chin strap)
Springer, Jerry (T. V. host/former mayor of Cincinnati)
Springfield, Dusty (singer)
Springfield, Rick (musician--The River)
Springstein, Bruce (The Boss) (musician--Pink Cadillac/E
Street band member--   Streets of
Philadelphia)
Sprinkel, Beryl (politician--economics)
Spyri, Johanna (author--Heidi)
Spyro Gyra (musical group--jazz)

St. Adela (William the Conqueror's daughter)
St. Aidan (monastery founder; Br.)
St. Alexander Nevsky/i (Grand Prince of
Novgorod/Kiev/Vladimir)
St. Anselm (founder of Scholasticism)
St. Bede (monk--calendar starting with Jesus)
St. Benedict (hermit)
St. Canute (patron saint of Denmark)
St. Claire (monk of Assisi)
St. Cyr, Jacques (designer--maple leaf on flag)
St. Cyril (doctor/apostle to the Slavs) (Saint of letters)
St. Damian (patriarch of Alexandria)
St. Denis, Ruth (choreographer)
St. Denys/Denis/Dennis (Bishop of Paris)
St. Eulalie (saint; Fr.)
St. Francis of Paola (friar--founder of R.C. Order of Minims)
St. Hilary of Poitiers (Doctor of the Church) (bishop)
St. Ignatius of Loyola (nee Inigo Lopez de Loyola)
(priest/theologian)
St. Isabel (Portugese)
St. Isidore of Seville (author--Etymologiae)
St. James. Lyn (race car driver)
St. Janurius (patron saint of Naples)
St. John Perse (Fernand Leger's pseudonym)
(diplomat/poet/nobelist; Fr.)
St. Johns, Adela Roger (journalist/author)
St. Leo (The Great) (pope that negotiated with Attila)
St. Marie, Buffy (singer)
St. Mark (Patron Saint of Venice)
St. Philip de Neri (Apostle of Rome) (religious leader)
St. Teresa of Avila (Mother Teresa) (missionary--Missionaries
of Charity founder)
St. Theresa of Avila (mystic/nun/author)
Stafford, Jo Elizabeth (singer--Stardust)
Stafford, Thomas P. (astronaut)
Stagg, Amos Alonzo (football)
Stahl, John M. (director/producer--Magnificent Obsession)
Stalin Josef (nee Iosif Dzhugashvili) (politician)
Staller, Ilona (actress--adult movies)

Stallone, Sylvester (Sly) (actor--Judge Dredd)
Stamberg, Susan (newswoman)
Stamos, John (actor--Grandfathered)
Stamp, Terence (actor--Poor Cow)
Stanford, Amasa Leland (industrialist/politician/university founder)
Stang, Arnold (comedian/actor)
Stanislaw, Lem (author; Pol.)
Stans, Maurice (politician)
Stansfield, Lisa (singer)
Stanton, David (politician)
Stanton, Edwin M. (politician)
Stanton, Elizabeth Cady (feminist)
Stanton, Harry Dean (actor--Repo Man)
Stanwyck, Barbara (nee--Ruby Stevens) (actress--Woman in Red, Annie Oakley, All I Desire)
Stapleton, Jean (actress--All in the Family, Aunt Mary)
Stapleton, Maureen (actress)
Stapp, Olivia (singer/opera director)
Stark, Ned (actor--Game of Thrones)
Starker, Janos (musician--cello)
Starkey, Zak (musician--drummer) (Ringo's son)
Starr Bart (football)
Starr, Belle (Myra Belle/ Myra Belle Shirley) (outlaw/Confederate leader)
Starr, Blaze (ecdysiast)
Starr, Edwin (singer--War)
Starr, Ellen Gates (social reformer/activist) (Jane Addam's partner)
Starr, Kay (singer--Wheel of Fortune)
Starr, Kenneth (judge)
Starr, Richard (Ringo) (musician--drummer--Beatles--It Don't Come Easy, With a Little Help From My Friends) (Zak Starkey's father)
Starship (musical group--Sara)
Stassen, Harold (politician)
Statius (poet)
Staub, Rusty (baseball)
Staubach, Roger (football)

Staunton, Imelda (actress--Harry Potter)
Stautner, Ernie (football)
Steadman, Robert (composer)
Steber, Eleanor (singer--soprano)
Steel, Danielle (author--H.R.H.)
Steele, Christopher (spy)
Steele, Michael (politician)
Steele, Richard (politician, essayist--The Tatler, Spectator) (Addison's co-author)
Steele, Shelby (author--The Content of Our Character--political)
Steele, Tommy (actor--Finian's Rainbow)
Steely Dan (musicians Walter Becker and Donald Fagan--A.J.A.)
Steen, Jan Havickszoon (painter--The Dancing Couple, Card Players Quarelling, The Feast of   St. Nicholas, The Cat Family; Dutch)
Steen, William (painter; Am.)
Stefani, Gwen (singer--Don't Speak)
Stefanik, Elise (politician)
Stegens, Craig (actor--Peter Gunn)
Steichen, Edward (photographer)
Steig, William (sculptor/cartoonist/illustrator/author--Shrek)
Steiger, Rod (actor--Capone)
Stein, Gertrude (author--The Lost Generation, The Autobiography of Alice B. Toklas)
Steinbeck, John Ernst (author--East of Eden (Adam Trask), To a God Unknown, The Pearl,   Cannery Row)
Steinbeck, Saul (cartoonist/illustrator)
Steinbrenner, George (businessman/New York Yankees owner) (Hal's father)
Steinbrenner, Hal (businessman/New York Yankees owner) (George's son)
Steine, Jill (politician--Green Party)
Steinem, Gloria (feminist/author--Revolution from Within)
Steiner, Maximilian (Max) (composer)
Steinhauer, Olen (author--The Tourist)
Steinway, Henry Engelhard (& Sons) (piano maker)
Sten, Anna (actress--silver screen--Nana)

Stendhal (Marie-Henri Beyle's pseudonym) (author--The Red
and the Black)
Stenerud, Jan (football)
Stengel, Casey (baseball/autobiographer--Casey At The Bat)
Stengel, Charles Dillon (Casey) (baseball)
Stephenson, Neal (author--The Baroque Cycle)
Stept, Sammy (Sam Ward's pseudonym) (composer--It
Seems Like Old Times)
Sterling, Ford (actor--Keystone Kops)
Stern, Daniel (actor/director--Wonder Years)
Stern, Howard (talkshow host)
Stern, Isaac (violinist)
Sterne, Laurence (author--Tristram Shandy, A Sentimental
Journey)
Stevens, Cat (singer)
Stevens, Connie (singer/actress--Hawaiian Eye)
Stevens, Craig (actor--Peter Gunn)
Stevens, Inger (actress)
Stevens, Kaye (singer)
Stevens, Ray (singer/songwriter--Santa Claus Is Watching
You)
Stevens, Rise (diva)
Stevens, Ruby (a.k.a. Barbara Stanwyck) (actress--Woman in
Red, Anie Oakley,   All I Desire)
Stevens, Ted (politician)
Stevens, Wallace (author)
Stevenson, Adlai Ewing (politician--We're Madly for Adlai)
Stevenson, Robert Louis (author--The Bottle Imp, Prince Otto)
Steve-O (T. V. co-host--Wildboyz)
Steves, Rick (author--travel)
Stewart, Alana (actress--Swift Shift/T.V. personality) (Rod's
wife)
Stewart, Donald Ogden (author)
Stewart, Ian (mathematician)
Stewart, James Maitland (Jimmy) (military officer/actor--
Seventh Heaven)
Stewart, Jon (satirist--political)
Stewart, Martha (business exec.)
Stewart, Michael (playwright--Hello Dolly)

Stewart, Patrick (actor--X-Men)
Stewart, Payne (golfer)
Stewart, Potter (justice)
Stewart, Rod (The Mod) (singer) (Alana's husband)
Stich, Michael, (tennis)
Stieb, Dave (baseball)
Stiers, David Ogden (actor--Mash)
Stiles, Ryan (actor)
Stiller, Ben (filmmaker/comedian/actor--Zoolander)
Stiller, Jerry (comedian/actor) (Anne Meara's husband)
Stimson, Henry Louis (politician)
Stine, Robert Lawrence (author--Goosebumps, Fear Street, Revenge R Us, Mostly   Ghostly)
Sting (Gordon Matthew Sumner's stage name) (poet/composer/singer) (band--The Police)
Stipe, Michael (musician/singer--R.E.M.)
Stockman, David (businessman/politician)
Stockton, Frank R. (author--The Lady)
Stockwell, Dean (actor--Shame, Quantum Leap)
Stojko, Elvis (figure skater)
Stokowsky, Leopold (conductor)
Stole, Mink (actress)
Stolle, Fred (tennis)
Stoltenberg, Jens (politician--Nor.)
Stoltz, Eric (actor)
Stoltz, Richard (actor)
Stone, Dee Wallace (actress)
Stone, Emma (actress--Easy A)
Stone, Ezra (actor)
Stone, Harlan Fiske (justice)
Stone, Joss (singer--soul)
Stone, Lewis Shepard (actor--Judge James Hardy)
Stone, Lucy (suffragette)
Stone, Matt (co-creator--South Park)
Stone, Milburn (actor--Gunsmoke)
Stone, Oliver (director--J. F. K., Platoon, Nixon, W (George W. Bush))
Stone, Sharon (actress--Sliver)
Stone, Sly (singer--rock)

Stonestreet, Eric (actor--Modern Family)
Stong, Phil (author--State Fair)
Stoopnagle, Col (radio personality--Snoopnagel & Bud)
Storch, Larry (actor--F Troop)
Storm, Gale (actress)
Storm, Lance (wrestler)
Storr, Rachel (Dr.) (theologian)
Stoss, Veit (sculptor)
Stossel, John (newsman--20/20)
Stoudemire, Amare (basketball)
Stout, Rex (author--mystery--Fer de Lance, Some Buried Caesar) (Nero Wolfe creator)
Stover, Russell (chocolateer)
Stowe, Harriet Beecher (author--Uncle Tom's Cabin, Dred, The Pearl of Orr's Island, The Minister's Wooing)
Stowe, Madeleine (actress)
Strabo (geographer)
Strachey, Giles Lytton (biographer/essayist/literary critic--Victorian era; Br.)
Strahovski, Yvonne (actress)
Strait, George (singer--country--Amarillo)
Strasberg, Lee (actor/director/acting teacher)
Strasberg, Susan (actress/acting teacher)
Stratas, Teresa (singer--soprano)
Stratus, Trish (wrestler)
Strauss, Johanne (composer--opera--Die Fledermaus)
Strauss, Louis L (historian/politician--A. E. C.)
Strauss, Richard (composer--Ariadne auf Naxos, Salome, Elektra, Der Rosenkavalier, Tod Und Verklarung, Arabella, Ein Heldenieben, Die Frau Ohne Schatten, Aus Italien, Eine Alpensinfonie)
Stravinsky, Igor (composer--Pianos for Wind Instruments, Agon, Card Party, The Nightingale)
Streep, Meryl (actress--A Cry in the Dark, Death Becomes Her, Sophie, The Iron Lady, Julia Child)
Street Singer (a.k.a. Arthur Tracy) (actor/singer--Marta)

Streeter, Edward (author--Father of the Bride/journalist--Dere Mable; Love Letters   of a Rookie)
Streisand, Barbra (singer/actress--Yentl, Duets, On A Clear Day, Nuts, A Love of Ours,   People)
Streit, Clarence (author--Union Now)
Stritch, Elaine (actress)
Stroh, Bernard (brewmaster)
Stroller, Mike (songwriter) (Jerry Leiber's partner)
Strong, Ken (football)
Stroud, Robert (Birdman of Alcatraz) (criminal/ornithologist)
Strug, Kerri (gymnast)
Strunk, William (author--Elements of Style)
Struthers, Sally (actress)
Stuart, Erwin (actor)
Stuart, Gilbert Charles (artist--portraits--Washington dollar bill)
Stuart, Jeb (General)
Stuart, Ruch (author--A Golden Wedding)
Stubbs, Levi (singer--Four Tops)
Sturgeon, Theodore (author--More Than Human)
Sturluson, Snorri (author--Edda)
Styne, Jule (composer--Funny Girl, Bells Are Ringing, Let it Snow, Gypsy)
Styron, William (author--Sophie's Choice, The Confessions of Nat Turner)
Styx (musical group--Babe, Mr. Roboto, Come Sail Away)
Sublett, John William (Bubbles) (vaudevillian/dancer--rhythm-soul tap)   (Ford Lee Washington's (Buck) partner)
Sudermann, Hermann (author--Frau Sorge)
Sue (Erie Canal mule)
Sugarhill Gang (musical group--Rapper's Delight)
Suggs, Louise (golf)
Sui, Anna (fashion designer)
Suleman, Nadya (octomom)
Sulla (politician; Caesar's predecessor)
Sullavan, Margaret (actress)
Sullivan, Anne (teacher) (Helen Keller's instructor)
Sullivan, Arthur (composer--Lost Chord, The Yeoman of the Guard)

Sullivan, Eric Per (actor)
Sullivan, John Lawrence (Boston Strong Boy) (boxer)
Sullivan, Kathy (singer)
Sulzberger, Arthur Ochs (publisher)
Sumac, Yma (The Peruvian Songbird) (singer 50's--exotica)
Summer, Cree (actress)
Summer, Donna (actress/singer--Bad Girls)
Summers, Lawrence (politician)
Summers, Mark (T.V. personality--Unwrapped)
Sumner, Charles (politician--abolitionist)
Sumner, Gordon Matthew (stage name--Sting)
(poet/composer/singer) (band--The Police)
Sun Yat-sen (politician/revolutionary leader; Chin.)
Sung, Alfred (fashion designer)
Sun-Ra (musician/bandleader--jazz)
Sununu, John (politician/political pundit)
Surrey, Earl of (Henry Howard) (poet--executed for treason;
Br.)
Susann, Jacqueline (author--Once Is Not Enough)
Sutclifffe, Stu (musician--early Beatle)
Sutherland, Donald (actor--Spys)
Sutherland, Joan Alston (Dame) (singer--soprano--opera--
Norma)
Sutherland, Kiefer (actor)
Sutter, Brent (hockey)
Sutton, Hal (golfer)
Sutton, William Francis (Willie) (bank robber/author--Where
the Money Was)
Suvari, Mena (actress--American Beauty, The Mysteries of
Pittsburgh)
Suzuki, Ichiro (baseball)
Swan, Craig (baseball)
Swan, Susan (author--The Last of the Golden Girls)
Swank, Hilary (actress--Amelia Earhart)
Swann, Lynn (football)
Swarthout, Gladys (singer--soprano)
Swayze, John Cameron (newsman)
Swayze, Patrick (actor--Red Dawn, Steel Dawn)
Sweeney, Daniel Bernard (actor--Fire in the Sky)

Sweeney, Julia (actress/comedian--S.N.L.)
Sweet, Sarah Blanche (actress)
Sweetnam, Skye (singer/songwriter/director/designer)
Sweig, Arnold (author)
Swenson, Inga (actress--Benson)
Swift, Jonathan (author--satire--A Modest Proposal, A Tale of a Tub)
Swift, Taylor (singer-songwriter)
Swinburne, Algeron Charles (critic/author/playwright/poet--Etude Realiste)
Swinton, Katherine Mathilda (Tilda) (model/actress--Burn After Reading)
Swit, Loretta (actress--M.A.S.H.)
Swope, Herbert Bayard (journalist/editor)
Sykes, George (Gen.) (army officer--Civil War)
Sykes, Wanda (actress/comedian)
Symington, William Stuart (Stu) (businessman/politician)
Syms, Sylvia (actress--Woman In a Dressing Gown)
Syms, Sylvia (saloon singer--jazz)
Synge, John Millington (playwright--Riders to the Sea, Playboy of the Western World, Deirdre of the Sorrows; Ir.)
Syngman, Rhee (politician; Kor.)
Szekely, Louis (C.K.) (comedian/editor/producer/director/writer/actor)
Szell, Georg (maestro)
Szewinska, Irena (runner/Olympian)

--T--

T. Booker (musician) (band & the M.G.'s)
T. Booker (nee Robert Booker Tio Huffman) (wrestler/promoter/color commentator)
T.L.C. (musical group--Waterfalls)
T'ugn, Hsuan (Chinese emperor)
Tadema, Alma (painter--Br.)
Tae-woo, Roh (politician; Kor.)

Taft, Lorado (sculptor)
Taft, Robert A. (politician--Taft-Hartley Act)
Tagore, Rabindranath (philosopher/poet--Farewell My
Friends/author/musician/   painter/playwright)
Tahari, Elie (fashion designer)
Taine, Hippolyte Adolphe (philosopher/historian/author/ literary
critic--Fr.)
Tajo, Italo (singer--bass)
Takei, George (actor--Star Trek--Sulu)
Tal, Mikhail (chess master)
Talbot, Fritz Badley (artist)
Talbot, Lyle (actor)
Talbot, Nita (actress)
Talbot, William (Father of Photography) (photographer)
Talese, Gay (author--Honor Thy Father, Unto the Sons, The
Kingdom & the Power,   Thy
Neighbour's Wife, Frank Sinatra Has a Cold, A Serendipiter's
Journey,   A Writer's Life)
Talib, Aqib (football)
Talking Heads (musical group--And She Was)
Tallchief, Maria (dancer--ballet)
Talmadge, Constance (actress)
Talmadge, Norma (actress)
Tamblyn, Amber (actress)
Tamblyn, Russ (dancer/actor--Tom Thumb)
Tamiroff, Akim (actor)
Tamm, Igor (physicist)
Tan, Amy (author--The Hundred Secret Senses, The
Bonesetter's Daughter, The Joy Luck Club,   Sagwa)
Tanaka, Masahiro (baseball)
Tanaka, Tomoyuki (director/producer--Godzilla)
Tancred (Norman crusade leader)
Tandy, Jessica (actress) (Hume Cronyn's Wife)
Taney, Roger Brooke (Supreme Court justice--Dred Scott)
Tanguy, Yves (artist)
Tani, Collette (actress--United States of Tara)
Tanquay, Eva (singer/dancer)
Tapper, Jake (newsman--C.N.N.)
Tarantino, Quentin (writer/director--Pulp Fiction)

Tarbell, Ida Minerva (author/journalist--muckraker)
Tarkington, Booth (author--Penrod, Seventeen, Magnificent Ambersons, In the Arena)
Tarkovskyk, Andrei (director)
Tarleton, Banastre (soldier/politician) (Cornwallis shipmate)
Tasman, Abel Janszoon (explorer; Dutch)
Tasso, Torquato (poet--Aminta, Jerusalem Delivered, Rinaldo--Renaissance--Este)
Tate, Allen (poet)
Tate, Donovan (actor)
Tate, Jeffrey (conductor)
Tate, Larenz (actor)
Tate, Nahum (poet)
Tate, Sharon (actress)
Tati, Jacques (director/comic/actor--Mon Oncle, Jour de Fete, Mr. Hulot's Holiday)
Tatu (musical group--All The Things She Said)
Tatulli, Mark (cartoonist--Heart of the City)
Tatum, Art (musician--slide piano--jazz)
Taurasi, Diana (basketball)
Tautou, Audrey (model/actress--Amelie)
Tavernier, Bertrand (director)
Taylor, Ann (designer)
Taylor, Billy (pianist--jazz)
Taylor, Charles Elmer (Rip) (actor/comedian)
Taylor, Deems (musicologist)
Taylor, Drew Hayden (playwright)
Taylor, Elizabeth (actress)
Taylor, Ike (football)
Taylor, James (singer--How Sweet It Is)
Taylor, John S. (publisher) (Moses Dodd's partner)
Taylor, Lili (actress--Six Feet Under, I Shot Andy Warhol, The Haunting)
Taylor, Nigel John (musician--bassist--Duran Duran)
Taylor, Niki (model/host--Make Me a Supermodel)
Taylor, Renee (actress--Nanny)
Taylor, Rod (actor)
Taylor, Tamara (actress--Bones)
Taylor, Zachary (politician)

Tchaikovsky, Peter Ilich (composer--Eugene Onegin, Capriccio Italien)
Te Kanawa, Kiri (diva; Maori)
Teabing, Leigh (Sir) (character--Da Vinci Code)
Teach, Marshall D. (pseudonym--Blackbeard)
Teale, Edwin Way (naturalist)
Tearle, Conway (actor--silent movies)
Teasdale, Sara (poet--suicidal--Dark of the Moon, Let It Be Forgotten)
Tebaldi, Renata (diva--soprano)
Tebow, Tim (football)
Tedder, Arthur (Air Marshal)
Teen, Harold (comedian)
Teens (musical group--pop)
Teeter, Lara (dancer/actor/singer/theater director/producer/professor)
Tegner, Esaias (author)
Teh-Chun, Chu (Zhu Degun/Zhu De) (painter--modernist)
Teheran, Julio (baseball)
Teigen, Chrissy (author/model/T.V. personality--Lip Sync Battle)
Telemann, Georg (composer)
Telfer, Dariel (author--The Caretakers)
Teller (magician--Penn & Teller)
Teller, Edward (physicist/inventor-- H bomb)
Teller, Henry Moore (politician)
Temple, Shirley (actress--Heidi, Our Little Girl)
Templeton, Alec (pianist)
Templewood, Hoare (Viscount) (politician)
Temptations (musical group--All I Need, Ain't Too Proud to Beg, Since I Lost My Baby)
Ten C C (musical group--The Things We Do For Love)
Ten Thousand Maniacs (musical group)
Tennant, Kylie (author)
Tennant, Veronica (dancer--ballet; Can.)
Tennant, Victoria (actress--All of Me)
Tenniel, John (illustrator--Alice in Wonderland)
Tennille, Toni (singer--Captain and Tennille)

Tennyson, Alfred Lord (poet--Enoch Arden, Maud, Flower in the Crannied Wall, Dora, Morte d'Arthur, Crossing the Bar, Geraint and Enit, The May Queen, Locksley Hall)
Tenuta, Judy (comedian)
Teo, Manti (football)
Tepper, Sheri Stewart (author--sci-fi)
Ter Haar, Bernard (poet)
Terence (author/poet--Where There's Life There's Hope; Roman)
Terhune, Albert Payson (author--Lad, a Dog, Loot)
Terkel, Studs (author--Working)
Tero, Lawrence (Mr. T.) (actor--A Team)
Terrell, Tammi (singer)
Terris, Susan (author--Author, Author)
Terry, Alice Ellen (Dame) (actress)
Terry, Eli (horologist)
Terry, Ellen (Dame) (actress)
Tertz, Abram (author)
Tesh, John (T. V. personality/pianist--A Deeper Faith)
Tesla (musical group--Edison's Medicine)
Tesla, Nikola (engineer/inventor--Chicago World's Fair City of Lights; Croatian)
Tevis, Walter (author--The Man Who Fell to Earth, Hustler)
Tewes, Lauren (actress--Love Boat)
Texada, Tia (actress--Third Watch)
Tey, Josephine (author--Brat Farrar, The Daughter of Time, Miss Pym Disposes)
Thackeray, William Makepeace (author--Vanity Fair, Barry Lyndon, Marquis of Steyne)
Thalberg, Irving Grant (The Boy Wonder) (producer--MGM)
Thales (philosopher)
Thang, Ton Doc (politician--Ho chi Minhy's successor)
Thant, U (diplomat--U. N. Chief) (Kurt Waldheim's predecessor)
Tharp, Twyla (choreographer--As Time Goes By)
Thaves, Bob (cartoonist--Frank and Ernest)
Thaxter, Celia (poet)
Thayer, Ernest (poet--Casey at the Bat)

Theiss, Brooke (actress)
Theron, Charlize (actress--Aeon Flux, Mad Max)
Theroux, Paul (author--The Happy Isles of Oceania, The Mosquito Coast)
Thibault, Jacques Anatole (pseudonym--Anatole France) (journalist/poet/author)
Thicke, Alan (actor/songwriter/T.V. host)
Thicke, Robin (singer--Blurred Lines)
Thiessen, Tiffany-Amber (actress)
Thieu, Nguyen Van (politician; Viet.)
Thirkell, Angela (author)
Thom, Ruth (actress)
Thomas, Ambroise (composer--opera--Hamlet)
Thomas, Brandon (playwright--Charlie's Aunt)
Thomas, Cal (political columnist)
Thomas, Danny (actor/comedian)
Thomas, Debra Janine (Debi) (figure skater)
Thomas, Dylan (poet/author--Under Milk Wood)
Thomas, Irma (singer)
Thomas, Isiah (basketball)
Thomas, Marlo (actress/author--Free to be You and Me)
Thomas, Norman (minister/pacifist/socialist--Socialists Party of America)
Thomas, Seth (horologist--clock maker/wire factory)
Thome, Jim (baseball)
Thompson, Emma (actress)
Thompson, Hunter Stockton (journalist/author)
Thompson, Kay (actress--Eloise)
Thompson, Kenan (actor--Kenan & Kel) (Kel Mitchell's partner)
Thompson, Lea (actress)
Thompson, Morton (newspaper journalist/screen playwright/author--Not As a Stranger)
Thompson, Sada (actress--Family)
Thompson, Tessa (actress--Creed, Selma)
Thomson, James (poet--Rule Britannia)
Thomson, Tom (painter--The Jack Pine)
Thoreau, Henry David (philosopher/diarist/author--Faith in a Seed, Walden, Civil Disobedience)

Thornburgh, Richard Lewis (Dick) (politician--Edwin Meese's successor)
Thorndike, Sybil (actress)
Thornton, Willie Mae (Big Mama) (singer--blues)
Thorp, Edward O. (author--Beat the Dealer)
Thorpe, Jim (decathlete/Olympian)
Three Dog Night (musical group--One, Try a Little Tenderness, Let Me Serenade You)
Throneberry, Marv (baseball)
Thurber, James (cartoonist/author--Is Sex Necessary, The Secret Life of Walter Mitty/   journalist/game inventor--Ghost)
Thurman, Nate (basketball)
Thurman, Uma (actress--The Truth About Cats and Dogs, Pulp Fiction)
Thurman, Wallace (author--Harlem)
Thurmond, Nate (basketball)
Thurmond, Strom (politician--senator)
Ti, Huang (Yellow Emperor) (politician)
Tiant, Luis (baseball)
Tibbets, Enola Gay (Paul Tibbets's mother)
Tibbets, Paul (pilot--Enola Gay)
Tiberius (politician) (Augustus predecessor)
Tiegs, Cheryl (model)
Tiepolo, Giovanni Battista (artist--Rococo--Labia Palace frescoes, The Crucifixion,   Adoration of the Magi)
Tierney, Gene (actress--Laura)

Tierney, Maura (actress)
Tikkanen, Esa (hockey)
Til Tuesday (pop group)
Tilden, Bill (tennis)
Tillis, Pam (singer--country)
Tillstrom, Burr (puppeteer--Kukla, Fran & Ollie)
Tilly, Meg (actress)
Tilton, Charlene (actress--Dallas)
Timbaland (musical group--The Way I Are)
Timberlake, Justin (singer--nsync)

Tintoretto, Jacopo Robusti (painter--The Miracle of St. Mark
Freeing the Slaves)
Tiny Tim (singer) (Tulip Victoria's father)
Tiomkin, Dimitri (composer/conductor)
Tippi (painter; Florentine)
Tiriac, Ion (tennis)
Tisch, Laurence Alan (Larry) (businessman/T.V. exec.--
C.B.S.)
Tiselius, Arne (chemist)
Titian (nee Tiziano Vecellio) (artist--Venus & Cupid, Ecce
Homo, Venus of Urbino)   Giovanni
Bellini's student)
Tito, Josip Broz (politician; Yugo.)
Titov, Gherman (cosmonaut)
Titov, Vladimir (cosmonaut)
Tittle, Yelberton Abraham (Y.A.) (football)
Titus (emporer of Rome 80-100 A. D.) (Vespasian's
successor/son)
Todd, Chuck (newsman)
Todd, Thelma (actress)
Toews, Miriam (author--A Boy of Good Breeding)
Toffler, Alvin (author--Future Shock/futurologist/sociologist)
Tognazzi, Ugo (actor)
Toguri, Iva (a.k.a. Tokyo Rose) (criminal)
Toklas, Alice (memoirist/author--cookbook) (Stein's
autobiography subject)
Tokyo Rose (nee Iva Toguri) (criminal)
Toland, John (biographer--Adolf Hitler)
Toler, Sidney (actor--Charlie Chan)
Toles, Tom (cartoonist--Randolph Itch)
Tolkien, John Ronald Reuel (author--The Lays of Beleriand,
The Hobbit, Lord of the Rings,   Lot R, Orc, The Two
Towers)
Toller, Ernst (playwright)
Tolstoy, Leo (author--The Death of Ivan Ilyich, What is Art?)
Tomba, Alberto (skier)
Tomei, Marisa (actress--The Wrestler, What Women Want,
Love is Strange, Before   the Devil
Knows You're Dead)

Tomislav (King) (founded Croatia)
Tomjanovich, Rudolph (Rudy) (basketball coach)
Tomlin, Lily (actress--All of Me)
Tone-Loc (born Anthony Terrell Smith) (actor/singer--rap--Wild Thing)
Toney, James (boxer)
Tony Toni Tone (musical group--Feels Good)
Toole, John Kennedy (author--A Confederacy of Dunces)
Toole, Kenneth Ross (author)
Toomey, Jim (cartoonist--Sherman's Lagoon)
Toomey, Regis (actor)
Toots, Shor (restauranteur)
Topol, Chaim/Haym (singer/voice artist/illustrator/film producer/actor--Tevye)
Tork, Peter (musician--The Monkees)
Torme, Mel (Velvet Fog) (singer--scat--The Christmas Song, Careless Hands/author--The Other   Side of the Rainbow) (autobiog.--It Wasn't All Velvet)
Torn, Rip (actor--Cross Creek, Heartland)
Torquato, Tasso (poet)
Torre, Joe (baseball)
Torrence, Gwen (runner--sprints)
Torres, Dara (swimmer/model/T.V. personality)
Torvill, Jayne (ice dancer)
Tosca (singer--Vissi d'Arte)
Toscanini, Arturo (conductor)
Tosh, Daniel (comedian)
Tosh, Peter (musician--reggae)
Tosti, Francesco Paolo (composer--Mattinata)
Totenberg, Nina (correspondent--National Public Radio)
Toth, Alex (cartoonist--Space Ghost)
Toth, Paul (baseball)
Toto (musical group--Rosanna, Africa, Hold the Line)
Toulouse-Lautrec, Henri de (artist)
Tov, Yisrael Baal Shem (rabbi--Hasidism founder)
Towne, Robert (screenwriter--Chinatown)
Toya (singer--I Do)
Toynbee, Arnold (historian/author--A Study of History)
Toyoda, Akio (business exec.--Toyota)

Tozzi, Giorgio (singer--basso)
T-Pain (record producer/singer/songwriter--Rappa Ternt Sanga)
Trabert, Tony (tennis)
Tracey, Doreen (Mouseketeer)
Tracy, Arthur (a.k.a. Street Singer) (actor/singer--Marta)
Tracy, Ellen (fashion designer)
Tracy, Spencer (actor--Captain Courageous, Dr. Jekyl, A Guy Named Joe, Tortilla Flats)
Traffic (musical group) (Steve Winwood's group)
Trainor, Meghan (singer-songwriter)
Trajan (Roman emperor--Nerva/Trajan/Hadrian's predecessor)
Travers, Mary (singer-songwriter--Peter Paul & Mary)
Travis, Merle (singer--country)
Travis, Nancy (actress--Three Men and a Lady)
Travis, Randy (singer--country)
Travolta, John (actor--Grease, Primary Colors, Saturday Night Live)
Traynor, Pie (baseball)
Treadway, Ty (actor)
Trebek, Alex (T. V. game show host)
Tree, Herbert Draper Beerbohm (actor/manager; Br.)
Trenet, Charles (singer/songwriter--La Mer)
Trenite, Gerard (poet--The Chaos)
Tresh, Tom (baseball)
Trevanian, Rodney Whitaker (author--Eiger Sanction, Loo Sanction)
Trevor, Claire (actress)
Trillin, Calvin (essayist--With All Disrespect)
Trilling, Lionel (critic)
Trillo, Manny (baseball)
Trinidad, Tito (boxer)
Tristano, Lennie (musician--jazz)
Tritt, Travis (singer--country--Here's a Quarter Call Someone Who Cares, The Whiskey Aint Workin/actor--Rio Diablo)
Troggs (musical group--Wild Thing)
Trojan (Nerva's successor)

Trollope, Anthony (author--The Eustace Diamond, The Barsetshire Novels, Phineas Finn, Lady Anne, Ayala's Angel)
Trotsky, Leon (nee Lev Bronstein) (politician; Ru.)
Troy, Deanna (actress--Star Trek T.N.G.)
Troyat, Henri (author)
Troyer, Verne (actor--Mini-Me)
Trudeau, Pierre (politician)
Truex, Ernest (actor)
Truffaut, Francois (director)
Trujillo, Rafael (politician; Dom. Rep.
Truman, Harrison S. (Harry) (politician/author--Mr. Citizen)
Trumbo, Dalton (screenwriter--Spartacus)
Trump, Donald (entrepreneur)
Trump, Ivana (author--The Best Is Yet to Come) (Donald's ex)
Trump, Ivanka (model/businesswoman)
Trump, Marla Maples (actress) (Donald's ex)
Tryon, Tom (author--The Other)
Tse, Lao (politician/philosopher)
Tseng, Yani (golfer)
Tse-Tung, Mao (politician)
Tsongas, Paul E. (politician)
Tubb, Ernest (singer)
Tuchman, Barbara (author--The Proud Tower)
Tucker, Sophie (Red Hot Mama) (singer)
Tucker, Tanya (singer)
Tufu (poet--Tang Dynasty)
Tull, Jethro (musician--Aqualung)
Tune, Tommy (actor/director/dancer/choreographer--Broadway, Nine)
Tunneil, Amlen (football)
Tunney, Gene (boxer)
Tunney, Robin (actor)
Tupper, Earl (founder of Tupperware)
Tureck, Rosalyn (pianist)
Turgenev, Ivan (author--Fathers and Sons)
Turin, Adela (author)
Turing, Alan (mathematician/inventor--digital machine)
Turner, Ike (singer)

Turner, Joseph Mallord William (painter--The Burning of the House of Lords   and Commons)
Turner, Lana (actress--Peyton Place)
Turner, Nat (negro slave/revolutionary leader)
Turner, Norv (football)
Turner, Ron (football)
Turner, Sherri (golfer)
Turner, Stansfield (Admiral) (director--C.I.A.)
Turner, Ted (media mogul)
Turner, Tina (singer) (autobiography--I Tina)
Turnesa, Doug (golfer)
Turnesa, Frank (golfer)
Turnesa, Jimmy (golfer)
Turnesa, Joe (golfer)
Turnesa, Mike (golfer)
Turnesa, Phil (golfer)
Turnesa, Willie (golfer)
Turow, Scott (author--The Laws of Our Fathers, Presumed Innocent, One L)
Turtles (musical group--Elenore)
Turturro, Aida (actress--Sopranos)
Tushingham, Rita (actress)
Tussaud, Marie (sculptor--wax)
Tutankhamen (King; Egyptian)
Twain, Mark (author--Puddin'head Wilson, Ah Sin, What is Man, A Tramp Abroad)   (biographer--Paine)
Twain, Shania (singer)
Tway, Bob (golfer)
Twisted Sister (musical group)
Twitty, Conway (singer--It's Only Make Believe)
Tycho, Brahe (astronomer)
Tye, Christopher (composer--Dundee)
Tyler, Aisha (actress--Lana, Friends/T.V. personality--The Talk, Whose Line is it Anyway)
Tyler, Anne (author--Patchwork Planet, The Accidental Tourist, Breathing Lessons)
Tyler, John (politician)
Tyler, Letitia (John's wife)
Tyler, Liv (actress--Armageddon)

Tyler, Steven (singer--Aerosmith)
Tynan, Kenneth (theater critic)
Tynan, Ronan (singer--God Bless America)
Tyner, McCoy (pianist--jazz)
Tyson, Cicely (actress--Sounder)
Tyson, Mike (Iron Mike) (boxer)
Tyson, Neil deGrasse (astrophysicist/author/science
commentator--Cosmos)
Tyson, Sylvia (singer)
Tyus, Wyomia (runner)
Tzara, Tristan (artist--dada)
Tzu, Sun (author--The Art of War)

--U--

Ubach, Alanna (actress)
Uccello, Paolo (painter; Florentine)
Udall, Mark (politician)
Udall, Morris King (Mo) (politician)
Udall, Stewart (Stu) (politician)
Udall, Tom (politician)
Uecker, Bob (sportscaster/actor--Mr. Belvedere)
Uemura, Naomi (explorer)
Uggams, Leslie (singer)
Ughi, Uto (musician--violin)
Ulanova, Galina (dancer--ballet)
Ulene, Art (physician)
Ullamn, Sybil (actress)
Ullman, Liv (actress--Sofie)
Ullman, Tracey (comedian)
Ulpianus, Domitius (jurist)
Ulric, Lenore (actress)
Ulrich, Lars (musician--drummer)

Ulyanov, Vladimir (Lenin) (politician)
Umeki, Miyoshi (actress--Sayonara)
Underwood, Blair (actor)
Underwood, Sheryl (comedian/T.V. personality--The Talk)
Ungar Stuart (Stu) (poker)
Unger, Caroline (singer--contralto)
Unger, Jim (cartoonist--Herman)
Unitas, Johnny (Golden Arm) (football)
Unruh, Jesse (politician)
Unseld, Wes (basketball)
Unser, Al (racecar driver)
Unser, Bobby (racecar driver)
Updike, John (author--Witches of Eastwick, A and P, Rabbit Run, Couples, A Month of Sundays, The Same Door)
Upton, Justin (baseball)
Upton, Melvin Emanuel (B. J.) (baseball)
Urbain, Gabriel (composer)
Urban, Keith (singer--country)
Ure, Mary (actress--Where Eagles Dare, Sons & Lovers)
Urey, Harold Clayton (chemist--isotopes--discovered deuterium/author--One World or None)
Urguhart, Jane (author)
Uriah Heep (musical group--rock)
Urich, Robert (actor--Spenser, Vegas)
Uris, Leon (author--Haj, Mila 18, Battle Cry, Trinity, A God in Ruins, Mitla Pass, Gunfight at the O.K. Corral, Redemption, The Angry Hills, Topaz) (hero--Ari)
Usher (singer--Arista Records)
Ussery, Bobby (jockey)
Ustinov, Peter (actor--Quo Vadis, Ashanti/playwright--Romanoff & Juliet)
Utley, Chase (baseball)
Utne, Eric (publisher/founder--New Age Journal)
Utrillo, Maurice (artist--Paris scenes)
Utterstrom, Sven (skier)
Utzon, Jom (architect--Sydney Opera House)

Vaccaro, Brenda (actress)
Vachel, Lindsay (poet)
Vaclav, Havel (author; Chech.)
Vadim, Roger (director--Barbarella)
Vague, Vera (a.k.a. Barbara Jo Allen) (actress)
Valazquez, Diego Rodriguez (painter--Las Meninas)
Valdez, Miguel Alman (politician; Mex.)
Valens, Ritchie (singer--Donna, Go Johnny Go) (biopic--La Bamba)
Valentine, Karen (actress--Room 222)
Valentino, Rudolph (actor--Blood & Sand) (Pola Negri's love)
Vallee, Rudy (singer)
Valletta, Amber (actress)
Valli, Alida (actress--Third Man)
Valli, Frankie (singer--Four Seasons, Grease, My Eyes Adored You)
Vallone, Raf (actor--The Italian Job)
Van Alen, William (architect)
Van Ark, Joan (actress)
Van Beethoven, Ludwig (composer/pianist--opus--Elise)
Van Buren, Abigail (Pauline Phillips's pseudonym) (Dear Abby) (advice columnist)
Van Cleef, Lee (oater/cowboy)
Van Damme, Jean-Claude (actor--Time Cop)
Van Delft, Johannes/Jan/Johan Meer) (painter)
Van der Beek, James (actor)
Van der Meer (Van Delft), Jan (artist; Dutch)
Van der Rohe, Mies (architect)
van der Waals, Johannes Diderik (physicist--force of attraction)
Van Der Weyden, Rogier (painter--The Annunciation)
Van Devere, Trish (actress)
Van Dien, Casper (actor--Tarzan)
van Dine, S. S. (Willard Huntington Wright's pseudonym) (author--Philo Vance)

Van Doren, Carl (author/editor--Jane Mecom, Benjamin Franklin) (Charles's uncle/Mark's   brother)
Van Doren, Charles (academic--quiz whiz) (Carl's nephew/Mark's brother)
Van Doren, Mamie (actress)
Van Doren, Mark (critic/teacher/poet) (Carl's brother, Charles's uncle)
Van Duyn, Mona (poet)
Van Dyck, Anthony (painter)
Van Dyke, Jerry (musician/actor/comedian) (Dick's brother)
Van Dyke, Richard (Dick) (comedian/actor) Jerry's brother)
Van Dyken, Amy (swimmer)
Van Exel, Nick (basketball)
van Eyck, Jan (painter; Flemish)
Van Gogh, Theo (art dealer/collector) (Vincent's brother)
Van Gogh, Theo (director/producer/actor/author) (Theo's grandson/Vincent's   great grandnephew)
Van Gogh, Vincent (painter--Bedroom at Arles, Irises, Starry Night Over the Rhone,   Lane in Autumn)
Van Halen (musical group--Hot for Teacher)
Van Halen, Alex (musician--drummer)
Van Halen, Eddie (singer/songwriter/producer)
Van Heusen, James (singer--All the Way)
van Leeuwenhoek, Anton (microbiologist/inventor--Microscope)
Van Loon, Hendrik Willem (author--Story of Mankind)
Van Noort, Adam (artist) (Ruben's teacher)
Van Oost, Jacob (painter)
Van Rijn/Ryn, Rembrandt Harmenszoon (painter--Des. From the Cross, Aristotle Con-   templating a Bust of Homer, The Rape of Ganymede)
Van Sant, Gus (director--To Die For)
Van Slyke, Andy (baseball)
Van Susteren, Greta (T. V. host)
Van Thieu, Nguyen (politician; Vietnam)
Van Vechten, Carl (author/photographer)
Van Vogt/Voght, Alfred Elton (author--sci-fi)
Van Winkle, Robert (stage name--Vanilla Ice) (singer)

Van Zandt, Steven (activist/actor/musician/singer/songwriter) (band--E. Street Band)
Van Zant, Ronnie (singer--Lynyrd Skynyrd band)
Vance, Cyrus (politician)
Vance, Vivian (actress)
Vanderbilt, Cornelius (industrialist)
Vandeweghe, Kiki (basketball)
Vanilla Ice (Robert Van Winkle's stage name) (singer)
Vannelli, Gino (singer)
Vanocur, Sander (Sandy) (journalist)
Vanzetti, Bartolomeo (anarchist) (Sacco's partner)
Vardalos, Nia (actress--My Big Fat Greek Wedding)
Varese, Edgar (composer--Hyperprism)
Varner, Jeff (Survivor participant)
Varney, Jim (actor--Ernest)
Vartan, Michael (actor--C.I.A., Agent Vaughn on Alias)
Vasarely, Victor (artist--op art--Zebra)
Vasari, Giorgio (painter/architect/historian/bibliographer--Michelangelo)
Vassar, Matthew (brewer)
Vaughan, Sarah (Sassy) (singer)
Vaughn, Mo (baseball)
Vaughn, Stevie Ray (musician--guitarist)
Vaughn, Vince (actor--Wedding Crasher)
Veale, Bob (baseball)
Veblen, Thorstein (economist/sociologist)
Vedder, Eddie (composer/musician--Pearl Jam)
Vedder, Elihu (painter)
Vee, Bobby (singer--Run to Him)
Vega, Alexa (singer/actress--Spy Kids)
Vega, Suzanne (singer--Luka)
Veidt, Conrad (actor--Casablanca)
Velazquez, Diego (painter--Lady with a Fan, Aesop)
Velez, Lupe (actress)
Veloz, Frank (dancer--ballroom) (Yolanda Casazza's husband)
Venner, Elsie (physician/author)
Ventimiglia, Milo (actor--Heroes)
Ventura, Jesse (wrestler/politician)

Venturi, Ken (golfer)
Verdi, Giuseppe (composer--opera--Ernani, Eri Tu, Otello, Celeste Aida, Giovanna d'Arco,   Bella Figlia Dell'Amore, Don Carlos, Otello, Ritorna Vincitor, Un Ballo in Mascera,   Rigoletto, O Mia Patria, La Traviata)
Verdon, Gwyneth (Gwen) (dancer/actress--Damn Yankees) (Bob Fosse's wife)
Verdugo, Elena (actress)
Vereen, Ben (actor/singer/dancer--Pippin)
Verity, Simon (sculptor/ stone carver--Cathedral of St. John the Divine)
Verlaine, Paul (poet--Clair de Lune)
Vermeer, Johannes (artist--A Maid Asleep, Woman with a Lute; Dutch)
Verne, Jules (author--Philias Fogg, Les Voyages Extraordinaires)
Veronese, Paolo (painter)
Versace, Gianni (fashion designer)
Vespasian (emporer of Rome 69-79 A. D.) (Titus's predecessor/father)
Vespucci, Amerigo (explorer)
Viaud, Louis Marie-Julien (pseudonym--Pierre Loti) (naval officer/author--Fin de Siecle)   (Anet's contemporary)
Vicade, George (comedian)
Vicario, Arantxa Sanchez (tennis)
Vicious, Sid (Sly) (born John Simon Ritchie) (musician--Sex Pistols)
Vickers, Jon (singer--tenor)
Victoria, Tulip (Tiny Tim's daughter)
Vidal, Gore (author--Burr, Myra Breckinridge)
Vidal, Thea (actress)
Vidor, King (director)
Vidov, Oleg (actor)
Vikander, Alicia (actress--Tomb Raider)
Vila, Bob (handyman/T.V. personality--This Old House)
Vilas, Guillermo (tennis)
Villa-Lobos, Heitor (composer)

Villechaize, Herve (actor--Fantasy Island)
Villella, Edward (dancer)
Villon, Francois (Gaston Duchamp's pseudonym) (poet)
Vima, Lisi (actress)
Vincent, Fay (baseball)
Vincent, Gene (singer--B-Bop-Alula)
Vincent, Norah (author--Adeline: A Novel of Virginia Woolf)
Vine, Barbara (pseudonym--Ruth Rendell) (author--crime--Inspector Wexford)
Vines, Amanda (actress--She's the Man)
Vinton, Bobby (singer--Blue on Blue)
Virgil (author--idylls--Aeneid) (hero-Aeneas)
Vishinsky, Andrei (politician/jurist/diplomat)
Vissi, Anna (singer)
Vitale, Dick (sportscaster)
Vitti, Monica (author)
Vittorini, Elio (author)
Vittorio, Alfieri (poet)
Vittorio, Desica (director)
Vivaldi, Antonio (The Red Priest) (priest/composer--Nisi Dominus)
Vivien, Renee (Musoe of the Violets) (poet)
Vizquel, Omar (baseball)
Vogel, Kenneth (author--Big Money/journalist--Politico)
Voight, Jon (actor)
Vollmer, Lula (nee Louisa Smith) (playwright--Sun-up)
Volta, Alessandro (scientist--ignition of methane/inventor--battery)
Voltaire (Francois Marie Arouet's pseudonym) (author--satire--Candide, Oreste)
Von Abner Eschenbach, Marie (author)
Von Auer, Leopold (violinist) (Efrem Zimbalist's/Mischa Elman's/Jscha Heifetz's/ Menuhin's teacher)
von Bayer, Adolf (chemist)
Von Behring, Emil (physiologist)
Von Braun, Eva (Hitler's wife)
von Braun, Wernher (inventor--rocketry)
von Bulow, Claus (aristocrat--murder suspect of wife Sonny)

Von Bulow, Hans (conductor/pianist)
Von Clausewitz, Karl (military theorist)
Von Flotow, Friedrich (composer)
Von Furstenberg, Egon (fashion designer)
von Klug, Gunther Adolf Ferdinand (German field marshal--
W.W.II)
von Linne, Carl (taxonomist)
von Losch, Maria Magdalena (a.k.a. Marlene Dietrich)
(actress--Just a Gigolo)
von Mohn, Hugo (botanist)
von Otter, Anne Sofie (singer--mezzo)
Von Papen, Franz Joseph (nobleman/diplomat)
Von Ribbentrop, Joachim (Foreign Minister of Nazi German)
Von Richthofen, Manfred (The Red Baron) (W.W.I. fighter
pilot; Ger.)
von Skoda, Emil Ritter (engineer/industrialist)
Von Spee, Maximilian Graf (Admiral; Ger.) (ship--Scharnhorst)
Von Sternberg, Josef (director)
Von Stroheim, Erich (actor/director/author--Greed)
Von Suppe, Franz (composer)
Von Sydow, Max (actor--The Exorcist; Swed.)
Von Tirpitz, Alfred (Admiral)
Von Trier, Lars (director)
von Weber, Karl Maria (composer--Der Freischutz, Oberon)
Von Zell, Harry (comedian--Burns & Allen's second banana)
Vonn, Lindsey (skier)
Vonnegut, Kurt (satirist/author--Fates Worse Than Death,
Slaughterhouse Five, The   Sirens of Titan/playwright--
       Happy Birthday Wanda June, Cat's Cradle)
Vorobyeva, Irina (athlete--runner)
Vought, Charles (cartoonist--Petey Dink, Betty)
Vreeland, Diana (magazine editor--fashion)
Vulcano, Sal (actor--Impractical Jokes)

--W--

Wade, John Francis (J.F.) (hymnist--Adeste Fideles)
Wade, Virginia (tennis)
Waggoner, Lyle (actor)
Wagner, Honus (baseball)
Wagner, Linsay (actress--Bionic Woman)
Wagner, Richard (composer--opera--Parsifal, Elsa's Dream, Das Rheingold, Ring Cycle, Rienzi,   Der Liegende Hollaender) (heroine--Isolde goddess--Erda/god--Wotan)   (autobiography--Mein Leben) (Cosima's husband)
Wagner, Robert Ferdinand (politician--N.Y.)
Wahl, Ken (actor--Wiseguy)
Wahlberg, Donald Edmond (Donnie) (singer/songwriter/actor/record producer/   movie producer)
Wahlberg, Mark (actor--Ted)
Waite, Ralph (politician/actor--The Waltons)
Waititi, Taika (director--Star Wars)
Waits, Tom (singer)
Waitz, Grete (marathon runner)
Wakefield, Ruth (inventor--Toll House Cookie recipe)
Wakefield, Tom (author)
Walcott, Derek (author)
Waldheim, Kurt (politician/diplomat) (U. Thant's successor)
Waldo, Peter (religious leader; Fr.)
Walesa, Lech (politician; Pol.)
Walker, Alice (author--The Color Purple)
Walker, Brian (cartoonist--Hi & Lois)
Walker, Esmond Cardon (Card) (C.E.O. Walt Disney Company) (Watson & Eisner's   predecessor)
Walker, Greg (cartoonist--Hi & Lois)
Walker, Herschel (football)
Walker, Hiram (distiller)
Walker, Junior (singer)
Walker, Kemba (basketball)
Walker, Mort (cartoonist--Beetle Bailey)
Walker, Nancy (actress--Rhoda)
Wallace, David Foster (author--The Infinite Jest)

Wallace, Dee (actress--E. T.)
Wallace, Henry Agard (politician)
Wallace, Ilo Browne (business owner--seed company)
(Henry's wife)
Wallace, Irving (author--The Man)
Wallace, Lew (Union General) (author--Ben Hur)
Wallace, Lila (publisher--Readers Digest/philanthropist)
Wallace-Stone, Dee (actresss)
Wallach, Eli (actor)
Wallechinsky, David (historian/T.V. commentator/author--Book
of Lists)
Wallenberg, Raoule (humanitarian)
Wallenda, Karl (circus performer)
Waller, Thomas Wright (Fats)
(comedian/pianist/composer/singer--jazz--
          One Never Knows Do One, Until the Real Thing
Comes Along)
Wallis, Harold Brent (Hal) (producer--Casa Blanca)
Wallis, John (clergyman/mathematician/inventor--infinity
symbol)
Walpole, Horace (author--Castle of Otranto)
Walsch, Neale Donald (author--Conversations with God)
Walsh, Enda (playwright)
Walsh, Joe (guitarist)
Walsh, John (T. V. personality--America's Most Wanted)
Walsh, Kerri (beach volleyball)
Walsh, Mary (comedian)
Walsh, Raoul (director)
Waltari, Mika (author)
Walton, Izaak (author--Complete Angler)
Waner, Lloyd (Little Poison) (baseball)
Waner, Paul Glee (Big Poison) (baseball)
Wang, Vera (fashion designer)
Wap, Fetty (singer--rap/hip-hop)
Warburg, Otto (physicist/Nobelist)
Ward, Anita (singer--Ring My Bell)
Ward, Artemus (Charles Farrar Browne's pseudonym) (author-
-humorist)

Ward, Arthur Henry (pseudonym--Sax Rohmer) (poet/songwriter/author--Dr. Fu Manchu)
Ward, Sam (pseudonym--Sammy Stept) (composer--It Seems Like Old Times)
Ward, Sela (actress--My Fellow Americans)
Warden, Jack (actor)
Wareheim, Eric (writer/director/comedian/actor)
Warhol, Andy (painter--pop art--A Set of Six Self-Portraits--Mao/co-founder--Interview Magazine/ film maker--Trash)
Warner, Albert (film studio founder--Warner Bros.)
Warner, Aron (producer--Shrek)
Warner, Harry (film studio founder--Warner Bros.)
Warner, Jack (film studio founder--Warner Bros.)
Warner, Sam (producer/film studio founder--Warner Bros.)
Warr, Thomas West De la (Baron) (colonialist; Br.)
Warren, Earl (Supreme Court justice)
Warren, Robert Penn (poet--first U. S. poet laureate)
Warwick, Dionne (singer--Alfie, Walk on By, I'll Never Fall In Love Again)
Washbourne, Mona (actress)
Washburne, Elihu (politician)
Washington, Denzel (actor--Eli, Hurricane Carter, Mississippi Masala, Malcolm X, Man on Fire, Training Day)
Washington, Dinah (Queen of the Harlem Blues) (singer)
Washington, Ford Lee (Buck) (musician/singer) (John W. Sublett's (Bubbles) partner)
Washington, George (American Cincinnatus) (farmer/land investor/politician)
Washington, Ned (composer--High Noon)
Wasikowska, Mia (actress--Alice in Wonderland)
Wass, Ted (actor--Blossom)
Wasserstein, Wendy (playwright)
Waterhouse, John (artist--The Awakening of Adonis)
Waterhouse, Keith (playwright--Billy Liar)
Waters, Alice (chef/author--The Art of Simple Food)
Waters, Ethel (singer--Am I Blue/actress--Beulah)
Waters, John (author/producer/director--Polyester)
Waters, Lou (newsman)

Waters, Muddy (musician/singer-songwriter--Hoochie Coochie Man)
Waterston, Sam (actor)
Watley, Jody (singer)
Watros, Cynthia (actress)
Watson, Bubba (golfer)
Watson, Emma (actress--Harry Potter)
Watson, James Dewey (biologist--D.N.A.)
Watson, Raymond (C.E.O. Walt Disney Company) (Eisner's predecessor/ Card's successor)
Watt, James (inventor/mechanical engineer)
Watteau, Jean-Antoine (painter--Embarkation of Cythera--rococo)
Watterson, Bill (cartoonist--Calvin & Hobbs)
Wattleton, Faye (feminist)
Watts, Alan (philosopher)
Watts, Andre (musician--piano)
Watts, Isaac (minister/theologian/hymnist--Horae Lyricae, Joy to the World)
Watts, Naomi (actress-Le Devorce, 21 Grams, Princess Diana)
Watts, Rolonda (talkshow host)
Waugh, Alec (author)
Waugh, Evelyn (author--Sword of Honour Trilogy, The Loved One)
Wawrinka, Stan (tennis)
Wayans, Damon (comedian/actor--Mo Money)
Wayans, Keenen Ivory (actor)
Wayans, Shawn (actor/producer/writer/comedian--Living Color)
Wayne, Anthony (General) (army officer/statesman/politician) (George Washington's officer)
Wayne, John (actor--Hatari, Rio Lobo, Flying Tigers, True Grit, Neath Arizona Skies, Quiet Man, Three Faces West, Back to Bataan, Honda)
Wayne, Lil (musician--rap)
Weatherford, Derek (swimmer)
Weathers, Carl (actor/director)
Weaver, Sigourney (actress--Alien, Avatar)

Webb, Anthony Jerome (Spud) (basketball)
Webb, Beatrice (socialist/economist/reformer--Fabian Society)
Webb, Chloe (actress--adult films)
Webb, Clifton (actor)
Webb, Delbert (Del) (realtor--Sun City)
Webb, Earl (#67) (baseball)
Webb, James (author--A Sense of Honor)
Webb, Jimmy (songwriter--Galveston)
Webb, Karrie (golfer)
Webb, Phyllis (poet)
Webb, Sidney (socialist/economist/reformer--Fabian Society)
Webber, Andrew Lloyd (composer--Evita)
Weber, Carl Maria von (composer--Der Freischutz)
Weber, Jake (actor)
Weber, Lois (director--silent films)
Weber, Max (artist)
Weber, Steven (actor--Jeffrey)
Webern, Anton (composer)
Webster, Daniel (politician)
Webster, John (dramatist--The Duchess of Malfi)
Webster, Noah (lexicographer--Webster Dictionary, Blue
Backed Speller/Spelling Book)
Webster, William Hedgcock (jurist--C.I.A. director)
Wechsler, David (psychologist--I. Q. Test)
Weems, Mason Locke (Parson) (author/fablist--Washington
cutting the cherry tree)
Weems, Ted (bandleader--Heartaches)
Weezer (musical group--Buddy Holly)
Wei, Wang (poet--Tang Dynasty)
Weil, Cynthia (songwriter--On Broadway) (co-writer/husband--
Barry Mann)
Weill, Kurt (composer--Speak Low, The Three Penny Opera,
Mack the Knife, September   Song)
(Anderson/Brecht's collaborator)
Weinberger, Caspar (politician)
Weiner, Matthew (writer/director/producer--Mad Men)
Weir, Peter (director--Dead Poet's Society, Picnic at Hanging
Rock)
Weiss, Eric (Houdini) (magician)

Weiss, Peter (playwright--Marat-Sade)
Weizman, Ezer (Gen.) (politician; Isr.)
Weizmann, Chaim (religious leader--Zionist)
Wek, Alek (model)
Welch, Joseph N. (army lawyer in McCarthy investigation)
Welch, Raquel (actress)
Weld, Tuesday (actress)
Weldon, Fay (author; Br.)
Weller, Peter (actor--RoboCop)
Welles, Orson (writer/director/producer/actor--Citizen Kane)
Wellesley, Arthur (Old Nosey) (Duke of Wellington)
Wellesz, Egon (composer)
Wellington (nee Arthus Wellesley) (Duke)
Wells, Clyde (politician; Nfld.)
Wells, Herbert George (author--Tono-Bungay, Ann Veronica)
Wells, Ida (activist)
Wells, Mary (singer--My Guy)
Wells, Orson (author--The Third Man, Long John
Silver/director--Mac Beth)
Wells, Rebecca (author--Ya-ya Sisterhood)
Welteroth (author/journalist/editor)
Welty, Eudora (author--Delta Wedding, The Optimist's
Daughter)
Wenders, Wim (director)
Weng, Will (puzzle editor)
Wenner, Jane (magazine publisher) (Jann's wife)
Wenner, Jann (magazine publisher) (Jane's husband)
Wentworth, Thomas (Earl of Strafford) (statesman)
Werner, Oscar (actor--Ship of Fools)
Wertmuller, Lina (filmmaker)
Wesley, Charles (hymnist--Glory to the New Born King, poet,
theologian--Methodist)   (John's brother)
Wesley, John (theologist--Methodism founder) (Charles's
brother)
Wess, Frank (musician--jazz)
Wesson, Tina (Survivor winner)
West, Adam (actor)
West, Benjamen (painter)
West, Cornel (philosopher/activist/author--Race Matters)

West, Dottie (singer--country)
West, Jessamyn (author)
West, Kanye (musician--rap, songwriter, producer, director, fashion designer) (label--   Def Jam)
West, Mae (actress--I'm No Angel, Every Day's A Holiday, She Done Him Wrong)
West, Nathanael (author--The Day of the Locusts)
West, Rebecca (author)
Westheimer, Ruth (Dr.) (sex therapist/host--Sexually Speaking)
Westinghouse, George (inventor--air brake)
Weston, Galen (entrepreneur--food sales)
Westover, Tara (author--Educated)
Weyl, Hermann (mathematician)
Weymouth, Martina Michelle (Tina) (musician--bassist--Talking Heads)
Whalen, Grover (New York's Official Greeter) (politician)
Wharton, Edith (author--The House of Mirth, Ethan Frome)
Wheaton, Wil (actor--Stand By Me)
Whedon, Joss (composer/writer/director--The Avengers/producer--Buffy)
Wheeler, Ella Wilcox (poet)
Whistler, James McNeill (etcher/painter--Old Battersea Bridge)
Whitaker, Forest (actor--Amin)
Whitcomb, Ian (singer-songwriter/record producer/actor)
White Stripes (musical group)
White, Alan (drummer--Yes)
White, Byron (football, justice)
White, Edmund (author--Travels in Gay America; Am.)
White, Elwyn Brooks (essayist--New Yorker/author--Stuart Little, Charlotte's Web, The Trumpet   of the Swan, Is Sex Necessary, Elements of Style)
White, Jack (musician/singer/songwriter--White Stripes)
White, Jaleel (actor--Urkel)
White, Meg (musician--drummer--White Stripes)
White, Onna (choreographer--Oliver)
White, Patrick (author--Voss, The Eye of the Storm)
White, Pearl (actress--The Perils of Pauline)
White, Shaun (snowboarder)

Whiteman, Paul (bandleader/composer--Rhapsody in Blue, Deep Purple/ musician--   violin)
Whitfield, Sharee (actress)
Whitman, Christie (politician--New Jersey governor)
Whitman, Margaret Cushing (Meg) (business exec.-- Ebay)
Whitman, Walt (poet--Song of Myself, Darest Thou Now, O Soul, I Sing the Body Electric,   Oh Captain My Captain) (muse--Erato)
Whitney, Eli (inventor--cotton gin)
Whittier, John Greenleaf (poet--Maud Muller)
Whitting, Margaret (singer--A Tree in the Meadow)
Who (musical group--Tommy, I'm Free)
Wicker, Thomas Grey (author--A Time to Die)
Widmark, Richard (producer/actor--Udo)
Wie, Michelle (golf)
Wiebe, Rudy (author--The Temptations of Big Bear)
Wiener, Norbert (cybernetics pioneer)
Wiesel, Elie (Eliezer) (author--NIght)
Wiest, Dianne (actress)
Wigand, Jeffrey (whistle-blower--tobacco)
Wiggin, Kate Douglas (author--children's)
Wiig, Kristen (actress/writer/comedian--S.N.L., Bridesmaids)
Wilander, Mats (tennis)
Wilbrand, Julius (inventor--T.N.T.)
Wilbur, Richard (translator/poet--Walking to Sleep)
Wilcox, Ella (poet)
Wilde, Cornel (actor/director)
Wilde, Oscar (author--Dorian Gray, Salome, The Garden of Eros, De Profundis)
Wilder, Alec (songwriter--While We Were Young)
Wilder, Gene (actor/writer/director/producer--Thursday's Game, The Woman in Red)
Wilder, Thorton (playwright/author--Our Town, The Skin of Our Teeth)
Wiles, Jason (actor--Third Watch)
Wilhelm, James Hoyt (baseball)
Wilhelm, Kate (author)
Wilkens, Lenny (basketball)

Will, George (newpaper columnist (op-ed)/journalist/author--
Men At Work)
Willard, Archibald MacNeal (painter--Spirit of 76)
Willard, Emma (educator/activist)
Willard, Jess (Pottawatomie Giant) (boxer)
William of Occam (philosopher/theologian)
William the Conqueror (First Norman King of England) (Henry
I &Adela's father)
Williams, Andy (singer)
Williams, Anson (actor--Happy Days)
Williams, Barry (actor--Brady Bunch)
Williams, Betty (activist/Nobelist--peace--Northern Ireland
Peace Movement)
Williams, Billy Dee (actor)
Williams, Charles Melvin (Cootie) (musician--jazz)
Williams, Deron (basketball)
Williams, Emlyn (dramatist/actor--The Corn is Green)
Williams, Esther (swimmer/actress)
Williams, John (musician--piano/conductor/composer--
Princess Leia's theme)
Williams, Micah Sierra (Katt) (actor/comedian/singer--rap)
Williams, Montel (T. V. host)
Williams, Otis (singer--The Temptations)
Williams, Ralph Vughan (composer--A Sea Symphony)
Williams, Robin (actor--Toys, Peter Pan)
Williams, Roger (The Founder of Providence) (religious
dissenter)
Williams, Serena (tennis)
Williams, Ted (baseball)
Williams, Tennessee (playwright--The Night of the Iguana,
Summer and Smoke,   Camino Real,
Suddenly Last Summer)
Williams, Thomas (Tom/Tennessee) (author/playwright)
Williams, Venus (tennis)
Williams, William Carlos (poet--Paterson)
Williamson, Henry (author--Tarka the Otter)
Williamson, Nicol (actor--Excalibur)
Willingham, Calder (author--End As A Man)
Willis, Bruce (actor--Death Becomes Her)

Willis, Chuck (singer--C.C. Rider)
Willis, Connie (author--sci-fi)
Wills, Chill (actor, singer)
Wilson, Angus (author)
Wilson, Ann (musician/songwriter--Heart band--These Dreams)
Wilson, Autust (playwright--Ma Rainey's Black Bottom)
Wilson, Demond (actor--Sanford & Sons)
Wilson, Dooley (actor/pianist)
Wilson, Earl (columnist)
Wilson, Edmund (author--Axel's Castle)
Wilson, Flip (comedian)
Wilson, Gahan (cartoonist--The Trouble with Harry)
Wilson, Jackie (singer--Am I The Man)
Wilson, Lanford (playwright--The Hot L Baltimore, Serendading Louie)
Wilson, Nancy (singer--You Don't Know How Glad I Am)
Wilson, Owen (screenwriter/actor--Royal Tenenbaums, Internship, The Darjeeling Limited)
Wilson, Pete (politician)
Wilson, Rainn Dietrich (comedian/writer/director/producer/activist/actor--The Office)
Wilson, Rebel Melanie (writer/producer/actor--Pitch Perfect)
Wilson, Sheree (producer/model/businesswoman/actress--Dallas, Walker Texas Ranger)
Wimsey, Peter (Lord) (author--Whole Body)
Win, Ne (politician; Burma)
Winans, Bebe (singer--I Found Love)
Winans, Cece (singer)
Winding, Kai (bandleader/trombonist)
Winehouse, Amy (singer--Rehab)
Winfield, Dave (baseball)
Winfrey, Oprah (actress/talkshow hostess)
Wingate, Orde Charles (Gen.) (Br. army officer who created Chindit missions)
Winger, Debra (actress)
Wings (musical group--Let 'em In, Jet) (Paul McCartney's band)

Winner, Septimus (songwriter--Oh Where, Oh Where Has My Little Dog Gone)
Winningham, Mare (actress)
Winslet, Kate (actress--Mildred Pierce)
Winslow, Ola (author)
Winsor, Kathleen (author--Forever Amber)
Winters, Shelley (actress--Polly Adler)
Wintour, Anna (editor--American Vogue)
Winwood, Steve (singer) (musical group--Traffic)
Wise, Isaac Mayer (rabbi--reformer)
Wise, Stephen Samuel (rabbi--Zionist/founded Jewish Institute of Religion)
Wiseman, Joseph (actor--Dr. No)
Wiseman, Len (director--Total Recall)
Wister, Owen (author--The Virginian)
Withers, Bill (singer--Use Me)
Witherspoon, Cora (comedienne)
Witherspoon, Reese (actress--Legally Blonde)
Witney, William (director--Master of the World)
Witt, Alicia (actress--Urban Legend)
Witt, Katerina (figure skater)
Wittgenstein, Ludwig (philosopher)
Wodehouse, Pelham G. (Sir) (author--Aunt Agatha, Aunt Dahlia/playwright/politician)
Wojtyla, Karol (Pope)
Wolfe, Thomas (Tom)(author--The Right Stuff, Electric Kool Aid Acid Test, Radical Chic,   A Man in Full, The Web and the Rock, Of Time and the River)
Wolfert, Ira (author)
Wolff, Michael (author/media observer)
Wolff, Tobias (author--This Boy's Life)
Wolitzer, Meg (author)
Womack, Leeann (singer--country)
Wonder, Stevie (nee Stevland Hardaway Morris) (record producer/songwriter/singer--   My Cherie Amour)
Wong, Ali (comedian/actress)
Wong, Anna May (actress--Bagdad)

Wong, Bradley Darryl (B. D.) (actor--Law & Order, Madame Butterfly)
Wons, Tony (radio personality)
Woo, John (director--Mission Impossible)
Woo, Roh Tae (General--R.O.K.)
Wood, Ed (director)
Wood, Edgar (author--Birds & Animals in the Rockies; Can.)
Wood, Elijah (actor)
Wood, Evan Rachel (actress--Thirteen)
Wood, Garfield (Gar) (The Boatbuilder) (entrepreneur/inventor)
Wood, Grant (artist)
Wood, Lana (actress--Peyton Place, Diamonds Are Forever)
Wood, Natalie (nee Natasha Gurdin) (actress)
Wood, Peggy (actress--Mama)
Wood, Ronnie (author--Rolling Stones)
Woodard, Alfre (actress--Crooklyn, Cross Creek, Primal Fear)
Woodard, Lynette (basketball--Harlem Globetrotters)
Woodbridge, Todd (tennis)
Wooden, John (basketball--U. C. L. A.)
Woods, Elin (Tiger's ex.)
Woods, Elle (actress--Legally Blonde)
Woods, Ilene (actress/singer/voice artist--Cinderella)
Woods, Jacqueline Ruth (Ilene) (singer/actress/voice artist--Cinderella)
Woods, James (actor)
Woods, Nan (actress)
Woods, Tiger (golfer) (Elin's husband)
Woodward, Bob (author/reporter--Watergate)
Woodward, Edward (actor)
Woodward, Joanne (actress--Rachel Rachel, Three Faces of Eve) (Paul Newman's wife)
Wooley, Sheb (singer)
Woolf, Adeline Virginia (author--Mrs. Dalloway, The Voyage Out, Orlando: A Biography,   A Room of One's Own, To the Lighthouse) (Leonard's wife)
Woolf, Leonard (politicial theorist/author--Downhill all the Way) (Bloomsbury Group)   (Virginia Woolf's husband)

Woollcott, Alec (critic--New Yorker magazine)
Woolley, Monty (actor)
Woolsey, James (lawyer--C. I. A.)

Woo-Shik, Choi (actor--Parasite)
Woosnam, Ian (golfer)
Wopat, Tom (actor--Dukes of Hazard)
Wordsworth, William (poet--Ode to Duty)
Work, Henry (composer--Grandfather's Clock)
Worley, Jo Anne (actress)
Worrel, Todd (baseball)
Worth, Irene (actress)
Wortman, Elmo (author)
Wouk, Herman (author--Winds of War, The Caine Mutiny,
Youngblood Hawke, City Boy)
Wray, Fay (actress-- King Kong)
Wren, Christopher (Sir) (architect)
Wren, Percival Christopher (P.C.) (author--Beau Geste)
Wright, James (politician) (Tip O'Neill's predecessor)
Wright, Orville (inventor)
Wright, Peter (spy)
Wright, Richard (author--Native Son)
Wright, Steven (comedian)
Wright, Teresa (actress)
Wright, Willard Huntington (pseudonym--S. S. van Dine)
(author--Philo Vance)
Wu, Roh Tae (politician; S. Korea)
Wuhrer, Kari (actress)
Wuinn, Aileen (actress)
Wyatt, Jane (actress--Father Knows Best, Star Trek--Amanda)
Wyatt, Rachel (author--Foreign Bodies)
Wyche, Charlie (football)
Wyeth, Andrew (visual artist/painter--realism--Christina's
World, Helga Pictures)
Wyeth, Jamie (painter) (Andrew's son/N.C.'s grandson)
Wyeth, Newell Convers (artist/illustrator) (Andrew's
father/Jamie's grandfather)
Wyle, Noah (actor--E. R.)
Wyler, William (director--Mrs. Miniver)

Wylie, Elinor (poet--The Little Clock)
Wyman, Bill (musician--Rolling Stones)
Wyman, Jane (actress--So Big, Dallas, Johnny Belinda)
Wynette, Tammy (singer--Stand By Your Man)
Wynn, Early (baseball)
Wynn, Ed (actor/comedian--The Perfect Fool)
Wynn, Keenan (actor--Dr. Strangelove)
Wynn, Nan (singer--big band)
Wynne, Arthur (inventor--crossword puzzle)
Wyss, John (author--Swiss Family Robinson)

--X--

Xerxes (king of Persia/victor at Thermopylae) (Greek invader)
Xiaoping, Deng (politician--Hua Guafeng's successor)
XTC (musical group--Skylarking, Oranges & Lemons)

--Y--

Yachty, Lil (singer-songwriter--Lil Boat)
Yagudin, Alexei (figure skater)
Yahoo Serious (nee Greg Pead) (composer/director/actor--Young Einstein)
Yale, Elihu (benefactor)
Yalow, Rosalyn (physicist)
Yamaguchi, Kristi (figure skater)
Yan, Martin (chef)
Yang, Andrew (politician)
Yankovic, Al (Weird Al) (parodist/singer--Eat It, Mandatory Fun)
Yanni (musician--Live at the Acropolis)
Yarborough, Cale (race car driver)
Yardbirds (musical group--For Your Love, I'm a Man)

Yarrow, Peter (author--Puff the Magic Dragon/singer--Peter, Paul & Mary)
Yasuhiro, Nakasone (politician; Jap.)
Yates, David (director--Harry Potter)
Yates, Peter (director--The Dresser, Breaking Away, Eleni, Bullitt)
Yates, Richard (author--Revolutionary Road, The Easter Parade)
Yatie, Cassie (actress)
Yat-sen, Sun (potitician--revolutionary; Chin.)
Ybarra, Thomas Russell (author--Young Man of Caracas)
Yeager, Chuck (astronaut)
Yearwood, Trisha (actress/singer--This Is Me You're Talking To)
Yeats, William Butler (poet--Easter 1916, Down By the Salley Garden, Sailing to Byzantium,   The Herne's Egg, The Lake   Isle of Innisfree, Lapis Lazuli, The Hour Glass)
Yehudi, Menuhin (musician--violin)
Yellen, Jack (screenwriter/lyricist--Ain't She Sweet)
Yellen, Janet (economist--Chair of the Federal Reserve)
Yeltsin, Boris (politician) (Naina's husband)
Yeltsin, Naina (Boris's wife)
Yeoh, Michelle (actress--Crouching Tiger, Hidden Dragon, Crazy Rich Asians)
Yepremian, Garo (football--kicker)
Yerby, Frank (author--The Foxes Harrow, A Rose for Ana Maria)
Yes (musical group--Owner of a Lonely Heart, Roundabout)
Yesenin, Sergei (poet)
Yevtushenko, Yergeny (poet--Babi Yar)
Yi, Soon (Woody Allen's wife, Andre Previn's adopted daughter)
Ying Yang Twins (musical group--rap/hip hop)
Yip, Vern (interior decorator--Trading Spaces)
Yo La Tengo (YLT) (musical group--Indie)
Yoakam, Dwight (singer--Honky Tonk Man)
York, Alvin (Sgt.) (W.W.I. soldier--most decorated)
York, Susannah (actress)
Yorke, Thom (singer--Radiohead)

Yoshida, Shigeru (politician; Jap.)
Yost, Dennis (singer--Classic IV--Spooky, Stormy, Traces)
Yost, Eddie (Walking Man) (baseball)
Yost, Fielding (football)
Yost, Ned (baseball)
Yothers, Tina (actress)
Young Rascals (musical group--How Can I Be Sure)
Young, Aden (actor--Rectify)
Young, Andre Romelle (a.k.a. Dr. Dre) (musician--rap)
Young, Burt (author/actor--Rocky; Br.)
Young, Cy (baseball)
Young, Dean (cartoonist--Blondie) (Chic's son)
Young, Gig (actor)
Young, Loretta (actress--Ramona)
Young, Murat Bernard (Chic) (cartoonist--Blondie) (Dean's
father)
Young, Neil (singer/songwriter--Ohio, Heart of Gold)
Young, Owen D. (business exec.--R.C.A. founder)
Young, Paul (singer--Every Time You Go Away)
Young, Sean (actress--Blade Runner)
Young, Stark (teacher/playwright/painter/essayist/literary
critic/translator/author--   So Red the
Rose)
Youngman, Hennie (comedian/violinist)
Yount, Erica Hill (journalist/co-host--Weekend Today)
Yousafzai, Malala (activist)
Ysaye, Eugene (musician--violin; Bel.)
Yuan, Hui (philosopher; Chin.)
Yuan, Liu (cartoonist)
Yugudin, Alexei (figure skater)
Yurick, Sol (author)
Yutang, Lin (author/transltor/linguist/inventor)

--Z--

Zadora, Pia (singer/actress--Butterfly)

Zagat, Nina (restaurant reviewer/co-founder--Zagat Restaurant Surveys)
Zagat, Tim (restaurant reviewer/co-founder--Zagat Restaurant Surveys)
Zager & Evans (musical group)
Zahn, Paula (journalist/newscaster)
Zane, Billy (actor--Dead Calm, Titanic)
Zanuck, Richard (producer--The Longest Day)
Zapata, Emiliano (revolutionary; Mex.)
Zappa, Frank (The Electric Don Quixote) (musician/songwriter--Valley Girls,director
          200 Motels) (Moon Unit's father)
Zappa, Moon Unit (musician/songwriter--Mothers of Invention) (Frank's daughter)
Zatopek, Emil (runner)
Zayak, Elaine (figure skater)
Zea, Fernando Botero (politician; Col.)
Zeeman, Pieter (physicist)
Zeffirelli, Franco (director)
Zeile, Todd (baseball)
Zellweger, Renee (director/actress--Me, Myself and Irene)
Zemeckis, Robert (director)
Zenger, John Peter (printer)
Zeno (philosopher--stoicism; Gr.)
Zermelo, Ernst (mathematician; Ger.)
Zetterling, Mai (actress)
Zhou, Litai (politician; China)
Zia, Mohammad (politician; Pak.)
Ziegfeld, Florenz (Flo) (impresario/producer--Rio Rita; Am.) (Anna Held's husband)
Ziegfeld, Helene Anna Held (singer/actress) (Florenz's wife)
Ziegler, Ron (politician)
Ziemba, Karen (actress)
Zimbalist, Efrem (actor--77 Sunset Strip, F.B.I.)
Zimbalist, Efrem (violinist) (Auer's pupil)
Zimmer, Hans (composer--Gladiator, Lion King)
Zimmer, Norma (L. Welk's Champagne Lady) (singer)
Zimmerman, Bob (author)
Znaimer, Moses (T. V. exec.--programming pioneer)

Zola, Emile Edouard (author--Germinal, Terese Raquin, Les Trois Villes, Nana,   J'Accuse, La Terre, The Dram Shop, The Sin of Father/La Faute de
        l'Abbe Mouret)
Zombies (musical group--She's Not There)
Zontang, Zuo (General Tso) (statesman/military leader)
Zorina, Vera (actress/choreographer/dancer--ballet)
Zoroaster (teacher--ancient Persia)
Zubin, Mehta (conductor)
Zuckerberg, Mark (computer programmer, internet entrepreneur, philanthropist)
Zuckerberg, Randi (internet entrepreneur/marketing director--Facebook)
Zukor, Adolph (business exec.--Paramount Pictures' founder)
Zulu, Shaka (African Napoleon) (warrior)
Zumwalt, Elmo (Admiral)
Zvereva, Natasha (tennis)
Zwingli, Ulrich (patriot/reformer; Swiss)
ZZ Top (musical group--Legs)